COASTAL
DEFENCES
of the
BRITISH
EMPIRE
in the Revolutionary &
Napoleonic Eras

For Staff Cdr David John Hayes RN (1950–2015)

COASTAL
DEFENCES
of the
BRITISH
EMPIRE

in the Revolutionary & Napoleonic Eras

DANIEL MacCANNELL

Pen & Sword
MILITARY

AN IMPRINT OF PEN & SWORD BOOKS LTD.
YORKSHIRE – PHILADELPHIA

First published in Great Britain in 2021 by
Pen & Sword Military
An imprint of
Pen & Sword Books Ltd
Yorkshire - Philadelphia

ISBN 978 1 52675 345 8

Typeset by SJmagic DESIGN SERVICES, India.
Printed and bound in India by Replika Press Pvt. Ltd.

Pen & Sword Books Ltd incorporates the Imprints of Pen & Sword Archaeology, Atlas,
Aviation, Battleground, Discovery, Family History, History, Maritime, Military, Naval,
Politics, Railways, Select, Transport, True Crime, Fiction, Frontline Books, Leo Cooper,
Praetorian Press, Seaforth Publishing, Wharncliffe and White Owl.

For a complete list of Pen & Sword titles please contact

PEN & SWORD BOOKS LIMITED
47 Church Street, Barnsley, South Yorkshire, S70 2AS, England
E-mail: enquiries@pen-and-sword.co.uk
Website: www.pen-and-sword.co.uk

or

PEN AND SWORD BOOKS
1950 Lawrence Rd, Havertown, PA 19083, USA
E-mail: uspen-and-sword@casematepublishers.com
Website: www.penandswordbooks.com

MIX
Paper from
responsible sources
FSC
www.fsc.org   FSC® C016779

CONTENTS

FOREWORD

The current populations of France and the United Kingdom are effectively identical in size. It is therefore usually forgotten that the former was, in the late eighteenth century, a demographic juggernaut. By the time Lord Cornwallis and Joseph Bonaparte concluded the short-lived Peace of Amiens in March 1802, France had more than three times the population of the UK, then including the twenty-six counties of southern Ireland. Moreover, Ireland's population today is only around 40 per cent higher than it was at that time, while England's has shot up sevenfold. Thus, as of 1796–98, when the French army and navy made multiple descents on the Emerald Isle aimed at fomenting revolution there, the English in England outnumbered the Irish in Ireland by as little as 3:2. Metropolitan France also boasted nearly half the population of the entire British Empire, India included. One curious effect of this was that, during the wars covered by this book, around one in eight adult males was serving in uniform in traditionally 'anti-militarist' Britain, a proportion three times higher than in 'militarist' France. The population imbalance also helps to explain Napoleon Bonaparte's belief that 'England was merely a small island – not unlike Corsica or Elba – which naturally belonged to France'.[1]

The 'island nation' concept was itself fairly new, however. When Edward VI, England's first unambiguously Protestant king, came to the throne in 1547, he inherited three land borders that had been in place for centuries. One separated the English colony in Ireland known as the Pale, roughly the modern counties of Louth, Meath, Dublin and Kildare, from the Irishry, who had their own aristocracy, language, and laws, and independent diplomatic and commercial relations, notably with Spain. A second border lay between the north of England and Scotland: the latter being, in some key respects, a French puppet state. And a third divided the twenty-square-mile English territory of Calais – containing the third-largest town in the kingdom, after Norwich and ahead of Bristol – from France itself. King Edward also ruled the city of Boulogne, captured from the French by his father in 1544. Just sixty years later, all this had changed beyond recognition: with Boulogne returned in 1550, Calais lost to a gargantuan French army in 1558, Scotland captured by home-grown pro-English Protestants in 1560, and the Irishry subjected to a brutally effective conquest, culminating in the 'Flight of the Earls' to Spanish Flanders in 1607. Only then, for the first time, did the political entity ruled from London have no land borders to defend; and only then did the funding of a standing navy emerge as a major political football.[2] As we shall see, the unaccustomed receipt of wholly adequate funding by the Royal Navy and Woolwich Arsenal during the decade of peace from 1783 to 1792, along with a welter of improvements in military and civil administration, would profoundly affect the course of the subsequent two decades of war.

The period covered by this book may at first seem odd, given that excellent ones on similar topics have tended to cover much longer periods (e.g. Norman

Longmate's *Island Fortress*) or much shorter ones (e.g. Richard Glover's *Britain at Bay*). My choice is rooted in contemporaries' lived experience. Numerous Britons who served as junior officers of the Ordnance, Army, and Royal Navy during the American War of Independence – notably including William Twiss, John Moore, and Horatio Nelson – had become senior ones by the start of the Napoleonic War. Joining the army in the ranks was usually for life; generals and admirals routinely served past the age of 70 if they were lucky enough to survive that long; and the service lives of ships, guns, and even earthworks could be measured in decades rather than years. Technological departures, even the famed Martello towers that will form such an important part of my narrative, tended to be incremental rather than revolutionary. Probably, the radical new clothing fashions of the first decade of the nineteenth century have produced an illusion of more major or rapid societal change than there actually was, at least on this side of the Channel.

Likewise, with regard to this book's geographic scope, I implicitly share William Pitt the Elder's view 'that the defence of the British Isles could not be conducted in isolation and that the defence of the homeland must form part of a worldwide strategy'.[3] For that reason, I have not shied away from detailed discussions of the lessons that British subjects learned from their efforts to defend, or indeed attack, coastal positions in any part of the world. In the process of researching this book, I also stumbled upon a surprisingly dense web of Swedish influences on the theories and practices of inshore naval combat that were adopted by both France and Britain.

Those peddling the notion of Britain 'standing alone against' Nazism are often rightly upbraided for forgetting or ignoring that the Britain of 1940 was merely the tip of a quasi-democratic Anglophone iceberg. But when the Peace of Amiens shattered in 1803, that berg had barely begun to coalesce. The Australian penal colony was still in its infancy; India, run by an unaccountable for-profit company; New Zealand, seen but not heard. South Africa had been taken from the Dutch just eight years before, and since returned to them. English Canada was filling up rapidly with economic refugees, many steeped in republican ideology, from an impoverished and broadly hostile United States. Sending the king to Ottawa and the fleet to Halifax and carrying on the war from there if things went belly-up in Europe was not yet a credible option. Worse, having formed an alliance with Austria against Prussia in the 1740s and with Prussia against Austria in the 1750s and 1760s, then fought against France, Spain and Holland simultaneously as recently as the 1780s, and attacked Denmark–Norway in 1801, Britain had no consistent allies in its own neighbourhood apart from Portugal, which was relatively insignificant economically and, for the time being, militarily.

Probably the best thing that could be said about the European scene was that – despite near-misses, such as the Ochakov Affair of 1791 – Britain had never gone to war against Russia: her only rival for the title of 'leading Western power' in a strictly military sense before the French Revolutionary War got underway.[4] But that, too, would change in 1807. In short, the brief interlude of peace between the French Revolutionary War and the Napoleonic War was a master-class in 'standing alone against…' that has never since been repeated, or repeatable. At the level of what used to be called mass psychology, or perhaps the psychology of the 'official mind', the horror of soloing a two-decade-long 'world war in all but name'[5] could have been decisive in the seemingly unconnected web of relatively minor decisions that led, over the subsequent century, to the flooding of the world with British people and institutions.[6] The forty years and specific topic covered by this book are therefore key to understanding some underappreciated aspects of the world as it now is, as well as fascinating in their own right. I hope the pages that follow will do them some justice.

I would particularly like to thank Vicky Dawson, not only for her consistent support for my writing career over the past thirteen years, but for first suggesting that I combine my interests in architectural and military history into a single project, of which this book is the result. Helena Ashton, Gary Birkett, Todd Braisted, Anna Brown, Bryony Chellew, Alan Chick, Duco Le Clercq, Peter Davidson, Louise Dolen, Evan Ellis, Andrew Elrick, Nancy Fosmire, Jarrett Gorin, Edward Hocknell, Dean MacCannell, Eleanor MacCannell, Juliet MacCannell, Matt Monos, Clemence O'Connor, Ralph O'Connor, Kim Segel, Catherine Simpson, and Daphne Wetmore are also owed my sincere thanks for materially helping with its more-or-less timely completion. And of the many others besides its dedicatee who guided my thinking on particular points of architecture, tactics, strategy, or ballistics, or simply encouraged me in the writing of it, thanks are particularly due to John Alford, Justine Ashley, Peter Bye-Jensen, Chris Cupson, Max Edelson, Gary Forder, Brian Huntington, Gavin Lenthall, Anemone Linthorst, Emily MacCannell, Kirsten Mckenzie, Frank Noble, Matt Robson, Hector Stamboulieh, H. Grant Timms, Harry Wadham, and John Watkins. Of course, its errors and omissions are purely my own fault.

Daniel MacCannell
St Martin's Plain Camp
February 2020

Nine-tenths of tactics are certain, and taught in books: but the irrational tenth is like the kingfisher flashing across the pool, and that is the test of generals.

–T. E. Lawrence

DEFENCE AGAINST WHAT?

The outbreak of war between Britain and thirteen of her American colonies in April 1775 created, among other things, a formidable pool of new enemy privateers who, up to that moment, would have counted as British in any war against another maritime power. Some 36,000 American colonists had served aboard these fast, state-licensed but *de facto* pirate vessels during the War of the Austrian Succession in the 1740s, during which the British side had captured 3,434 merchant ships, or some 200 more than it had lost in the same fashion to the chiefly French and Spanish enemy. Of the British tally, one-fourth of all captures, worth £7.5 million (£15.7 billion at today's prices), had been taken by Americans.[1]

Many eighteenth-century privateers boasted top speeds of 12 knots, comparable to that of the fastest ship in the Royal Navy (the forty-gun fifth-rate HMS *Endymion*) and considerably faster than second-rate ships of the line mounting ninety to ninety-eight guns. This loose modern interpretation of a 1799 Bermuda-built Royal Navy 'advice boat' for rapid ship-to-shore communication gives a sense of the size, sharply raked mast(s), and extraordinarily long bowsprit of a typical Bermudian or Virginian privateer.

As compared to their western Atlantic counterparts, French privateers could be very large indeed. The thirty-two-gun fifth-rate HMS *Arethusa*, which carried a crew of 270, began life in Le Havre as a purpose-built privateer called the *Pèlerine*.

Individual rebelled colonies were quick off the mark, licensing as many as 1,151 privateer voyages on their own authority, but it took the Continental Congress nearly a year to launch its privateer war. In the spring of 1776, it enacted that American skippers

> may, by Force of Arms, attack, subdue, and take all Ships and other Vessels belonging to the Inhabitants of Great Britain, on the high seas, or between high-water and low-water Marks, except Ships and Vessels bringing Persons who intend to settle and reside in the United Colonies, or bringing Arms, Ammunition or Warlike Stores to the said Colonies, for the Use of such Inhabitants thereof as are Friends to the American Cause[.][2]

Privateers' activity, the naval equivalent of commission-only sales work, was funded almost entirely by the sale of captured ships and goods, sometimes supplemented by ransom payments. '[E]mbedded in a broader political economy of violence which needed and actively promoted "private" violence in a broader pursuit of power',[3] privateering was so efficient economically that, by its existence, it may actually have increased the frequency with which wars were fought.[4] And as well as the gratification of seeing their enemies' seaborne communications cut and economies damaged, the licensing government received a cut of each prize-ship and prize-cargo sold, via taxation of between 10 and 40 per cent.[5] After 1693, English privateers were even able to claim half the value of English ships as prize money, provided that such vessels had first been captured and held by the enemy for at least four days.[6] More than 50,000 Americans would take up privateering on one side or the other in the War of Independence, which would last well into the 1780s, and rebel privateering vessels of warship-like sizes outnumbered those of George Washington's official navy by at least 4:1.[7]

Crucially, because privateers of all nations roamed as far and wide as the merchant fleets they preyed on, their attacks were not limited to active war zones. They also often occurred within sight of shore – as the Continental Congress's reference to 'high-water and low-water Marks' implied; and when the opportunity arose, they could develop into amphibious hit-and-run attacks on British colonial and even British mainland towns. In part, it was this extreme geographic range, with its inbuilt element of surprise, that made privateer-licensing such an 'effective means of waging war', analogous to the submarine warfare of the early twentieth century, and a 'militarily efficient means of projecting national power [... that] reduced the demand for a standing national navy'.[8]

In the colonies that remained loyal to Britain in and after 1775, privateer raids on settlements began immediately. There was a spectacular one at Fort Frederick (on the site of Saint John, New Brunswick, Canada) in August of that year, leading to the burning of the fort and the capture of a British supply ship, three soldiers, three civilian adults, and five children. A hundred tons of livestock destined for the British garrison of Boston, 400 miles to the southwest, were also taken. In the same month, the Philadelphian ship *Lady Catherine* deprived Bermuda, then undefended, of around 90 per cent of its stock of gunpowder.[9] The next year, an American privateer even managed to capture a troop transport carrying half a battalion of Fraser's Highlanders.[10] Moreover, such attacks continued even after the war had effectively come to an end. Annapolis Royal in Nova Scotia was temporarily seized in August 1781 by the crews of two Yankee privateer schooners, who 'proceeded to plunder every house, store and shop of what goods, provisions, furniture, plate, bedding, cloathing, &c., were to be found [...] taking even their wearing apparel, so as not to leave them a second shirt, and the buckles out of the ladies' shoes'.[11] Lunenburg, Nova Scotia, was similarly invaded by the crews of four American privateers in July 1782, more than eight months after the Yorktown campaign had effectively ended British hopes of victory in the Western Hemisphere.

Within sight of Britain itself, privateer actions were commonplace after 1778, not least because the rebels' roughly 2,700 letters of marque included ones 'issued by Benjamin Franklin in Paris to mostly Irishmen who plied the waters around the British Isles'.[12] Three of these ships licensed by Franklin took 114 prizes during a fifteen-month period in 1779–80.[13] But even regular forces were well known to indulge in privateer-like escapades by both land and sea. In September 1778, for instance, an amphibious force under British Maj.-Gen. Charles Grey took more than 10,000 sheep, cattle, and pigs and £950 in cash from the civilian population of Martha's Vineyard, Massachusetts, which was undefended at the time.[14]

Dunkirk was the traditional nerve centre of enemy privateering efforts, but French corsair captains also had full access to Norwegian ports including Bergen, Egersund, and Stavanger, among other places around Europe, at this time. Nor were privateers alone in mounting coastal raids on the British Isles, of various intensities. In April 1778, the northwest English port of Whitehaven was raided by a landing party of US Navy sailors and marines, its fort captured and its shore battery of long-range 32-pounder guns 'spiked' to render them inoperable before an attempt was made to burn all 200 or so ships at anchor there.[15] This could easily have resulted in mass civilian casualties, given that most of these vessels – and the warehouses close beside them – were loaded with a smorgasbord of inflammables: 'coal for Dublin [...] rum, sugar and tobacco'.[16] Thankfully, one of the raiders named David Freeman, a secret loyalist to Britain or perhaps just a humanitarian, alerted the local fire brigade and populace in time. The town and most of its merchant fleet were saved, and at least one of the spiked cannon was apparently returned to working order before the disappointed Americans had even fled the harbour.[17] Nevertheless, the incident sent 'shock waves' across the British Isles, 'completely out of proportion with the mere few hundred pounds' worth of damage actually caused [... and] awakened everyone to the threat of invasion',[18] France and the rebels having concluded a commercial and defensive alliance two months earlier. Anyone seeking to understand the coastal defence of British territory in the Georgian era should bear in mind that privateer and

Canadian hooked rug depicting the burning of the blockhouse at Lunenburg, Nova Scotia, by the Americans in July 1782, the last major privateer attack of the War of Independence.

'privateer-like' raids,[19] rather than invasions in strength, had long been seen as the primary threat, at least in the sense that their occurrence was inevitable rather than merely possible.

Early in King George III's reign, the relative informality of the privateering profession was matched by that of British arrangements to defend against it. The 'principle that local defence should be financed by local efforts' was so strong that, when Sunderland failed to raise sufficient funds for gunpowder, the government reclaimed the guns and shot it had provided to the town in 1778.[20] An eight-gun battery was erected in Banff on the northern coast of Scotland because the Massachusetts privateer *Tartar* had taken two British prizes within sight of the town; yet, despite being made mostly of turf, this fortification was completed only four years after the fact. The Meikle Battery in the major fishing port of Peterhead, Aberdeenshire, was remembered in the 1850s as having contained seven brass cannon recovered from a wrecked ship of the 1588 Spanish Armada,[21] though it seems unlikely that such weapons would have been retained when the battery was comprehensively rebuilt in 1780 'in response to the threat of privateer raids during the American War of Independence [...] in the form of a half moon surrounded by a palisade, with a guard house'.[22] Irrespective of their age and whether they had been recovered from the sea, however, Scottish seaports' shore-defence weapons were served almost exclusively by civilians, albeit 'sometimes directed by retired sailors'.[23] And as in Scotland, so in the south of England, where numerous shore batteries 'were demanded, paid for, and manned, by the townships concerned', with only the guns, projectiles, and requisite loading equipment such as sponges and rammers being supplied by the government's powerful and notoriously stingy Board of Ordnance.[24] Not for nothing did the second half of Lt John Ardesoif RN's popular *Introduction to Marine Fortifications and Gunnery* (1772) aim to explain 'Every useful part of Gunnery [...] in so simple a Manner' that it could be understood even by persons of 'the meanest Capacity'.[25]

A greater spur to defence than the previous year's Whitehaven episode occurred at eleven o'clock in the morning on 1 May 1779, when St Ouen's Bay on the west coast of Jersey was attacked by 'Five French Ships of War, several Bomb-Vessels, and Fifty Boats', supported by 'Cutters and Small Craft [... firing] Grape Shot'.[26] The situation was saved, in Lt-Gov. Moses Corbet's words, only by 'the spirited March of the 78th, and the Militia of the Island, with some few of the Artillery [...] which we were able to drag through the heavy Sands'. Only around twenty Frenchmen got ashore and were captured, and a roughly equal number drowned when their boat sank,[27] though whether this was caused by a British cannonball or the victims' poor seamanship remains a matter of debate. The only British casualties were caused by the bursting of one of their own cannon: a chronic problem during this war, to which we shall return in a later chapter.

Revenge by the Royal Navy was swift. On the night of 12–13 May, His Majesty's ships *Cabot*, *Experiment*, *Fortune*, *Pallas*, and *Unicorn* pursued a large part of the would-be French invasion force into Cancale Bay, just to the east of Saint-Malo. The British division's commander, Capt. Sir James Wallace, elected simply to ignore the threat from the powerful French shore batteries, on the grounds that if they fired at his ships 'they would probably hit the French [ones] as well'.

Though vindicated in that opinion, he was soon attacked by a group of local Breton militia who started 'pounding away with howitzers[28] and cannon from the beach'.[29] Having run aground, Sir James's fifty-gun[30] *Experiment* was fortunately pointing in the right direction to engage this impromptu defensive position in 'a ferocious cannonade' lasting three quarters of an hour, destroying it completely for the loss of two of her own men killed and thirteen wounded. The damage sustained by the *Experiment* was severe, but she was still capable of sailing home when the tide rose. Of the four largest French ships present, two were damaged beyond repair and a third was sailed back to England and pressed into naval service, the Channel Islands thus being 'saved from further molestation by this particular squadron'.[31]

Inspections conducted on the British mainland in the immediate wake of the 1779 'Motions of the Enemy' around Jersey revealed, alongside questionable structures and inexpert personnel, 'suspect' powder, rotten gun-carriages, and rusty cannonballs.[32] Portsmouth, being full of soldiers, was able to spare two infantrymen per company to re-train as coastal gunners, but most towns had to make do with 'practically untrained' militiamen, dockyard workers, and other civilians 'inclinable to learn how to load, point and fire'.[33] In a promising new expedient, volunteer troops were raised explicitly for 'the defence of the coast-line' in places including Plymouth, Falmouth, and the principal ports of Scotland and Ireland.[34] In London, volunteers came forward from the American loyalist refugee community, the staff of the Board of Works, and two groups of theatre technicians, among other bodies; and the national total was equivalent in size to at least twenty-two regular army battalions.[35] In the Scottish and Irish cases, however, volunteering 'raised an awkward constitutional question; for, however praiseworthy their object, and whatever their value in times of emergency, such combinations were illegal'.[36]

It was against such defences and defenders, accurately described by one civilian observer as 'thinly scattered' and 'problematical',[37] that France and Spain planned to hurl their Great Armada of 1779. Consisting of some 400 transports and sixty-six ships of the line, it was ordered to descend on southern England with 47,000 troops collected from Normandy and Brittany. Lack of specific knowledge of Britain's defences was not high on the enemy's list of obstacles. '[U]nder pretence of curiosity, grown fashionable amongst them for the first time', as Horace Walpole cattily put it,[38] French officers

> had been at work in England all through 1767 and 1768, surveying the southern coast and taking note of the country and of the best military positions inland; and there were even traces of a joint design of France and Spain to surprise and burn the dockyards at Portsmouth and Plymouth.[39]

At that time, in Walpole's view, '[e]xcept Portsmouth and Plymouth, we had not a fortification in South Britain that could afford us time to recover from the panic of the first successful invasion'.[40] Worse, a disguised French engineer officer was in 1779 able to tour the specific targets of the invasion, and found that Portsmouth's fortifications – while strong in themselves – were severely undermanned, while Wight and Gosport had even fewer defenders, and the Portsea Lines no garrison at all. He recommended a phased attack, in which Wight would be secured by 20,000 troops (4,000 in the first wave) and Gosport by a separate group of at least 6,000, who once installed there would use two dozen mortars to deny the use of Portsmouth's dockyard to its rightful owners. Two-thirds of this Gosport force would then assault Fort Cumberland, supported by naval gunfire. Another 5,000 troops, crossing over from Wight in small boats, would capture the Portsea Lines from behind; and lastly, the full army would cross over from France and Wight to take the remainder of Portsmouth in a formal siege.[41]

The manning problems revealed in the spy's report reflected that '[m]ost of the regular army was in North America, and arms, ammunition, and warlike stores for home defence were in very short supply'.[42] The Armada was also lucky that the British Channel Fleet was patrolling between Ushant and Scilly, far to the west of the projected scene of action, and was, in any case, only three dozen strong. An Ordnance official who rushed to Hampshire and the Isle of Wight,[43] which emerged much later as the enemy fleet's primary targets, found sixteenth-century Calshot Castle 'much out of repair', its gun-carriages 'broken down'; the 6-pounder carriages at its near-contemporary, Hurst Castle, 'decayed'; and medieval Carisbrook Castle '[d]ismantled and being used as a hospital'.[44] Remediation of such problems across the south of England was, by eighteenth-century standards, swift. Emplacements for six new 12-pounders were added to Dover Castle; four redoubts containing a total of six heavy[45] and twenty-two light cannon were built on Guernsey; and thirty shore batteries, with more than 150 light guns in all, were newly constructed from Mevagissey, Cornwall, in the west to Broadstairs, Kent, in the east, and north as far as the Caister Heights, just beyond Great Yarmouth. 'Large quantities of stores were sent out from the Tower', while 'palisades, fascines, and pickets for defending the batteries against land attack' were made locally.[46] In Tunbridge Wells, some women took to wearing military uniforms, which one observer thought betokened their willingness to 'drive the French back [...] if they invade'.[47] Minds were presumably concentrated by the fact that, on 24 June, the operation that would eventually come to be known as the Great Siege of Gibraltar had commenced with a Spanish blockade of that critically important British territory, gateway between the Atlantic and the Mediterranean.

On 14 August, the Franco-Spanish fleet[48] sent a flotilla under American colours to Ireland as a diversion. While the British authorities failed to take the bait, their defence planning was critically undermined by a plausible but unfounded assumption that the invasion's primary target was Plymouth, and therefore that it was probably headed for Cawsand Bay.[49] This suspected landing site was immediately ordered reinforced with three redoubts on the foreshore and six new batteries, totalling twenty heavy and twenty-eight light pieces. In case of an attack on London from the east, Coxheath in Kent and Warley in Essex became the sites of tented camps[50] for 16,000 men in total, of whom two-thirds were militia. The defences of Portsmouth were also improved somewhat, with eight 18-pounder guns added to Priddy's Hard, and fieldworks built on Southsea Common.[51]

In the event, Britain's bacon would be saved by three factors, none of her own making. The first was French indecisiveness regarding whether they should proceed to their original targets in Hampshire or instead, as a prelude to the isolation and occupation of the whole of Cornwall, attack Falmouth – whose garrison consisted chiefly of 2,000 tin-miners issued with pikes, the long unwieldy spears that had been deemed obsolete by the regular army during the reign of Queen Anne more than seven decades previously.[52] The second was the outbreak of scurvy, typhus, and smallpox in the enemy fleet. On Adm. D'Orvilliers's flagship alone, out of 1,100 men, 621 fell ill and sixty-one died.[53] The third factor was '[a]n easterly gale […] which, blowing hard for several days, drove the combined fleet out of the Channel'.[54] As a spur to recruiting in England, the effect of the Great Armada had been enormous. In July and August, wealthy patrons paid for the raising of fourteen new regiments of regular infantry for general service; three regiments of the home-service regulars known as fencibles; and a light dragoon regiment, as well as large numbers of drafts for pre-existing battalions.

The next year and a half did not go quite so well. In the following month, Britain was defeated by the Spanish on land in British West Florida (encompassing southern parts of the now-US states of Louisiana, Mississippi, and Alabama, as well as the Florida Panhandle). This territory would be ceded permanently at the end of the war. She also lost two ships and more than fifty men to the American navy in a battle off Flamborough Head, Yorkshire.

During the Battle of Flamborough Head, 22 September 1779, the British heavy frigate *Serapis* was captured by Americans in a smaller ship that attached itself to her side, below the minimum level of a broadside – a tactic that would famously be repeated by the British sloop *Speedy* against the Spanish heavy frigate *Gamo* in 1801. By modern standards, Georgian-era guns' capacity to be aimed in the vertical plane was miniscule, a fact that affected tactics on land and sea in numerous ways.

The port of Leith, by Edinburgh, 'which had no coast-defences' at the time, was threatened with destruction on 13 September by 'a Franco-American squadron of five ships with embarked about 120 French marines', and was spared only due to 'contrary winds'.[55] The port of Fishguard in Wales, defended only by some Gentlemen Volunteers, was raided on 15 September 1779. On that occasion, the Dunkirk-based American privateer *Black Prince*, 'crewed by a mixed collection of Irish and English smugglers', was driven off by a more patriotic cannon-armed smuggler at anchor there. A fort would be built in direct response in 1781, though not armed until 1785, two years after the American war ended, and then somewhat ineffectually, with eight 9-pounders and a paltry sixteen rounds of ammunition.[56] Despite the findings of a 1756 report by a colonel of Engineers[57] 'that six forts and gun batteries were required to properly defend the area', there was 'no military defence work of any substance between St David's Head and Cardiff' forty years later.[58] Swansea, which pleaded for guns in the American War after losing fourteen vessels to privateers in one week ('almost at our doors') would not receive any until 1803.[59] Even St Ouen's Bay, the 1779 attack on which was the immediate spur to coastal-defence reform, would not receive a battery until 1787, and Leith Fort would not be completed until six years after that.[60]

Among Britain's overseas possessions, the Bahamas remained 'defenceless' in 1782, despite a 1776 raid.[61] At Pensacola, the harbour had no defence-works at all, presumably due to the local dearth of building materials and tools, and thus it 'lay at the mercy of any single privateer'.[62] Jamaica, with an economy comparable in size to that of all thirteen rebel colonies put together, appears to have had no specialist coast artillerymen at any time in its history down to the end of 1779 – partly because yellow fever was known to 'destroy a unit without it suffering any battle casualties whatsoever' within two years,[63] but partly because its Assembly 'would not vote a penny [...] for repair of the fortifications'.[64] On comparatively unimportant Tobago, on the other hand, there *were* gunners, as

> some perfectly useless fortifications had been constructed at great expense, with more guns than there were men to work them [...]. To keep such bodies of men and such numbers of guns in indefensible stations was simply to court attack[.][65]

That attack duly came in May 1781, and the French landing was unopposed.

Similarly, but on a larger scale, the 230 guns and mortars of Minorca, a key British Mediterranean possession since 1713, had only 280 artillerymen to operate them. In practice, the crew of each gun in a garrison usually numbered six men, to allow it to continue to fight if up to 50 per cent casualties were sustained. Thus, the number of specialist gunners on Minorca was 410 short of the bare minimum required to operate all the heavy weapons in their arsenal simultaneously.[66] For the main strong-point there, Fort St Philip, this meant that a 'party of seamen and a contingent from the infantry were required as "additional gunners" to complete the gun detachments'.[67]

Appointed Master-General of the Ordnance in 1784, the third duke of Richmond – a descendant of King Charles II by his mistress Louise de Kérouaille – was an 'abrasive personality', prone to nepotism and widely mistrusted due to his radical anti-colonialist and pro-American views. Nevertheless, he was a talented administrator who prepared Plymouth 'against a regular siege' in 1784, the first year of peace following the American War, and lobbied hard – but unsuccessfully – for the building of 'comprehensive land defences against French attack' in 1785–86.[68]

Meanwhile, in Gibraltar, the British, Hanoverian, and Corsican defenders were chronically hungry and increasingly suffering from scurvy, yet managed to thwart an attack by Spanish fireships on HMS *Enterprise* and HMS *Panther* in the harbour in June. By this point, no supply convoy from England had succeeded in breaching the Spanish blockade of Gibraltar in five and a half months, and a gruelling ten more would pass before the arrival of the next. There were 303 heavy and 149 light guns in the territory, not including mortars and howitzers, but never as many as 500 artillerymen, so again the infantry, marines, and others had to pitch in. As we have seen, such arrangements were widespread, but they were also a cause for concern, insofar as aiming was 'by direct line of sight' and thus 'still relied mainly on the experience of the gunners for accuracy'.[69]

Late 1780 also saw warfare intensify in southern India, and a small British East India Company army thoroughly defeated at the First Battle of Pollilur by rocket-armed troops of the pro-French Hyder Ali, ruler of Mysore – for whom, incidentally, the celebrated American sixteen-gun privateer sloop *Hyder Ally* was named. That October in the Caribbean, seven British warships were dismasted and more than a dozen wrecked or lost without trace in the worst hurricane ever recorded, which did £1 million (£1.9 billion) in damage to private property on Barbados alone.[70] Worse, only one French ship, the thirty-two-gun *Junon*, suffered the same fate. And in December, tensions that had simmered for at least a year between Britain and the neutral Dutch Republic over their rival definitions of contraband war materiel

In this Dutch cartoon, a man in a nightshirt, representing Britain, is attacked by personifications of enemies including the League of Armed Neutrality formed in 1780. Grasped by a Swede and a Dane, Britain has a fool's cap placed on his head by a Frenchman, and manacles on his ankles by a Dutchman, as an American steals his clothing and a Russian prepares to club him.

erupted into armed conflict, adding Holland's fleet to the enemy side of the ledger in what was looking increasingly like a global war in which Britain had no path to victory. As Army historian J. W. Fortescue put it, a limited police action begun in 1775 for the preservation of imperial order had mutated into a 'gigantic struggle [...] for sheer national existence'.[71]

The following year opened with a vivid and lethal lesson in what could and would happen if French troops got ashore. At around ten o'clock in the evening on 5 January, with Jersey's garrison indulging in Twelfth Night celebrations and its naval squadron away attacking the Dutch, 'more than two thousand men [...] composed of the Volunteers of Luxembourg, and of piquets from the regiments in garrison at St Malo and its environs'[72] set out from Granville-sur-Mer for the island's southeastern tip. '[W]ith much difficulty', they reached

> the Violet Bank, which stretches a considerable way into the sea at low water and forms the southern extremity of Grouville Bay [...and] landed, with between seven and eight hundred troops, at a place called Platte Rocher, near La Roque Point, on which there was a small redoubt with two pieces of cannon mounted[.][73]

Led by Gen. the Baron de Rullecourt and an Indian prince named Mir Sayyad, the attackers had two aims: first, to seize the island, which had long been a convenient base for British privateers who struck as far away as the coasts of the Thirteen Colonies; and to divert, to the defence or recapture of Jersey, British resources that might otherwise be used to relieve Gibraltar. Some 600 of the invaders were not able to land at all, presumably due to contrary winds or tides; and another 200 to 400 were reportedly drowned on approach, when four of their boats and one privateer were wrecked on the rocks, despite help from a renegade pilot who had fled the island for France to evade a murder charge.

Since the previous French descent of 1779, Jersey had acquired a web of guard-houses, batteries, and small forts, defended by a half-battalion of Glasgow volunteers who had been brought into the line as the 83rd Foot; a half-battalion of regular army Highlanders; a whole regular battalion from Yorkshire; and 700 of the semi-retired regulars who, though 'Invalids' in the parlance of the time, were generally quite capable in defensive roles. Nevertheless, the regular units' colonels were on Christmas leave on the British mainland, and 'the militia guard of the island were so deficient in vigilance, and so totally neglectful of their duty, that the French effected their landing with the utmost privacy'.[74] Soon, without having fired a shot, between 500 and 900 French had made it overland to the island's capital, St Helier, seized two of its guns, and set up camp in the market square (now Royal Square). They also captured Lt-Gov. Corbet, whom they told to sign a surrender of the whole island, drafted by de Rullecourt, 'on pain of firing the Town, and putting the Inhabitants to the Sword'.[75] Corbet did so; but he had either already sent word to the British troops in Elizabeth Castle to resist to the last, or Capt. Mulcaster, the chief engineer, had formed his own opinion that the invaders could be beaten back.[76] In the event, Mulcaster answered a follow-up demand to surrender the castle with a well-aimed roundshot that killed several Frenchmen; and Maj. Francis Peirson, just 24 years old but the senior officer at St Peter's Barracks, also decided to ignore the surrender order, even if doing so cost him his commission.

As de Rullecourt had hoped, the British counter-attackers approaching through the narrow streets were not able to bring their full firepower to bear on the main French camp in the square. They did, however, manhandle a howitzer into the Grande Rue (now Broad Street) that cut down large numbers of the invaders. The French use of their captured British pieces, on the other hand, was ineffective:

> [W]hen the King's troops had got within forty yards of them, they fired one of them; but so ill did they take aim, that the shot went over the column. They attempted to fire the other gun; but the troops advancing briskly, the French soldiers attending the cannon abandoned them, and fled into the guard house[.][77]

After a fierce battle lasting only fifteen minutes, the market square was retaken for the loss of six British regulars killed and twenty-nine wounded. Maj. Peirson was among the dead, shot through the heart with a musket ball, an incident commemorated in an epic painting by Massachusetts-born British artist John Singleton Copley. Four were also killed, and twenty wounded, among the various units of Jersey Militia there.[78]

The larger of the two land engagements comprising the Battle of Jersey was immortalised in John Singleton Copley's *The Death of Major Peirson, 6 January 1781* (1783). One of the roughly one-third of Americans who had a settled preference for British rule, Copley was in London when the War of Independence broke out and simply never went home again.

Nine members of the East Regiment of Jersey Militia were wounded in a separate action at Platte Rocque, where de Rullecourt had left a substantial rearguard to prevent the loss of his boats. Having seized the guns and guardhouse there, this body of at least a hundred men tried to fire at an approaching force of some 500 led by Capt. William Campbell, but apparently were unable to operate their captured guns. They were then overwhelmed by the grenadier company of the 83rd, who killed twenty-one, for the loss of six killed and eight wounded of their own. The total haul of French prisoners across the two engagements was about 600, including eighty who had been wounded in the market square. The hundred or more French dead included their commander, de Rullecourt. Not for the last time, a combination of luck and pluck had saved a key strategic position – though it would be hard to argue that the sheer number of Jersey's defenders was inadequate to purpose.

Not long after this, the Spanish besiegers of Gibraltar launched a swarm of small, flat-bottomed galleys in the town of Algeciras, each armed with a single immense 36-pounder cannon. These curious vessels fanned out to demolish storehouses and workshops in Gibraltar's dockyard, damage British ships at anchor, and deliver enfilade fire into the main, northward-facing British defensive lines from the west.[79] And, over a period of six weeks in the spring, by dint of firing more than 75,000 rounds into it from boats and shore batteries, the besiegers 'almost entirely destroyed the town of Gibraltar'.[80] Thankfully, due to the tremendous strength of the defences, both natural and artificial, the enemy managed to kill only twenty-three British gunners. Nevertheless,

> the ruin of the houses brought about the most serious danger [...] for the fall of the buildings revealed large stores of wine and provisions which had been accumulated by the merchants. The hungry troops at once fell upon the booty, and for seven days they gave themselves up to an orgie among the wine-casks, and became absolutely unmanageable. By merciless use of the lash and of the gallows [Gov. George] Eliott restored discipline and order; and the garrison returned to patient endurance of the bombardment.[81]

This was far from being an isolated episode. Any eighteenth-century military unit might, even under heavy fire, dissolve into a mob of drunken looters; and this was something all good commanders had to prepare for as best they could. Even ideologically motivated insurgents, like the Americans in the midst of the Battle of Eutaw Springs in 1781, would on occasion drop whatever they were doing if an opportunity to get drunk presented itself.

The Sortie Made by the Garrison of Gibraltar in the Morning of 27 November 1781, a 1789 oil painting by John Trumbull. The night attack in question undid fourteen months' worth of Spanish siege works and inflicted £2 million in damage, or about £3.3 billion in modern terms. The Roxburghshire-born British governor, Gen. George Eliott – depicted at centre right in a gold-laced hat – was educated in Holland and France and served briefly in the Prussian army before earning a British Engineers commission in 1739. Two decades later, he was 'appointed to command a brigade of cavalry intended for amphibious operations against the French coast'.[82] Eliott's aide-de-camp, the artist and inventor George Koehler, stands immediately to his right.

By the end of January 1782, having been under siege for five months by more than 10,000 French and Spanish troops with 200 cannon of their own, British-held Fort St Philip, Minorca, was 'in ruins, a great number of the guns destroyed or dismounted, and the garrison reduced by the enemy's fire, disease, and starvation to a mere remnant'.[83] And soon after Minorca finally fell on 4 February, nearly the whole enemy force that had taken it was added to the strength of the besiegers of the Rock of Gibraltar, who then consisted of 4,000 French as well as around 21,000 Spanish, as against fewer than 6,000 defenders.

These allies soon agreed that a radical, integrated plan for finally overwhelming Gov. Eliott's forces was called for. Their new commander, the Duc de Crillon, conqueror of Minorca, provided it.

> The main attack [...] was to be an amphibious operation launched against the waterfront between the Old Mole and Europa Point, the southernmost point of Gibraltar. A corps of about 3,300 men under General Cagigal, a Spaniard, was to be embarked at Algeciras in small boats covered by large planks on hinges which on unfolding would form ramps for disembarkation. This landing was to be prepared and covered by the fire of the combined fleet [of fifty sail of the line] under Admiral de Cordova and [...] floating batteries designed by the French engineer [Gen. Jean le Micheaud] d'Arcon.[84]

Ten in number, the floating batteries were constructed from warships of between 600 and 1,400 tons, i.e. in British parlance, fourth-rate ships of the line and frigates, with protective roofs of wet hides and two of their three masts removed. Beneath each roof was a supply of water 'from which numerous pipes, like the veins of the human body, circulated through the sides of the ship, giving a constant supply of water to every part, and keeping the wood continually saturated'.[85] On the broadside that would face the enemy, each vessel had between six and twenty-one 'heavy brass cannon of new manufacture'[86] and a three-foot-thick layer of extra wooden armour, filled with wet sand and backed by a layer of waterlogged cork. The floating batteries' bombardment would be supplemented by that of ninety 'gun and mortar-boats and bomb-ketches'.[87] The detailed orders given to the grenadiers, chasseurs, and dragoons of the first landing wave, and the Catalonian volunteers of the second, seem to bespeak de Crillon's confidence on the eve of battle – though other senior officers mocked him for supposing that Gibraltar might hold out for as much as two weeks after the floating batteries were brought to bear.[88]

Patiently, and with equal confidence, Eliott prepared his hungry troops, by now outnumbered 6:1, for the final showdown. Though he had not arrived as governor until 1777, he was aware of a series of gunnery experiments carried out in the territory in 1771. These established that, even after cooling in the air for four minutes and then being plunged into cold water three times, a 24-pound cannonball that had been red-hot when fired could set a woodpile aflame in seven minutes – and then reignite it less than an hour after the initial fire was put out. A 32-pound ball, meanwhile, was found to be still too hot to handle after twenty-one hours. Accidents to those firing such projectiles were prevented either by wetting the normal wadding, or using turf in its place, though ramming and loading remained 'a lively business – to say the least'.[89] Eliott therefore saw to it that his main batteries were equipped with braziers and fuel so that they could use this technique against an amphibious assault whenever it might arrive. However, having observed a significant quantity of combustible building material in the Spanish lines to their north, the British officers elected to try out red-hot rounds for counter-battery fire during the enemy landward guns' six-day softening-up operation. '[T]he effect exceeded their most hopeful expectations', with two Spanish batteries being silenced temporarily, and one permanently.[90]

On the great day itself, 13 September 1782, watched by 'countless thousands of spectators [...] from all parts of Spain',[91] the enemy's shore batteries, fleet, and floating batteries all commenced firing, causing immense damage and death on the Old Mole and at the King's, Orange, and South bastions. Six Royal Artillery officers including the most senior then surviving, Maj. Lewis, were hit. Yet, all but ignoring both the enemy's conventional warships to the west and their vast numbers of troops (with between 170 and 200 guns) to the north, the British forces concentrated all their fire on the floating batteries, 'with the deliberate coolness and precision of school practice', as Eliott put it afterwards.[92] Four exhausting hours would pass, during which 'the whole heaven was obscured by the curling

A key coastal-defence innovation of the 1780s was the Koehler garrison carriage, which allowed the depression of guns' barrels to 70 degrees, enabling them to engage ships close inshore from a height. It was named for Woolwich-born Lt George Koehler RA, who invented it at Gibraltar at the height of the Great Siege. Credit for the life-saving idea of tunnelling into the Rock during the siege belongs to Sgt-Maj. Henry Ince of the Soldier Artificers (as Gibraltar's non-commissioned Engineers were called at that date). Even assisted by blasting, making one 4 feet wide by 6 feet high took seven man-weeks per yard.

clouds of smoke [...] fitfully illumined by the flashes'.[93] But at long last, beginning with d'Arcon's own ship, the twenty-one-gun *Talla Piedra*, and Adm. Moreno's flagship, the twenty-one-gun *Pastora*, the floating batteries 'were ruthlessly and systematically destroyed' by Eliott's 'tremendous counter-bombardment'.[94] If, as various sources have suggested, only ninety-six of the fortress's guns were able to engage the enemy vessels, and they fired 40,000 rounds, mostly by four in the morning on 14 September, they were undoubtedly operating at the limits of metallurgical and human endurance: firing nearly one-and-a-half times faster than the British guns at Waterloo,[95] an engagement which – at nine and a half hours – was also less than half as long. Regardless of the number of artillery pieces actually involved, the action accounted for a significant proportion of all the ammunition fired by the defenders during the siege as a whole.

By the time it finally ended, on 7 February 1783, the Great Siege of Gibraltar rated, in terms of numbers of troops engaged, by far the largest action of the American War of Independence, not to mention one of the longest sieges in the history of the world. The British and their allies had lost just over a thousand men dead or permanently disabled by enemy action or disease – less than half the number of French and Spanish killed or taken prisoner on the night of 13–14 September 1782 alone.[96] For defenders and attackers alike, it had been a veritable university of coastal defence.[97]

Lt Koehler's own picture of the King's Bastion during the siege. His Fortifications exam at Woolwich in 1779 was remembered for 'the completest series of drawings ever produced at the Academy'.[98] Having served as artillery commander and, latterly, overall military chief of an ill-fated Belgian revolt against Austria in 1790, he would die of plague, aged 42, while serving as an advisor to the Ottoman army in the Holy Land.

Contemporary British caricature of the Franco-Spanish general Louis des Balbes de Berton de Crillon, 1st Duke of Mahón and 2nd Duke of Crillon (1717–96), who in 1781–82 deprived the British of Minorca, their key Mediterranean privateering base, but subsequently failed to eject them from Gibraltar. The cartoon is noteworthy for its depiction of the red-hot cannonballs, with their trails of smoke, that the British defenders used to burn and sink his 'incombustible' and 'insubmergible' floating batteries.

The explosion of a floating battery from the perspective of the Spanish siege lines.

A highly atmospheric engraving by Archibald Robertson of confused small-boat combat around the enemy's doomed floating batteries, after a painting by William Hamilton.

Various lessons could be gleaned from French descents in force on British possessions in the 1770s and 1780s. One especially noteworthy episode took place in December 1778 on St Lucia in the West Indies, which ten British infantry battalions and a smattering of gunners barely had time to occupy before they were counterattacked by a French fleet of twelve ships of the line, carrying 7,000 troops.[99] In the initial phase, the newly British-manned fortress guns in the island's capital, Port Castries, supplemented by fire from Royal Navy ships in the harbour below, were able to drive the French off. But the enemy only went as far as Vigie, immediately to the north of the harbour, before disembarking 'the main body of their infantry' and several field guns, and moving against Castries again, via a subsidiary position with six light guns manned by the British 5th Foot and fourteen flank companies detached from other battalions. Most of these defenders were veterans of the battles of Brooklyn Heights, Fort Washington, and Brandywine, and 'probably without any exception the finest troops in the world'.[100] As the French attack went in,

> [t]hen was seen the potency of the tactics learned in America. Advancing in skirmishing order and keeping themselves always under cover, the light companies maintained at close range a most destructive fire upon the heavy French columns. If the enemy attempted to extend, they threatened a charge with the bayonet; when the French closed up, they were already extended and pouring in a galling fusillade; when the French advanced with solidity and

determination they fell back and disappeared, but only to renew their fire, themselves invisible, from every direction.[101]

The French in Vigie outnumbered the British by nearly 10:1, and unlike the defenders were supported by naval gunfire. Nevertheless, they were fought to a standstill, losing 1,600 killed and 'grievously' wounded – a number larger by several hundred than the entire British force that opposed them. At last they withdrew in disorder, unaware that the British side's musket ammunition had just run out.[102]

As well as the tenacious defensive fighting power of British regular infantry and artillery, even when in unfamiliar, barely prepared positions, the St Lucia episode reflected the symbiosis of fleets and naval bases. That is, without the support of the British ships, Port Castries would likely have fallen to the first, direct assault, or been easily starved out; but had the port not been strongly held by friendly troops, the Royal Navy would have had little rationale for being there. Something of a truism at the operational level, this also held in the sphere of grand strategy. As K. W. Maurice-Jones explained, the

> startling series of losses of [British-held] coast fortresses and forts, both in the West Indies and Western Florida, during the period 1778–82 shows that, though a defended naval base – or protected harbour – may provide a safe refuge for a fleet in which to carry out repairs and take in munitions and supplies, should that fleet lose superiority in the surrounding waters for any appreciable time, the safety of that base is seriously endangered. An enemy fleet in command of the sea may transport at leisure an expeditionary force, which once landed, can set about reducing the base without fear of interruption, and the defending power, being inferior at sea, can do nothing to save it.[103]

Slightly different lessons could be gleaned from Maj.-Gen. Sir Robert Pigot, Bt's equally spirited, but much better planned, defence of Aquidneck Island in the colony of Rhode Island against French and American forces in July and August of the same year. John Innes's company of the Royal Artillery particularly distinguished itself in this action, losing thirty-five killed and wounded; and the defence was further assisted by the superb eye for ground and meticulous map-making skills of the chief engineer, Abraham D'Aubant, about whom we will hear more later.[104] Pigot's measures included driving all livestock from the island within his defensive lines (described by the French commander as 'well entrenched'); cutting down orchards; and destroying wheeled vehicles. This approach, sometimes referred to as 'driving the country', had been commanded in England by a 'scaremongering proclamation' when a French invasion was expected in 1756,[105] and would again controversially be advocated as a primary method of defence on England's south coast, as we shall see.[106] The Battle of Rhode Island also showed that shore batteries and field-artillery units working together – in this case, American ones located at Bristol Neck and Turkey Hill, respectively – were, if competently manned, more than capable of putting frigates, troop transports and galleys to flight.

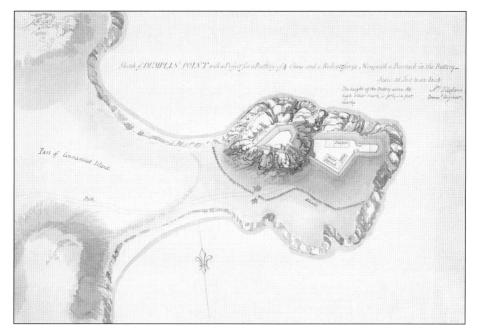

Plan by Abraham D'Aubant for a four-gun, ninety-man fort on a headland of Conanicut Island, part of the defences of the colony of Rhode Island against the French and rebels. D'Aubant noted that its battery was 'forty six feet, nearly' above the high-water mark.

THE ROLE OF FORTS IN COASTAL DEFENCE TO 1783

The early modern period represented a new era in the design and use of shore forts, amid a wider escalation in the importance, sophistication, and cost of fortifications more generally: a phenomenon often described as amounting to a 'military revolution'.[1] The key new departure was the *trace italienne*, a type of fortress consisting primarily of rammed earth, in geometric patterns and specific angles designed to ensure that

With the notable exception of sixteenth-century Berwick, then a border fortress, the few English applications of the *trace italienne* tended to be small, and aimed at preventing coastal strong-points being surprised from the rear. This aerial view of Tilbury Fort on the north bank of the Thames clearly shows its slanting, low, earth-packed walls, which were intended to absorb rather than withstand bombardment, and angled to allow its various parts to give covering fire to one another if attacked from the landward side. Like Southsea Castle on Portsea Island in Hampshire, Tilbury had been a Tudor 'Device Fort', but was rebuilt as a *trace* in the 1670s.

Angled bastions, a nod toward the true *trace*, were often added to small square forts in British possessions overseas, which would thereafter be referred to as 'star forts'. This 1:330 scale pen-and-ink and watercolour plan of a fairly typical example, Fort George on the southwestern tip of Manhattan Island, dates from some point between 1771 and 1777.

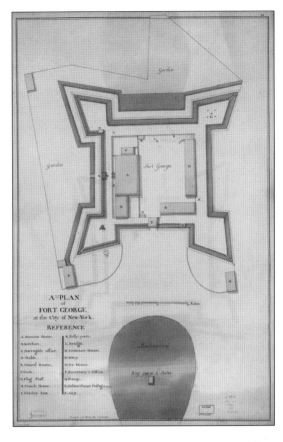

A PLAN of FORT GEORGE at the City of New-York.
REFERENCE

most projectiles would either bounce clear or bury themselves harmlessly in its substance. Inevitably, such structures' footprints were many multiples of the size of the relatively narrow and vertical stone artillery forts that had preceded them. Moreover, 'measured by its impact on society' through increased taxation in both money and labour, and the rising power of the state relative to the individual, the *trace italienne* would constitute 'the most important piece of military technology in modern European history'.[2] Neuf-Brisach alone, upon its completion in 1705, had required around 10,000 man-years of work. Such fortified positions 'anchored political power, contained supplies, [and] controlled communication routes', and how many one gained or lost was a key indicator of strategic success or failure.[3]

They were also scarcely seen in Britain, a fact that by itself could do much to explain that country's status as the 'Land of the Free' relative to its Bourbon and Habsburg rivals.[4] The key exception proving this rule was the fortification of Berwick-upon-Tweed, begun by Sir Richard Lee and Capt. William Pelham around 1555,[5] which eventually became one of the most expensive single projects of the Tudor age – the northern border of England having been, in effect, a land border with France since medieval times, and a rather hotly contested one since 1544.[6]

The apotheosis of these super-dreadnoughts of the land would occur in the Low Countries during the siege-mad wars of Louis XIV, who died in 1715, but they would remain militarily significant for generations afterwards. Their vanishing rarity in Britain and Ireland on a per-square-mile basis, however, reflects the lack of seriousness with which, prior to the period covered by this book, our islands' rulers and armies took the possibility of having to fight massive engagements on home soil – despite serious threats of invasion having been made in 1708, 1722, 1744, 1756, 1759, and 1762, and sizeable numbers of foreign troops having actually been landed in 1688, 1719, and 1745, and 1760.

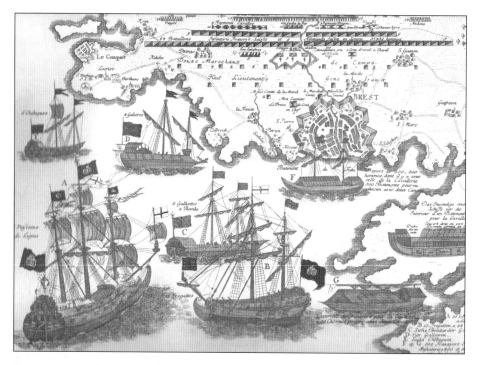

Contemporary illustration of diverse types of invasion craft assembled at Brest in 1759, also showing the mighty *trace italienne* landward defences of the naval base. The Royal Naval Dockyard at Plymouth was founded at the outset of the French Wars in 1690 because its main predecessor, Portsmouth, 'was too far east to service a fleet blockading the main French base at Brest'.[7]

Though 'the firepower of many individual ships of the line [...] surpassed that of entire armies',[8] bringing such power to bear on specific onshore targets was another story entirely. Writing in the early 1770s, a time of peace when French spying was nevertheless known to be rife, British naval officer John Ardesoif noted that

> [t]here is a considerable advantage in fortifying on high rocks, or eminences of any kind, near the entrance of an harbour or place of anchorage, as men of war cannot bring their guns to any degree of elevation to hurt such works but on the contrary, the ships['] decks are totally exposed to them[.][9]

This deceptively simple problem had important strategic implications. As historian Jeremy Black has pointed out, the eighteenth century was often marked by a 'mismatch between governmental decisions to [...] build up naval strength' and the actual bringing to bear of naval power on an enemy.[10]

Where high cliffs or hills were not available, Ardesoif recommended that shore batteries for the defence of naval facilities be 'as low and near the surface of the earth as the ground could permit', with walkways 'two feet lower than the level of

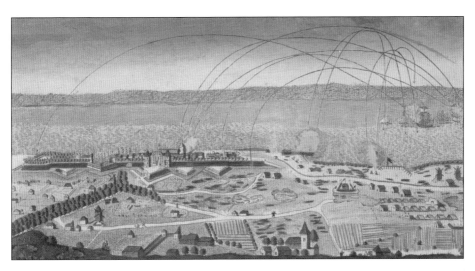

Hand-coloured magic-lantern slide of Rear-Adm. George Rodney's bombardment of the French invasion barges at Le Havre, 3–5 July 1759. As well as many of the invasion craft, Rodney's bomb-vessels destroyed nearly a hundred houses, inflicting an estimated £400,000 in damage or about £900 million at today's prices.

the ground'; and if they included a set of inner works from which flat-trajectory gunfire would be directed out over the outer works, the former should be no more than six feet taller than the latter, 'as forts liable to be attacked by shipping cannot be too snug'. In that passage, Ardesoif was, in effect, advocating a shore-to-ship version of the American ship-to-ship tactics that would later be used at the Battle of Flamborough Head: whereby the weaker party could achieve victory simply by being so close to sea level that its opponent's guns could not be 'dipped' enough to fire back (p. 18). Low-lying fortifications of this type, Ardesoif said, should also ideally have 'regular slope from [...] two feet above the platform' to the sea or harbour, which should be not less than eighty fathoms (i.e. slightly under 500 feet) away, on the grounds that this would 'admit of great shelter to the men'. However, in certain circumstances – such as when their purpose was to prevent river-crossings by large groups of small enemy boats – batteries needed to be 'within the distance of a pistol shot from the water side', probably meaning about twenty yards. He considered howitzers to be especially useful weapons against landing boats.[11]

Earthworks were to be 18 feet thick in a 'clay or binding soil' or 22 feet thick in 'a light and sandy one', and 'well rammed'. However, even if such advice were followed, 'no single battery whatever [...] can stand the fire of two or three line of battle ships, where they can be brought within point blank shot', unless of course it is 'situated too high for the ships['] guns['] greatest elevation'.[12] It is important to note here, however, that Ardesoif's reference to 'two or three' ships reflected the received wisdom that a single shore battery of four to six guns, if suitably constructed and manned, *was* a match for *one* ship of the line. As Ardesoif lamented,

Major John James attacking Capt. Ardesoif.

Rebel officer John James tries to kill Capt. John Ardesoif RN with a chair, Williamsburg, South Carolina, July 1780.

> every sea-officer must be as good a judge as myself that the present mode of working guns cannot produce any great degree of certainty in their direction toward the object [… due to] the complicated motion of the ship, which alters her position so suddenly, that a gun well pointed in one instant may be several degrees wide of the object the next[.][13]

The recommended lateral space between a gun and its immediate neighbour in a shore battery was 18–20 feet, and the embrasures through which they fired were to be 2 feet wide at the muzzle of the weapon, spreading to 9 feet at the opposite, enemy-facing side of the structure. Allowing for tapering-off of the earthwork at each end of the battery, this meant that a six-gun variant would be the length of 20 toises: a builders' term referring to a cube of solid matter 6 feet long on a side. Ideally, any battery would also be given the extra protection of a ditch, beginning 3–4 feet from its face, 6 feet deep and 10 broad, out of which the earth for building it would mostly have come. If warships were within a harbour and in a fit state to help with its defence, they should be drawn up stem to stern in a concave line that allowed them to focus as much as possible of their firepower on the harbour entrance. The ships forming such a crescent should also have gaps between them of 101 yards,[14] so that an attacker using fireships 'may be obliged to burn each ship singly'.[15] Ardesoif also advised naval officers tasked with protecting anchorages to prepare their own defensive fireships.[16]

His book also addressed head-on the problem the French sailors would later experience during the fight against Sir James Wallace in Cancale Bay (p. 15): that once enemy ships are close enough to one's own to grapple and board them, shore batteries are 'rendered useless' due to the danger of friendly fire. The best way to mitigate such a problem was for boats to 'attend along-side to take your people out [… and] for both officers and men to make for the next ship, or the shore'.[17] This was, in fact, what the French crews at Cancale did, although they seemingly failed to communicate this fact to the gunners ashore; and while mocked for their cowardice by some modern observers, their behaviour was a standard response to the situation they found themselves in. That is, if a ship cannot possibly be saved from capture, even by being intentionally sunk by friendly shore batteries, it is far better that it be lost empty than lost with a trained crew on board.

Ardesoif's defensive system included ground plans that were intended to improve upon those of the leading *trace italienne* architects of a century earlier, specifically in harbourside contexts. One of his recommendations 'contrary to all former rules' was that some batteries be constructed 'rather below the surface, sloping the earth inwards'. This, he said, would allow the defenders 'to point the guns at the masts, yards, and rigging of the shipping in their approach, which may prove […] the most effectual method of disabling them from pursuing the plan laid down for their attack'.[18] Such variations aside, however, it remained – like most other such complex formal systems – heavily based on detailed and accurate angular measurement.

In practice, crude improvised defences could be highly effective. In August 1777 in Machias, Massachusetts,[19] three dozen local militia manning rough earthen breastworks mounted with small guns borrowed from the local privateering fraternity succeeded in driving off a force of more than a hundred British marines,[20] who were subsequently only able to land under cover of dense fog. Eventually, the British prevailed, destroying stores that had been destined for a rebel invasion of Nova Scotia. Nine days later, 400 miles to the southwest in Setauket, New York, some 250 loyalists occupying breastworks, 6 feet high and perhaps a hundred in diameter, that they had thrown up round a local church were attacked by twice their number of rebels. Again, the only artillery available to the defenders was a handful of small anti-personnel swivel-guns of the type normally mounted on boats; but they prevailed, and Setauket was never attacked in such strength again.

Properly prepared fortifications, meanwhile, could be nigh impossible to break into. It would not have escaped the attention of subsequent generations of British defence planners that the rebel-occupied fort on Mud Island in the Delaware River at Philadelphia held out for fifty-one days in the autumn of 1777 against a combined attack by the Royal Navy and shore-based heavy artillery. The latter was commanded by no less a personage than Gibraltar-born Capt. John Montresor, chief engineer of the British forces in North America, who in 1771 had designed the very fort he was now attacking. Cheaply but ruggedly built, mostly of earth and wood, it is thought to have mounted twenty-six cannon, mostly 18-pounders with some smaller pieces and one larger, and it was never defended by more than 500 troops at any point in the siege. Due to damage inflicted by Mud Island's gunners, the eighteen-gun sloop HMS *Merlin* was scuttled by its own crew, and the sixty-four-gun ship of the line HMS *Augusta* exploded spectacularly, with a report that was heard thirty miles away and broke windows across the city. During October, Montresor's two 32-pounders, six 24-pounders, an 18-pounder, two howitzers and three mortars proved unable to batter his fort down from a range of just 500 yards. Even when the besiegers' complement of 32-pounders was increased to six, and of 24-pounders to twelve, the fort was not wrecked sufficiently for an infantry assault until Montresor received close support from the specialist shore-bombardment vessel HMS *Vigilant*, supplemented by broadsides from five warships farther out.

Just as spectacularly, Gen. Francis McLean's 600 or 700 troops occupying Britain's small, freshly built Fort George on the central Maine coast's Majabigwaduce Peninsula held out against overwhelming odds for three weeks in 1779, before the Royal Navy arrived and destroyed nearly all of the forty-three vessels of the Massachusetts invasion fleet. Ranking as the worst American naval disaster until Pearl Harbor, it was an ignominious end to 'the largest amphibious expedition of the American Revolution', and 'virtually marked the end of the Continental Navy'.[21] It was also the first action seen by the visionary future general John Moore, who served under McLean as a 17-year-old junior officer of the 82nd Foot, which had been raised in Lanarkshire just two years earlier.

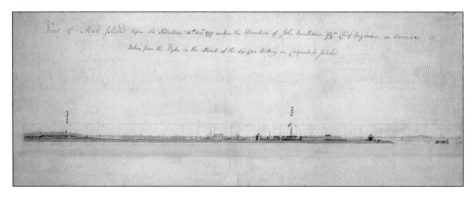

Mud Island Fort, Philadelphia, held out for fifty-one days in 1777 against forces led by the man who had designed it six years earlier.

Fort George, on the heights above present-day Castine, Maine, measured just 200 feet on a side, but held out against incredible odds for three weeks in 1779. Strategically important both as a source of masting timber for the Royal Navy and as a refuge for loyalists, it would be the last place in the Thirteen Colonies to be evacuated, in 1784. Thereafter, 'Britain was dependent upon supplies of hardwoods, mast timber and hemp from the Baltic region', with great masts from Russia accounting for 83 per cent of all such imports in 1796.[22]

In July 1779, Cdre Sir George Collier, an accomplished playwright[23] and hero of the Machias expedition as well as a 2,000-man raid on Hampton Roads that destroyed more than a hundred American ships at anchor or building, mounted another amphibious expedition of impressive size. This time, 2,600 British, Hessian and American loyalist troops, including my ancestor Darling Whelpley, targeted the shore of Connecticut. The rebel towns there, in spite of or because of their status as leading centres of both rebel army recruitment and anti-British privateering, were virtually undefended at the time. Having captured the three-year-old, poorly supplied Black Rock Fort by New Haven and taking its nineteen defenders prisoner, the raiders moved on to Fairfield, and, in what was widely regarded as a war crime even in those unscrupulous and violent days, destroyed nearly the whole town: including two churches, a school, and eighty-three private residences, as well as all targets of even tangential military or mercantile significance.[24] Three days later, again ineffectually opposed by a handful of local militia, they repeated this performance at Norwalk. British casualties for the whole expedition, including thirty-two men reported missing, were less than 6 per cent. But in one of the war's last engagements in the northern colonies, on 6 September 1781, the attackers did not get off so lightly. At Fort Griswold, above Groton, Connecticut – another notorious privateer base – 800 British, Hessian and loyalist troops with two light artillery pieces overwhelmed the 165 American defenders, but only at the cost of 24 per cent casualties,[25] a loss 'disproportionate to the object attained' both tactically and strategically.[26]

In practice, where defenders were present within small fortifications, be it in Whitehaven or Jersey or Dominica or Long Island,[27] it was the element of surprise, and not the forts' structure or armament, that was generally the key determinant of casualties among the attackers. It should also be noted that a large bribe was offered to the British commander of Minorca for its surrender in the summer

Nassau in the Bahamas was, in theory, defended by sixty-three guns, but had only around a hundred relatively unmotivated militiamen to man them. Unsurprisingly, British artillery played little part in the defence of the island in March 1776, when it was seized and held for more than a week by US marines desperately hunting for gunpowder.

Dating from the 1820s, these 24-pounder cannon can be seen at Fort Phoenix in Fairhaven, Massachusetts, a privateering base during the American War of 1775–83 and scene of that conflict's first naval battle. The as-yet unnamed fort's original armament was destroyed by British troops in September 1778, after its defenders had fired ineffectually at the British troopships and fled.

of 1781, but 'indignantly rejected'; while the French, by the same method, actually secured St Eustatius in November of the same year, and Cuddalore in India the following spring.[28]

Amid a general lack of will and resources to fortify British and Irish coastal towns in the manner of Continental cities, the idea of a new chain of simple, inexpensive round towers as a primary coastal-defence technique – generally assumed to have arrived with the Martellos of the following century – was not merely proposed, but executed in 1778–79 on Guernsey and Jersey. Gen. Henry Seymour Conway, Governor of Jersey from 1772, is rightly or wrongly credited with having conceived these early defensive towers. An occasional cross-dresser and rumoured lover of his cousin Horace Walpole, Conway had famously captured the Castle of Waldeck in 1762 by the ruse of 'marching up with scaling ladders' despite being out of ammunition.

At no point in modern times, however, had England relied wholly on the 'wooden walls' of her navy for coastal defence. Whereas medieval castles had acted primarily as residences, the forts constructed beginning in the fifteenth century 'were purely military [...] designed to mount artillery to sink or drive off enemy warships and invaders'; and the new parts of Dartmouth Castle added between

One of the twenty-three 'Conway towers' built for the coastal defence of Jersey in the last two decades of the eighteenth century. Four had been completed by the time of the French landing of January 1781, but were not near the scene of the action. They would have 12-pounder carronades added to their roofs in the Napoleonic period.

The purpose-built fifteenth-century artillery fort attached to Dartmouth Castle, Devon, painted by Paul Sandby in 1794.

Ground-floor embrasure on the landward side of Sandgate Castle, Kent. Dating from the reign of Henry VIII, Sandgate would be remodelled on the lines of a Martello tower more than two and a half centuries later.

1486 and 1495 were 'purpose-built for "ship-killing" guns',[29] of which there seem to have been sixteen by the latter year.[30]

Unlike in many aspects of warfare and technology generally, early Tudor England was not behindhand in this. Gun-loops 'coeval with the walls' did not appear anywhere until the last quarter of the fifteenth century, and then were always on the ground-floor level, because the cannon of the age 'could not be [...] dipped so as to attack those below'.[31] This first installation of cannon in castles was rapidly followed, in the first half of the following century, by the 'complete disseverance between domestic and military structures', and a corresponding separation of the military-leadership caste from the landed aristocracy: key markers of modernity.[32]

The cause of this rapid change is not difficult to deduce. The 1470–1521 rebuilding of the Fortress of Rhodes in the eastern Mediterranean had been among the first projects to make comprehensive use of gunpowder artillery for coastal defence; and the consistently successful use of shore-based guns against ships during the defence of Rhodes against the Ottomans in May-August 1480 was an international news event of the first rank of importance, undoubtedly playing a role in the decline

A giant granite-ball-firing mortar used by the Christian defenders of Rhodes, late fifteenth century. Into the period covered by this book, a few stone-firing mortars continued in British and Ottoman service on land, and lead-firing swivel guns were used by the Royal Navy.

of the knightly prejudice against firearms. In England by that time, solid metal shot had largely replaced the stone and iron-hooped stone projectiles that had predominated a century earlier, and which often broke up harmlessly when used against stone targets. It was not yet clear, however, that iron made better shot than lead, bronze, or even lead-dipped stone.

In England, Dartmouth Castle notwithstanding, '"artillery forts" really came into their own under King Henry VIII', whose string of 'Device Forts' built between 1539 and 1547 represented 'the first co-ordinated scheme of national defence since Roman times'.[33] At least forty-three in number[34] and costing £376,000, or around £92 billion at today's prices if reckoned as a proportion of national economic output (but, in fact, funded largely out of monastic confiscations), they were a mixed bag of true castles, blockhouses, and earthworks, covering the south coast from Falmouth to Kent, as well as other parts of the country including Hull, Tilbury, and Milford Haven. Only Hampshire and Sussex were actually attacked by the French at the time, in revenge for Henry's successful capture of Boulogne, and in each case, longbow-armed militia were able to repel the invaders in field engagements.[35] An English officer at Boulogne explained to a French counterpart two years later that, though England's fortifications had never been stronger, 'it is not England's profession to trust in lime and stone' to repel invaders, but rather in infantry battles 'without end' in the fields and woods.[36] With this in mind, it is perhaps less surprising that many Device Forts, including those at Brightlingsea in Essex and East Cowes on the Isle of Wight, were decommissioned almost immediately, and have since vanished without trace. At the other extreme, however, Calshot Castle at the entrance to Southampton Water remained in active military use into the 1960s.

In the early Stuart era, the art of fortification 'stagnated' and only in Portsmouth, the Isle of Wight, Chatham, Harwich, and Hull did the defences actually improve.[37] Pirates based in Morocco routinely raided the relatively defenceless West Country, taking hundreds of prisoners away to uncertain fates.[38] In 1633,

> the Lord Chief Justice himself had to go to Ireland 'by Scotland' rather than Bristol due to rumours of pirate activity, and Captain Thomas James of the Ninth Whelp – one of just two warships then dedicated to patrolling the Irish coasts – felt the need to report 'no Turks' at Kinsale in May and September of the same year.[39]

The Puritan regime of the 1650s would build just two round artillery towers, Mount Batten at Plymouth and 'Cromwell's Castle' at New Grimsby in the Scilly Isles, both mounting multiple small pieces fired through embrasures.[40] And Charles II's reign was marked by 'great activity in defending the coast', but mostly via the repair and improvement of existing structures rather than the creation of new ones.[41] In short, nothing so systematic as the Device Forts would follow until the Martello programme of the 1800s; and it is therefore not especially surprising that the above-mentioned Ordnance Inspectors' reports of 1779 featured Henrician-era fortifications so prominently. Two-fifths of the original Device Forts seem to have been in active use at the time.

The fifteenth-century Siege of Rhodes, with an early artillery tower in the foreground.

Above and opposite: Deal Castle, Kent (top left), Calshot Castle, Hampshire (bottom left), and Sandgate Castle, Kent (right) were all built in 1539–40. With other 'Device Forts' from the reign of Henry VIII, they were deemed militarily significant even long after the period covered by this book. Sandgate successfully repelled Dutch raiders in September 1652, and Calshot mounted nine modern 18-pounder guns and four smaller pieces as of 1779.

It is also worth noting that the only Dutch overseas possession to be attacked by the British, but not taken, during the Anglo-Dutch War of 1780–84 was the slave-trading post of Elmina in what is now Ghana.[42] Its two forts, St George and Coenraadsburg, dated from the late fifteenth and mid seventeenth centuries, respectively. It would therefore be unwise to dismiss the incorporation of similarly aged structures into British defence plans as foredoomed to failure. On the other hand, it may have been the mutual fire support provided by the two forts at Elmina that proved insurmountable to the attackers, who dealt in short order with three isolated forts of the same general age as Coenraadsburg, as well as two

Incorruptible and therefore chronically in debt, William Pitt the Younger (prime minister 1783–1801 and 1804–06) utilised his *ex officio* right as Lord Warden of the Cinque Ports to live in the Device Fort at Walmer, a fact gently mocked in this 1803 cartoon by P. Roberts.

significantly newer ones: Fort Lijdzaamheid at Apam, and Fort de Goede Hoop in Awutu Senya. All five of the Dutch Gold Coast forts that fell mounted between eighteen and thirty-two cannon.

Lastly, mention should be made of the wooden blockhouse and stockade on the New Jersey side of the Hudson River at Bull's Ferry. Not strictly speaking in a coastal position, it may, nevertheless, have played a role in King George's thinking about coastal defence in future wars. On the night of 20–21 July 1780, it was attacked from the landward side by Pennsylvania regulars, 1,800 strong, with six 6-pounder field guns and a howitzer. But the post's garrison, comprising just seventy members of Capt. Thomas Ward's Loyal Refugee Volunteers – perhaps with some members of the Black Pioneers[43] – prevailed, and even took several prisoners, despite enduring a ninety-minute cannonade from 160 yards that pierced their walls in fifty or more places, causing 30 per cent casualties and the loss of their own two guns, followed by a two-battalion assault.[44] The action, described by Fortescue as '[t]he most gallant feat of the whole war', prompted the sovereign's 'special thanks'.[45] At the level of force sizes and capabilities, though not architecture, a key part of the Martello idea had been born.

On 20 February 1782, the medieval and seventeenth-century forts at Elmina on the Dutch Gold Coast withstood an attack by 500 British soldiers, despite the support of broadsides from the fifty-gun HMS *Leander*.

Underappreciated ancestors of the Martello tower were the 1770–71 'Gun Towers' of Fort Niagara, which was occupied by white, black and Mohawk loyalist forces throughout the American War of Independence. Snow-roofs of similar design to the one shown here were added to the Canadian Martellos of the 1790s, which (with those of South Africa) were among the first to appear on British territory.

3

'MAKING PROVISION [...] AGAINST A FUTURE WAR',[1] 1784–93

In the 'prosperous and optimistic' mid-1780s, Britain had an energetic and diligent king, not yet aged 50; a very young and able prime minister; and a new – and, as yet, unique – Industrial Revolution, driven in surprisingly large measure by the Royal Navy's need to remain ready for war at all times.[2] Not yet a democracy, but less undemocratic than most of its European rivals, its status as a major power was nearly brand new and still open to challenge, being derived almost solely from the miraculous outcome of the so-called Seven Years War of 1754–63.

Students of British military history will be well acquainted with the cycle of strategic victory followed by complacency, budgetary cutbacks, doctrinal ossification, and an inevitable string of early defeats in the next war against a re-energised version of the same foe. But this cycle was broken in the 1780s, not least because the war of 1775–83 against rebel elements in the Thirteen Colonies, and latterly France, Spain, and Holland, had ended in catastrophe. This time, the defeated yet reinvigorated nation leaping up Hydra-like into the next global conflict would be Britain herself.

Instead of being 'slashed, as was usual after an eighteenth-century war', the Royal Navy's annual budget was increased from £7 million in 1783, to around £9.5 million the following year, and nearly £12 million in 1785.[3] As historian Paul Webb has noted, '[i]n a peacetime ministry devoted to economy it is remarkable, indeed almost unprecedented [...] that the navy received virtually all the money it needed'.[4] In 1784, the first full year of peace, the combined budget for all three services – Navy, Army, and Ordnance – was £13.8 million, nearly treble the equivalent figure for the first year after the Seven Years War, despite no inflation to speak of having occurred in the meantime.[5]

Prime Minister William Pitt the Younger, perhaps inspired by the Spanish attackers of Gibraltar in 1782, 'took a personal interest' in the design of 'small shallow-draught vessels, armed with a single large gun' for the defence of that territory, procuring plans for them from the father of naval architecture, the Swedish Adm. Fredrik af Chapman (both of whose parents had been English), in November 1787.[6] Built at Deptford, they were trialled in 1788.[7] The Provincial Marine, a distant ancestor of the Royal Canadian Navy comprising Royal Navy sailors, British soldiers, and Canadian civilians, was first assigned a permanent base on the Great Lakes in 1785.[8] The value of the British economy roughly doubled between 1780 and 1800, with output per person rising by 9 per cent over each of the two decades in question; and it was this fundamental economic strength, more than any other factor, that would allow Britain, from 1 February 1793, to pursue and eventually, to win, its longest war since medieval times.[9] Nevertheless, it is inescapable that Pitt, with the help of Adm. Sir Charles Middleton, master-general the Duke of Richmond, postmaster John Palmer and their legions of

Unlike Royal Navy ones, British land service gun-carriages were always painted grey or grey-green and, where otherwise similar to naval carriages, had iron rather than wooden wheels. However, in both the garrison and sea-service cases, these small wheels were technically known as 'trucks', the minimum threshold for use of the word 'wheel' in the British forces of the time being a diameter of 20 inches. Nothing prevented the use of field carriages in fortresses, apart from the fear that they would make the guns much easier for an enemy to steal.

hardworking underlings, made 'fundamental improvements [...] to the country's capacity to wage war' over the ten years down to 1793.[10]

Another pivotal figure in the country's preparation for the next war was Thomas Blomefield. Son of a Kentish clergyman, and conceivably related to the two prominent Elizabethan alchemists of the same surname, Blomefield joined the brand-new eighty-gun ship of the line HMS *Cambridge* as a midshipman, aged 11. At 13, however, he entered the Royal Military Academy, Woolwich, and was commissioned into the Royal Artillery eleven months later, having excelled at mathematics and chemistry. With the formation of the Royal Marine Artillery still nearly fifty years in the future, the mortars of the Royal Navy's 'bomb ketches' were still commanded by officers of the land forces,[11] and it was on one of these vessels that Blomefield saw his first action: in Admiral Rodney's fifty-hour continuous bombardment of the Duc de Choiseul's invasion fleet at Le Havre in July 1759 (illustrated, p. 35). From this point, Blomefield was increasingly seen as 'a specialist in water-borne artillery', and served on another bomb vessel during the successful British siege of Havana, Cuba in 1762.[12] In the years of peace prior to the outbreak of the American War of Independence, '[m]uch of his time was taken up with experiments in gunnery' but he returned to active service in 1776, mostly supervising the construction of floating lake-batteries for the defence of Canada, to his own designs.[13] At the request of Gen. John Burgoyne, he also set about designing a gun-carriage suitable for use on both water and land. But it was back in England that Blomefield, now a captain, would make his greatest impact, for wartime experience had led the British government to recognise the 'great need for stricter military supervision of armaments manufacture, and in particular the proofing of guns at Woolwich before their use in the field'.[14] Thus, in 1780, the new post of Inspector of Artillery was created for him,

> and in his first year he condemned as many as 496 pieces of ordnance in proof. The widespread problem of 'bursting' led him to visit various foundries to examine the metals used, and to the consideration of instruments for better measuring the strength and accuracy of guns. The value of his efforts was quickly apparent and under a royal warrant of 24 January 1783 [...] the artillery workshops, gun butts, and proof office were placed under Blomefield's entire control [... and his] responsibilities included periodic surveys of the strength and condition of coastal artillery.[15]

It would be hard to overstate the complexity and labour-intensiveness of British gunfounding in this period.

> The first stage of the process was to create an exact model of the gun, mortar, or howitzer that was to be cast. This was built up upon a tapered wooden spindle [...] set upon a wooden turning frame and covered with grease or soap to aid in its eventual removal from the mould. Beginning at the breech end, workmen began winding a plaited straw rope around it. [... Prof. Isaac] Landmann[16] depicted the turning frame as separate, but most other works showed it sitting atop a brick firebox in which a fire would be lit to dry the mould during the next stage. Over top of the rope or cord armature, workmen began to plaster on a composition [...] of clay, sand, horsedung, and water, well beaten and mixed to give it a smooth and homogeneous consistency. Layers were put on by hand, each dried over a fire, until somewhat more than the required dimensions were reached. Then a wooden stickle board or pattern of the profile of the piece [...] was held against the model to smooth and shape it as it was turned on the frame. Finally the model was coated with wax or a solution of wood ashes in water to prevent it from adhering to the mould. With the aid of a trunnion gauge that ensured that the trunnions were level and at right angles to the axis of the model, wooden replicas of the trunnions, well greased, were attached by long iron skewers or nails. Finally wax models of [...] the vent shell, and of the arms of the monarch and of the Master-General of the Ordnance were made in permanent moulds and attached in their proper place by iron skewers.[17]

Only then could the mould, a negative image of the model, be constructed from it via a similarly arcane series of steps, this time including liberal amounts of 'cow's hair'.[18]

It would also be hard to overstate the haphazardness of the process's metallurgical side. Amid the outsourcing, technological stasis, 'lethargy and incompetence' that marked the latter part of the forty-three-year reign of Andrew Schalch (d. 1776) as master of the Royal Brass Foundry at Woolwich, much of the raw material for new artillery pieces consisted of old and worn-out or otherwise unacceptable guns, often foreign-made, their exact compositions unknown.[19] In the case of so-called 'brass' ordnance – which was, in fact, a degenerate sort of bronze containing surprisingly high percentages of zinc, and even lead – the man in charge of the smelter, operating essentially on instinct, would throw extra ingots of copper and tin into the mix if he didn't like the look of it, while skimming off the dross 'with a large wooden rake'.[20] Blomefield

> entered into his job with great vigour and subjected the pieces to rigorous proofs. According to his proposed regulations for iron ordnance, should one gun in 10 burst, then the whole number submitted from that cast would be rejected immediately. If a smaller proportion failed, then the inspector could select two other guns which had been cast immediately before and after the burst gun, and fire each 20 times with the service charge. If either of them failed, the inspector could reject the whole batch [...]. Such rigour was not appreciated by the contractors and a less demanding solution was worked out. If any gun were to burst, then all the guns of that batch would be subjected to a third proof, using the same charge as in the first two proofs.[21]

However, positive change predated Blomefield's appearance on the scene. Indeed, in hindsight, it is quite astonishing that Britain fought and won the War of the Spanish Succession (1701–14) with essentially the same *ad hoc* field- and siege-artillery arrangements that had prevailed since early Tudor times. Gunners in fortresses, too, had begun the eighteenth century with 'an almost civilian status [...] not subject to the orders of the officers commanding the army garrison'.[22] With that in mind, the century can be seen as an era of steady professionalisation of the British artillery arm, beginning with the foundation of the Royal Regiment of Artillery and Royal Brass Foundry, both in 1716. Over the following eight years, Col John Armstrong and the long-serving Danish mercenary Albert Borgard strove 'to design a complete system of artillery' for the British forces, albeit with mixed success.[23] This was followed by the formation of the Company of Gentleman Cadets in 1744; the nationalisation of the Waltham gunpowder mills in 1787, leading to improvements in powder's quality and reductions in its cost; the near-standardisation of both gun and carriage types by 1790; the formation of the first troops of horse artillery[24] in 1793; and the dying-out by 1799 of the Stuart-era practice of allocating each army battalion two guns, each served by seventeen specially selected infantrymen.[25]

Between 1722 and 1771, the Royal Artillery would grow from two companies to four battalions, implying a twentyfold increase in manpower. A similar drive for improvement in artillery organisation and tactics was also afoot in pre-revolutionary France; and while that country's revolutionary regime boasted 'the best artillery in Europe', it was only because they had inherited it from the army of Louis XVI, as reformed particularly by Jean-Baptiste Gribeauval following his service with then-leaders the Austrians in the Seven Years War.[26] It is also true that the 'ballistics revolution' led by Benjamin Robins FRS, Bernard Forest de Bélidor and Leonhard Euler was essentially complete by the early 1750s. And importantly,

A carronade on a simple 'rear chock' garrison carriage. On land, these low-velocity weapons of moderate accuracy and range – in capability, differing from true cannon much as shotguns differ from rifles – were used mainly for flanking fire or in confined spaces. Along with low cost, one of their advantages was that they required fewer gunners than cannon of the same calibre. Ships armed exclusively with them were found wanting in battle, albeit not before Sir James Yeo's misadventures on Lake Ontario in 1813.

the novel Swiss technique of casting each gun 'in the solid' and drilling out its bore afterwards using a horse-powered drill[27] had replaced the old German bore-in-cast system in England for both 'brass' and iron guns by the end of the 1770s, i.e. before Blomefield's appointment.[28]

The low-velocity and low-cost yet deadly guns known as carronades – though famed for their later association with Martello and Conway towers – were designed as early as 1776, based on scientific proposals made by Robins in the 1740s for a new type of gun whose 'barrel length and charge weight [would] provide the minimum muzzle velocity to destroy only the target in question'.[29] Spherical case shot, about which we shall hear more in Chapter 5, was perfected in 1784 by Lt Henry Shrapnel RA, whose name it would later bear.[30] George Koehler's invention of a remarkable garrison carriage during the Great Siege of Gibraltar has already been discussed, and, as we have seen, the Franco-Spanish forces in the same siege elaborately re-designed ships and boats specifically for coastal attack. It was presumably this long background of Enlightenment innovation that led Maurice-Jones, in his magisterial history of British coastal artillery, to stress the *lack* of technological change that occurred specifically during the ten years that separated the end of the American War of Independence from the opening of the great war with France.[31] But, in any case, Britain's relentless pursuit of better-quality guns and powder via a more scientific approach in the 1780s, together with major improvements in field-artillery carriages, the Swedish-inspired design of specialist small craft for inshore defensive fighting, and the Indian-inspired emergence of rockets as a moderately effective weapon for both land and naval forces, are perhaps even more significant in light of Prof. Jeremy Black's assessment that 'across most of the world, there was relatively little difference in warmaking between 1700 and 1800'.[32]

Promoted to major-general in 1803, Thomas Blomefield did arguably more than anyone to transform the Royal Arsenal from a 'miscellaneous collection of small craft-based workshops' into 'an institution of national importance with the beginnings of a modern factory-based system' over the final two decades of the eighteenth century. He designed this model for a 13-inch land-service mortar in 1795.[33]

A Blomefield 12-pounder. Still commonly seen, skeletonised iron garrison carriages like this one were more weather-resistant than their wooden counterparts, but had no other advantages: being more expensive, more prone to irreparable battle damage, and more likely to injure their own crews if damaged. Thus, whenever war broke out, every British garrison gun not already mounted on a wooden carriage was re-mounted on one for the duration. The wood was 'in all cases [...] selected for the job it had to do', with oak, elm, and ash all being used within the same carriage.[34] In distant stations, however, garrison carriages could be improvised out of local materials, as is known to have happened at Vandivasi in India in 1780.

The key area in which British preparations can be said to have fallen short during most of the interwar period of 1784–93 was shore-based personnel. In the forty-three domestic coastal strong-points that were the responsibility of the Board of Ordnance rather than of local authorities in 1789, there were only 212 permanently resident specialist gunners, all classified as Invalids. Of these gunners, two-fifths were in the Channel Islands and Scillies; and of the 128 on the British mainland, nearly a third were concentrated in Plymouth, Portsmouth, and Sheerness. Nineteen stations – including Brighton, Camber Castle, Calshot Castle, Holy Island, Lowestoft, and Liverpool – had only one artilleryman apiece.[35] There were also thirty companies of Invalid infantry, but they, too, were disproportionately posted to Jersey, Guernsey, the Scillies, and Plymouth.[36] 'In all cases "additional gunners" for manning the "great guns" had to be found from the infantry garrison or from some other source, suitable or otherwise.'[37]

Distant stations were better supplied with personnel than home ones. In 1789, Newfoundland, Nova Scotia, New Brunswick and Quebec had seven non-Invalid coastal-defence artillery companies between them, with a combined paper strength of around 1,000, not including wives and children. The West Indies had another seven, which were headquartered on Jamaica (three), Grenada (two), Dominica, and St Vincent; and Gibraltar had six. However, the men and their families, compared to their home-service counterparts, were ill-used: for them, 'the Board of Ordnance was much too mean ever to provide proper clothing, decent accommodation, or sufficient money to purchase adequate rations', and their officers' correspondence with it was 'one long, continuous plea for more money, more equipment, [and] more stores to furnish the bare necessities of existence'.[38] Likewise, Britain's West Indian fortifications themselves, 'where not in a ruinous condition [...] were sadly out of repair' already at the start of the war in the 1770s,[39] and only more so by its end.

The army *per se*, of which the Artillery and Engineers would not form a part until the abolition of the Board of Ordnance in the 1850s, was not in much better shape. Recruitment – generally for life – was a perennial problem; and even after terms of enlistment of three years, five years, and for the duration of the war were introduced, few if any battalions departed for America, let alone arrived, with their 'normal' complement of men. This was because of 'the unpopularity of the conflict' as well as soldiers' low pay.[40]

The usual remedy was to recruit in the Highlands and the south of Ireland, where civilian life was harder than in other parts of the country. Yet, even with sharp increases in the bounty-money payable to a man on joining, and widespread flouting of the standards for general health, height, age, criminal records, and so on, the British infantry and cavalry in mid-1775 had been a mere 'fragment' of their paper strength of 33,000.[41] Including volunteers, 'embodied' militia, and mercenaries hired in Germany, this 'nominal total' would stand at 207,000 by the end of 1780, and 191,000 one year later, after hostilities on the American mainland had ceased.[42] Interestingly, this was not far from the 200,000 that – according to French Gen. Charles Dumouriez, a 'deep thinker' and 'one of the greatest military experts of the warlike age in which he lived' – would make England equal to repelling any possible invasion, provided only that the Royal Navy not be allowed to fall into decline.[43] Of course, Dumouriez meant actual numbers of soldiers in England, and not inflated, theoretical numbers pertaining to every far-flung point of the empire.

In any case, in 1783, peace having broken out everywhere except the East Indies, the establishment was reduced to 48,000 (exclusive of artillery), of whom just 17,000 were to serve in Britain, 12,000 in Ireland, and 3,000 at Gibraltar. For those attempting to calculate the army's size, then or now, it did not help that the use of fictitious soldiers was required by its arcane, even bizarre, accounting system, which encouraged 'dishonesty [...] almost impossible of detection', from the most obscure captain up to the paymaster of the forces: a politician, usually of cabinet rank, who routinely trousered the bank interest earned on his office's credit balance of more than £400,000.[44] Among the first actions of the reformist Pitt government, elected in early 1784, were the long-overdue rectification of the paymaster's worst abuses, and the simplification of the army's accounting system as a whole. Many small improvements were carried out simultaneously. For example, tropical-weight uniforms for units being posted to the East and West Indies were first adopted in 1787. In temperate climates, the infantry's stiff linen gaiters were replaced by warmer, softer woollen ones; and bulky or weighty pieces of equipment such as grenadiers' swords and light infantrymen's powder horns were dispensed with, if it was found that they 'were never used in the late war'.[45] In place of these useless burdens, the number of cartridges carried was increased, reflecting that measures taken to increase infantrymen's rate of fire had succeeded.[46] Experiments with rifled as opposed to smoothbore personal weapons for the infantry and cavalry, begun on the eve of the American War by Patrick Ferguson and others, continued.[47] In 1787 a proposal was also made to double the size of each infantry battalion, to 660 men, by increasing the number of companies from eight to eleven and the number of men in each company from forty-two to sixty, though, in the event, a ten-company structure was preferred, and in actuality, companies usually numbered around forty-six all ranks.[48] The following year, desertion was made punishable by death;[49] and Col David Dundas began drafting the army's first really effective drill manual, which would be introduced in early 1792, curing a previous state of affairs in which every regiment's colonel developed his own system of battalion- and company-level field movements according to his own 'damned whims'.[50]

In some respects, however, the new government was initially quite unlucky: notably, in the sphere of Army and Ordnance recruitment. As conflict loomed with Louis XVI's France in 1787 over its meddling in the internal affairs of Holland, and when Spain seized British settlers on Vancouver Island in 1789, no one could argue that the prospective enemy were 'fellow Britons' like the Americans.[51] Nevertheless, nowhere near the desired number of new recruits could be obtained in England and Wales, this time due to 'a raising of the general standard of comfort and luxury' in every walk of life other than the military itself.[52] This problem – if that is the right word – would persist throughout the remaining period covered by this book. As the commander-in-chief would remark, on the Continent,

> there is comparatively speaking little or no trade or manufactures and consequently little means for the Employment of the Population otherwise than in agriculture, [so] the Pay and advantages of a soldier are equal if not superior to that of the Handicraftsman [... but English wages are] exceedingly high[.][53]

Recruitment headaches were compounded in 1790, when the growth of the Royal Navy outran its pool of marines. This meant that nearly 2,500 ordinary infantrymen – a number equal to 21 per cent of the entire effective strength of the army then on the British mainland – had to serve aboard warships.[54] Army shortfalls were partially redressed in 1792, when

> more liberal regulations were issued as to [pay] stoppages for clothing, and a weekly allowance of bread was added to the pittance of pay which passed under the name of subsistence. The general result was that the soldier not only received food enough to keep him alive, but the magnificent sum of 18s. 10½d. per year [i.e. £1,302 in today's money ...] over and above all deductions for food and clothing.[55]

The second policy area where the new government at first fell flat was the development of infrastructure for the defence of the coastline:

> In vain Pitt appealed to the precedents of centuries; in vain Samuel, Lord Hood, pleaded with all the weight of his great naval reputation that the function of British ships was to seek out the enemy's fleet and not to protect British ports; in vain three distinguished Captains of the Navy pushed Hood's argument yet further, urging that in case of hostilities with France England should always take the offensive, and affirming that many failures of the past war might have been averted if more ships could have been released for service at sea. [...I]ncredible though it may appear, the arguments of the Opposition were based on constitutional grounds. [...] Fortifications, said Pitt's opponents, must of course be manned if they were to be of service; but how could this be done without increase of the regular army, or at least without isolation of the militia within them from the rest of the community? [... And William] Windham, not foreseeing that one day he would be Secretary-at-War at a very critical time, boldly averred that it was not worth while to spend money on fortifications.[56]

Nevertheless, beginning in 1787, Pitt managed to obtain funds for the strengthening of port defences in the West Indies, and to form a new corps of 600 non-commissioned Engineers on the model of the Soldier Artificers of Gibraltar. As usual, this had to be achieved in the teeth of opposition from the Whigs, Charles James Fox MP chief among them.

In any case, to say that Britain was unusually well prepared for war by the early 1790s is not to suggest that her probable future enemies were ill-prepared. Both Spain and France ruled somewhat more colonial territory at the end of the American War than at the beginning, and the latter's navy and artillery were as good as ever. Of key intelligence and strategic interest, therefore, was the French scheme to build a new naval base at Cherbourg, which – unlike Brest – they would be able to leave in a strong westerly or southwesterly wind.[57] It would also avoid the problems of Calais, Boulogne, Dieppe, Le Havre, Harfleur, and Saint-Malo, which were then 'each too small to contain a transport fleet large enough to move an army', and which 'all suffered from narrow entrances which complicated departure on a single tide'.[58] A naval base at Cherbourg would also have the advantage of being nearer to Portsmouth, a perennial top-three French invasion target.

Though it had boasted a mighty fortress during the Hundred Years War, Cherbourg was by the mid-seventeenth century a sleepy village with a shallow harbour. Plans to develop it into a commercial port town were scuppered by British troops under 73-year-old Irish Lt-Gen. Thomas Bligh who, having landed unopposed at Urville, stormed Cherbourg in August 1758 and stayed there for a week, comprehensively dismantling its military and commercial infrastructure. But in 1775, Dumouriez chose Cherbourg over Le Havre and La Hougue 'as the great naval centre of the future'.[59] Two years later, he was made its governor, and tasked with making that dream a reality.

The main idea was to enlarge Cherbourg's harbour area roughly sixfold by building an enormously long breakwater from the Île Pelée, lying to the northeast of the town (and since connected to the mainland by landfill), across to Querqueville in the northwest. After considering and rejecting the use of ships' hulks and large bare rocks, the projectors decided to make the breakwater out of ninety immense purpose-built wooden cones, 100 feet in diameter at the base and 65 feet tall, with rocks inside. The area between this line of cones and the natural shoreline would then be dredged to about eleven fathoms. It was in the midst of this complex engineering project that Dumouriez began crafting plans for the expedition against England that would go down in history as the Great Armada of 1779.

John Jeffries, a Massachusetts-born British Army surgeon, flew the Channel in a balloon in January 1785 and lived to tell the tale. His partner in the expedition, Jean-Pierre Blanchard, conducted the first successful parachute experiments later that year using dogs, and would survive an emergency parachute jump from a balloon in 1793.

Problematic artillery, controversial fortifications, personnel shortages and the King of France's implicitly hostile dockyard-building projects were not the only factors affecting British defence planning in the 1780s, however. On 4 August 1784, a serious riot broke out in London when a planned balloon ascent by the Chevalier de Moret did not occur. De Moret's failure could have been due to his haste to beat rival aeronauts Robert Sheldon and Vincenzo Lunardi into the sky. In the event, Sheldon's balloon caught fire, so the credit for the 'First Aerial Voyage in England'[60] went to Lunardi, who took off from the London Artillery Ground on 15 September. After briefly touching down in a cornfield in North Mymms, Hertfordshire – where he threw out a badly behaved cat – Lunardi came to rest at Stanton Green End, twenty-four miles from his starting point, 'where some farm labourers mistook him for the devil'.[61] However, his possible status as the Fiend did not deter the Honourable Artillery Company from enrolling him, citing his 'ingenuity and laudable intrepidity': evidence that the military potential of manned ballooning was already apparent to some in England.[62] James Sadler, an amateur chemist in Oxford who achieved 'the first ascent by any English aeronaut' nineteen days after Lunardi's flight, was later 'much involved in improving naval ordnance' and steam engines.[63] He would also form a corps of sharpshooters and design a primitive armoured fighting vehicle, armed with two 3-pounder cannon (illustrated p. 129), during an invasion scare of the following decade.[64]

It has been suggested that the invention of the manned balloon was itself motivated by military considerations. According to an oration given at leading aeronaut Joseph Montgolfier's funeral,

> One evening in November 1782 [... Montgolfier] was idly contemplating a print on the wall of his sitting room depicting the long siege of Gibraltar. [...] Impregnable by land, impregnable by sea – might not Gibraltar be taken from the air? The evenings were growing cool in Avignon. A fire burned in the grate. Surely the force that carried particles of smoke up the flue could be confined and harnessed to lift conveyances and float men[.][65]

Moreover, 'as soon as the balloon was proved practicable [...] flight across the English Channel was talked of'; and despite various misadventures, Frenchman Jean-Pierre Blanchard and American loyalist Dr John Jeffries actually achieved it, surviving the two-and-a-half hour crossing from Dover Castle to the Fôret de Guînes near Calais in early January 1785.[66] The first use of a balloon for artillery-spotting in battle, by a twenty-six-man specialist unit of French army engineers, would occur as early as June 1794.

Via Jonathan Swift's classic 1726 satirical novel *Gulliver's Travels*, the idea of a manmade, hideously oppressive force descending from the English sky was called into service in the 1786 parliamentary debate on the Duke of Richmond's proposed scheme for south-coast invasion preparedness. Amid a wider opposition argument 'that large fortifications would lead to an "unconstitutional" militarization of British society',[67] one contemporary critic wailed,

> [a] Master General, with his Committee of Engineers, like the Laputan philosophers in their flying island might hover over the kingdom in their

Contemporary image of the successful Jeffries-Blanchard cross-Channel balloon flight of 1785.

Ordnance balloon, descend in a moment, and seize on any man's house and domain [...]. The country Gentlemen would find their terraces converted into bastions, their slopes into glacis, their pleasure grounds into horn works and crown works to which they have hitherto borne an irreconcilable aversion.[68]

The House being deadlocked 169 to 169 over Richmond's proposals, despite the prime minister's support for them, the speaker voted them down.[69] In the event, it would be another decade before the Army, Ordnance, and Home Office all agreed even on which areas of the coast were most under threat.[70] Yet, as historian Sven Widmalm notes, Richmond 'returned from his defeat [...] with a new, subtler and more successful scheme for militarization: the Ordnance Survey [which ...] would provide essential information to "a resistance, which is not confined to particular spots, but is capable of operating every where"'.[71] Surely, this was a fitting way to prepare for war against a future enemy who seemed on the verge of being able to land *anywhere*.

Theory and practice of amphibious operations in the eighteenth century

To have any hope of being effective, of course, the siting, design, and armament of fortifications – be they large or small – had to take account of what an enemy might actually do near them, or to them. Data on this was scarce, however, since the European powers of the eighteenth century 'found amphibious operations very difficult'.[1] A key moment was the formulation of a 'policy of Descents' by Prime Minister William Pitt the Elder in the 1750s. Its implementation commenced with Gen. Bligh's destruction of Cherbourg discussed above, which was hailed in the press as the first successful coastal attack against France by England since medieval times (the Renaissance English troops who took Boulogne having come by land from Calais).

The Cherbourg raid was followed up with a massive one on Saint-Malo, aimed at diverting French troops from the main seat of war in Germany, discouraging privateers, and spreading alarm and despondency among the French populace. The land element of this force, again commanded by Bligh, included ten line infantry battalions; some light cavalry; 400 artillerymen; and one battalion from each of the three regiments of Foot Guards. By the end of their second day ashore, it became clear that Saint-Malo was impregnable, but by then the weather was too awful to permit re-embarkation of all the troops in their small flat-bottomed boats. Thus, it was decided that the fleet would rendezvous with the remainder of the army a few days later at Saint-Cast, which was less than ten miles away by sea, but more than twenty by road. In the event, fighting all the way against French militia, the British soldiers took four days to reach Saint-Cast, and were critically short of supplies by day three. Unaware that they were being followed by a larger and fresher French army commanded by the Marquis d'Aubigné, they embarked their heavy equipment first, and thus were almost all still on the beach when the French bombardment began, sinking three boats. After fighting fiercely amid the sand dunes, supported by the fire of Royal Navy frigates and bomb-ketches, the bulk of the British managed to escape; but a rearguard formed of 1st Bn, 1st Foot Guards and the grenadier companies of various line battalions was driven into the surf and annihilated, half killed and the rest captured. The 'policy of Descents' was over almost before it had begun. Interestingly, in light of subsequent events, one of Bligh's only prominent defenders in the wake of the fiasco was the future King George III.

A sort of ghost in the machine of all subsequent thinking on amphibious warfare, notably by two influential British counter-invasion theorists of the 1790s, Alexander Dirom and George Hanger, was the Welsh Jacobite officer and author Henry Humphrey Evans Lloyd, who may have coined the term.[2] Indeed, Lloyd's reputation as 'the father of the principles of modern warfare' still stands, largely on the strength of his eloquent *History of the Late War in Germany* (1766), with its

Contemporary print of the Saint-Cast disaster, by Nicolas Ozanne.

numerous later expansions and translations, and his 1779 anti-invasion manual, *A Rhapsody of the Present System of French Politics*. Son of a poor Merioneth vicar, Lloyd could not afford to serve as an officer of British infantry, but attained a French engineer's commission on the strength of his drawing ability, and in the 1740s, 'disguised as a clergyman [...] reconnoitred the south English coast in anticipation of a possible French invasion'. By 1756, however, he could have been working for his native country as a spy, as he certainly was in 1768 when he organised clandestine British peacetime support for the Corsican resistance to the French. By this point, he had served in three different armies, becoming a major-general in Austria, and retained this rank when he subsequently fought for Russia against the Ottomans and Sweden.[3] Specifically, his commentaries on opposed river crossings were taken as gospel with regard to the importance of meeting invaders as near as possible to the landing beaches, which – if such beaches' identity could be guessed at in advance – should be prepared with 'retrenchments, abbatis,[4] &c [...] every difficulty which art and nature could oppose'.[5] Interestingly, one of the few consequential military figures of the nineteenth or twentieth centuries to reject Lloyd's principles outright was Napoleon Bonaparte.

Notable examples of the difficulties of amphibious warfare occurred during the Russo-Turkish conflict of 1768–74, when the Russians and their allies failed to capture the Georgian port of Poti; and in the Spanish amphibious assault on Algiers in 1775, during which coastal sand appears to have played a vital defensive role.[6] British warships were completely unopposed by rebel vessels at Boston in the same year, but their bombardment of an entrenched position on Breed's Hill had 'little effect owing to the extreme elevation'; three successive frontal attacks by British infantry and marines eventually secured it, but only at a cost of 42 per cent casualties.[7] A direct amphibious assault on Fort Moultrie at Charleston, South Carolina, in 1776 was even less fortunate. The British ships

> engaged the American batteries at long range, the intention being that the troops should wade ashore through the shoals and carry the fort by storm. The result was a serious reverse. The shoals were found to be unfordable, and the squadron after ten hours' firing withdrew, heavily punished by the great guns of the fort, with the loss of one ship burned and over two hundred men killed and wounded. The loss of the Americans was trifling[.][8]

At Whitehaven in the spring of 1779, the same low tide that had stranded the British merchant fleet helplessly in the mud, ripe for destruction, meant that the American marines had to row towards the shore for so long that all their incendiary lanterns went out, a factor that helped save the town. The following month on Jersey, as we have seen, the sand slowed, but did not prevent, the local militia and 78th Foot bringing their field guns into position; but so few of the attackers actually got ashore on that occasion, and for so short a time, that its effect on them can only be guessed at. And a French and American attempt to seize Savannah, Georgia, from its much smaller British and loyalist garrison that October failed in part because one of its columns lost its way in a swamp shrouded in mist, and was badly mauled by the city's artillery as soon as the mist cleared. Certainly, the 1780 invasion of swampy Nicaragua was the costliest action of the entire American War, whether measured in terms of sheer numbers of British dead (c. 1,100) or dead as a proportion of those engaged (77 per cent), though this was down to tropical diseases more than enemy action.[9] Lack of knowledge of the local topography of the sea bed, or its known dangers, also often made disembarkation much harder. At Whitehaven, as also two decades later in the hostile-but-unopposed French landing at Marabur, Egypt, troops' nightmarish journeys in open boats from their seagoing vessels to the shore were measured in hours per mile rather than miles per hour.[10]

Perhaps most significantly, for our purposes, the largest naval battle ever fought on the Baltic Sea – and one of the largest, in terms of sheer numbers of vessels engaged, in the history of the world – took place at Svensksund on 9–10 July 1790 between the Russian Coastal Fleet and Swedish forces led by the militarily and socially elite Arméns Flotta (literally 'navy of the army'), which boasted an astonishing array of specialist craft for inshore fighting, some designed by af Chapman, that will be described in a later chapter. The battle was won handily by the Swedes, despite the Russian vessels having more men and twice as many guns; but crucially, for purposes of the present discussion, it only had to be fought in the first place because Sweden had just tried and failed to take the Russian-held coastal town of Vyborg.

The innate difficulty of amphibious operations, however, did not inevitably lead to their failure. In addition to the various examples of coastal forts taken by force or surprise that were presented in previous chapters, it should be borne in mind that the Russians had mounted successful galley raids on coastal Sweden

Svensksund, 1790, with Russian galleys in the foreground.

in 1719, and eighteen years later used a thousand boats to move 40,000 men across the Sea of Azov. The town and medieval castle of Carrickfergus in the northeast of Ireland had been taken and held for five days by 800 French regulars carried in three frigates under a privateer commodore in early 1760.[11] Havana was taken in 1762, along with one-fifth of the Spanish navy, by nearly 13,000 British regulars (not counting marines) who had been conveyed there from Spithead and Martinique aboard a fleet of twenty-two ships of the line and more than 150 other vessels. The American infantry and artillery blockading the city of Quebec were surprised and routed in May 1776 by a force of 200 British infantry landed from river-craft; and in September, the same type of shore bombardment that had failed to clear Breed's Hill the year before 'sent the Americans flying out of their entrenchments' at low-lying Kip's Bay in Manhattan.[12]

In October 1779, 'a mere handful of troops from Jamaica' confronted by the Honduran fortress of Omoa, which had 18-foot-thick stone walls, decided that a siege would be fruitless and so decided to storm it instead, despite being outnumbered 2:1 by its Spanish defenders. Paralysing the latter with fear at 'the sheer audacity of the enterprise', they succeeded: burning the adjoining town and carrying off 'the gold of Guatemala, together with ships and cargoes worth three millions of dollars [...] bloodlessly'.[13] And in April 1780, a British naval squadron and force of 7,000 troops simply rushed past the previously indomitable Fort Moultrie and proceeded directly to Charleston.[14] The fort surrendered to the besiegers less than a month later, and the port five days after that, when it was threatened with red-hot shot. More than 5,000 Americans were made prisoners of war, ending the Continental Army as a force to be reckoned with in the Carolinas.

Most eighteenth-century plans for cross-Channel 'Descents' focused in the first instance on securing a single, major dockyard town such as Portsmouth or Brest. As such, it is worth repeating this cogent passage by Fortescue, relating to a point

A May 1780 French view of Fort Moultrie, Sullivan's Island, South Carolina.

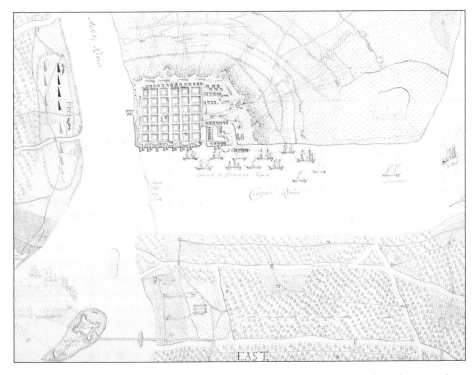

Fort Moultrie bombarding the British fleet, from a 1:11,500 pen-and-ink and watercolour map of the 1780 Siege of Charleston. It was probably drawn during or soon after the events by Lt Finnegan of the 16th Foot, a regiment that had been stationed mostly in Florida since 1767.

in the American War when the British forces had abandoned Boston, Rhode Island, and Philadelphia, but had made themselves virtually unassailable in the environs of New York City.

[T]he British could be sure of working much mischief by [… brief, small-scale raids], whereas the Americans could do nothing except by attack on New York, which implied a great and formidable effort. But if the British undertook serious operations to southward, or at any point remote from New York, the whole situation was altered, since each new British post offered to the enemy a fresh point for attack. A new base must first be taken and held; and if any advance into the interior was to be effective, the captured territory and the lines of communication must be sufficiently guarded. In a word, two complete armies would be needed[.][15]

Translated into European terms, this meant that conquest of an enemy country would *not* follow as night follows day merely because one captured a naval base on its mainland – even if it were the largest such base, and even if its civilian inhabitants proved more sympathetic to the invaders than to their own government. Rather, success would depend on the capture of other bridgeheads, and/or an immediate, well-organised thrust into the interior with forces that were, at least locally, overwhelming.

From this, it was relatively straightforward to infer that future invaders might strike in multiple places simultaneously, including some that were not major naval dockyards. Thus, unsurprisingly, rulers around the world were by the end of the century expressing a new-found interest in systematic coastal defence. Tipu Sultan, who succeeded Hyder Ali in 1782, used 'fixed coastal defence batteries and forts' to protect his harbours against naval attacks, apparently in a new departure for Mysore; and in Japan, the coast was first fortified, in response to a perceived threat from Russia, in 1792.[16]

On the other hand, even European powers 'well oiled […] with war experience'[17] at the end of the 1790s would have been hard pressed to organise or fund successful seaborne invasions of other such nations on the scale envisioned by Fortescue's 'two complete armies' strategy. Down to the Second World War, the most ambitious scheme for a British invasion of the French mainland was hatched in 1799, and involved taking and keeping the French city and naval base of Brest. In detail, it reflected that – despite their many admirable qualities, notably including a capacity for sustained hard work – the politicians of the 1790s often 'avoided expert military counsel' and 'were unwilling to understand the limited capacity of the British military machine'.[18] Only 15 per cent of Britain's merchant marine comprised ships of more than 200 tons, and therefore of any potential value as transports. Nevertheless, '[m]ost' of the ships employed in Britain's fifty or more successful amphibious captures of enemy territory between 1793 and 1815 would be hired merchantmen.[19] In practice, excluding warship escorts, two tons of shipping were required for each British man or horse being sent on a 'conjunct expedition', the contemporary term for an amphibious landing; and the scheme to take Brest was projected to require 70,000 troops. In the event, this was a number both too large for the available number of ships (and quantity of food), yet too small to guarantee the achievement of any further objective such as the permanent seizure of the wider province of Brittany or the restoration of the French monarchy there.

Clearly, only one lesson had been learnt from the 1793 British, French monarchist, Spanish, Sardinian, and Neapolitan occupation of France's Mediterranean port and arsenal of Toulon, 'to be held in trust for King Lewis the Seventeenth until the end of the war'.[20] Of dubious validity, this lesson was that 70,000 defenders might hold an enemy naval base indefinitely – though up to 17,000, with the support of much of the town's populace, had ignominiously failed to hold one for as much as four months, facing perhaps as few as 30,000 relatively ill-disciplined French for most of that time.[21]

> Sir Charles Grey, when consulted by Pitt as to the force that would be required [to hold Toulon], declared that fifty thousand good soldiers would be no more than adequate; upon which Pitt dismissed him with the remark that he hoped that a smaller force would suffice. Probably he rested his opinion on Lord Hood's phrase about ending the war with six thousand men [based in Toulon], which was of course nonsense, and nonsense of a kind which naval officers at that period were far too ready to talk and Ministers to hear.[22]

It did not help on that occasion that the enemy commander was a 24-year-old artillery major named Napoleon Bonaparte, already on his way to becoming one of the greatest tacticians in the history of the world, and one of its most notorious monsters. After the allied forces and 14,877 of Toulon's most ardently monarchist inhabitants had evacuated it by sea, accidentally setting much of it alight as they went, hundreds of the remaining townspeople were executed, some apparently by cannon-fire, and thousands more simply murdered.[23] As Walter Scott would later note,

> It was upon this night of terror, conflagration, tears, and blood, that the star of Napoleon first ascended the horizon; and though it gleamed over many a scene of horror ere it set, it may be doubtful whether its light was ever blended with those of one more dreadful.[24]

Interestingly, the siege of Toulon was one of only two occasions on which Bonaparte personally faced British opponents on a battlefield, the other, of course, being Waterloo. In the immediate aftermath of the siege, he was entrusted with

> surveying and fortifying the sea-coast of the Mediterranean; a very troublesome task, as it involved many disputes with the local authorities of small towns and villages, and even hamlets, all of whom wished to have batteries erected for their own special protection, without regard for the general safety.[25]

Part of the motivation for this may have been that the British army and fleet who had been defeated at Toulon retreated only as far as Hyères, a mere twenty miles to the east, where they stayed unmolested for five weeks.

The question of food for amphibious operations, briefly alluded to above, was as critically important as that of merchant-shipping capacity. As historian Roger Knight has pointed out, spikes in food-price-related unrest in England coincided with 'major amphibious expeditions setting out from British ports to the West Indies, the Mediterranean and the Baltic'.[26] That is, the government's attempts to satisfy tens of thousands of soldiers', sailors' and horses' present and future nutritional requirements led to localised near-famines in the hinterlands of those ports. Tellingly, the British half of a 38,000-man Anglo-Russian seaborne descent

The defence of the broadly anti-republican French port of Toulon was centred not on the city walls, but on a fifteen-mile ring of detached forts in the surrounding hills. To reduce one of these, Maj. Napoleon Bonaparte built a battery of eight 24-pounders and four mortars in secret, concealed by an olive grove. It was so well-sited that when its existence was discovered, 2,300 allied defenders sallied forth to destroy it, in a confused action that led to the capture of the British commander-in-chief, shown here. This was followed less than three weeks later by the loss of two other forts and, as a result, the collapse of the entire allied position. The abandonment of outlying defence-works that could be re-purposed for offence had also contributed to the fall of Yorktown, Virginia, in 1781.

'Buonaparte massacreing fifteen hundred persons at Toulon' by Robert Ker Porter.

Royal Artilleryman and infantry soldier in an 'open' battery at Fort Townshend, commanding the harbour of St John's, Newfoundland, in 1795.

on Holland in 1799 – which, unlike the Brest operation, actually occurred – was expected to consume not less than 13.3 million pounds of oats, wheat and rye.[27] But this is not to say that depriving the civilian population of food ensured that the forces themselves were fed well. The British expedition sent to capture the Cape of Good Hope in 1795 risked starvation, but fortunately were able to intercept some friendly ships laden with Indian wheat bound for Britain. Sir Ralph Abercromby's successful amphibious assault on Egypt in March 1801, requiring 20,000 rations per day, was somewhat beyond the range of direct resupply from the UK, and thus only possible thanks to Britain's recently acquired bases on Malta (which was itself not self-sufficient in food) and Sicily (which was).

'Conjuncts' were far and away 'the most complex and costly operations attempted by the British state' in the period covered by this book, and therefore overseen at cabinet level; yet, despite mighty efforts, 'massive conjunct expeditions involving over 100,000 tons of merchant shipping were beyond the resources of the country, its inter-service relations or its communication systems'.[28] This meant that, even at the British state's peak of efficiency within the period covered by this book, a maximum of 50,000 men and animals could have been conveyed to any one point abroad in any one lift. Moreover, even if more could have been sent, the relative puniness of the British Army's cavalry arm would have made deep penetration into the heart of Europe difficult or impossible. Thus, it was only after Britain's *de facto* acquisition of Portugal in 1808[29] that she and her allies would be able to tackle the French empire on land, year after year. However, this is not to suggest that the Peninsular War of the following six years was devoid of gallant small-boat and amphibious actions, which, in fact, were numerous.[30]

Bonaparte suffered from no shortage of cavalry; and it is probably worth mentioning here that the maximum number of troops he contemplated landing in England at any one time, 167,000, exceeded by 32,000 the grand total of British troops that were successfully sent by sea *anywhere* during the whole of the French Revolutionary War.[31] Coupled with command of the Channel, or even naval parity there, such a number would almost certainly have been sufficient to both hold an English naval base or large coastal town indefinitely, *and* to defeat a conventional British home army in the field.

But we are getting ahead of ourselves. I will conclude this chapter by pointing out that Britons, both at the time and more recently, who have scoffed at France's strange accumulation and assortment of small and small-ish watercraft for the purpose of invading the south of England could do worse than to consider what actually happened at Aboukir Bay, Egypt, in March 1801. With their ships unable to approach nearer than two miles to the shore due to shallows, the vanguard of the 16,000-man British invasion force was sent in three waves: the first consisting of '3,000 men in fifty-eight flat-bottomed boats, supported on each side by cutters with 6-pounders mounted in their bows'; the second, of eighty-four smaller boats, carrying a total of 2,500 troops; and the third, of 'fourteen launches, towed by thirty-seven cutters, carrying the [army's field] guns'.[32] Several boats were sunk and many men killed or wounded by the 'the guns in the castle of Aboukir'[33] and the twelve field guns of the defending French general, Louis Friant, who was fairly sure he would prevail. Yet, most of the attacking force 'remained calm, and [...] formed up in perfect order on the beach' before routing the 2,500 enemy infantry and cavalry who opposed them.[34] It cannot have escaped Bonaparte's notice that an amphibious force outnumbering local defenders by just 3:2 in the first wave, and having a roughly equal number of artillery pieces that could actually be brought to bear, swept all before it in minutes. And if this feat was logistically possible at a remove of 1,200 leagues from the homeland, surely it was possible at just nine, the distance from Boulogne to Dover.[35]

The Landing of British Troops at Aboukir, 8 March 1801 by Philip James de Loutherbourg, National Galleries of Scotland.

5

Powder and Shot

In the five years following the outbreak of war between Britain and Revolutionary France in 1793, French landings in the British Isles and rumours thereof would come so thick and fast that it is time that we pause to consider the capabilities and drawbacks of the artillery weapons and ammunition of both sides. First, it should be noted that guns from different countries identified as having the same weight of projectile would not necessarily be inter-operable. One reason for this was that the weight of a pound varied substantially from one country to another, and even from city to city, meaning that a French 8-pounder projectile based on the Paris pound of 1.093 British pounds weighed nearly as much as an English 9-pounder one. Bonaparte, when preparing a cross-Channel invasion attempt in the autumn of 1797, took pains to ensure that his troops' guns were 'of the same calibre as the English field-pieces, so that, once in the country, we may be able to use their cannon-balls'[1] – 'may' perhaps being the operative word. A less easily surmounted difficulty for any French invaders would have been ensuring an adequate supply of horses to draw not only their artillery's guns, but its whole panoply of ammunition waggons, mobile forges, spare-wheel carts, and so forth. For the gun alone, the smallest team used in wartime by any country other than Russia comprised six horses.[2] Including its horses and limber, a typical field gun took up 60 linear feet of road space, rendering the shipping of each one a complex affair indeed; thus, claims that an entire eight-gun, 100-man French field artillery company and its horses could have been carried in a single 70-foot *bateau cannonière* seem farfetched.[3]

Defenders of coasts in this period had the advantage that all nations' musket cartridges were 'mere paper envelopes containing a musket ball and a charge of powder', and any soldier who was immersed during a disembarkation from ships' boats or other small craft was, in effect, 'disarmed of everything but his bayonet' until issued with fresh ammunition.[4] Keeping barrels of powder dry while landing them from boats was likewise important. However, gunpowder that became unfit for use through damp or the passage of time was not altogether ruined, but could have its saltpetre extracted and reused in fresh batches. The major ingredient of gunpowder by both weight and value, petre – also known as nitre – is a naturally occurring mineral form of potassium nitrate, which in Georgian times could be manufactured, but in practice was found mostly in India. It was purchased from the British East India Company at fixed rates of £38. 10s per ton in peacetime and £45 per ton in wartime,[5] the aim being to maintain a peacetime stock of 80,000 barrels (i.e. nearly 3,600 tons) of prepared gunpowder in Britain, the Isle of Man, Jersey, and Guernsey. More than a third of this total stockpile seems to have been kept in the Tower of London.[6] A key site for the refining of raw petre into saltpetre was the Royal Laboratory at Woolwich, which (like the Tower) would *ipso facto* have been an important strategic target for French invaders. Approval of the finished powder by Ordnance officers took place in the Grand

Field-artillery practice, with the new, 1806 incarnation of the Royal Military Academy, Woolwich, occupying the right background.

Magazine at Purfleet. Often, the powder was found wanting; an inspection of the fleet at Plymouth in 1799 conducted by Blomefield and Gen. Sir William Congreve the Elder found that only four barrels of powder aboard were 'well-prepared'.[7]

Guns were hungry beasts. In the major sieges of the latter part of this period, the British side alone consumed *per hour* twenty-two to twenty-five 100lb barrels of gunpowder. The British government therefore acquired at least 8,000 barrels per year during peacetime, and four to five times that much during each year of the American War of Independence. The three chief storehouses of naval gunpowder in Britain prior to the French Revolutionary War were at Upnor Castle on the Medway; Priddy's Hard near Gosport; and the Grand Magazine. However, a new facility at Tipner Point on the east side of Portsmouth Harbour was added beginning in 1789.[8]

The question of how much powder ought to be used was a live one in the mid-eighteenth century, and the subject of various experiments. Some conducted with French 24-pounders at Metz in 1740 'found that nine pounds of powder produced commonly as much effect as ten, twelve, fourteen, and even of sixteen pounds'.[9] In part, this was because less than the whole quantity of powder had time to ignite before the ball left the barrel. But more importantly, because no clear division existed between the barrel and the chamber, the physical bulk of larger quantities of powder always, in effect, shortened the barrel and thus offset the increase in velocity that might otherwise have been achieved through more propellant being used. After 1764, when the British military reduced the maximum charge of powder from half to one-third of shot-weight, a single firing of a 12-pounder gun consumed 3–4lb of powder, and of a 24-pounder, twice that much.

Howitzers aside, the field guns of both Britain and France travelled with 275 to 400 rounds of ammunition apiece, and seldom ran out in combat, given that this would have been a sufficient amount for two to four hours of uninterrupted

A typical Continental field-gun on the march, by Aleksander Zauerveid, 1813.

Aquatint of British heavy guns on siege carriages, 1804, by F. C. Lewis and J. Powell after a drawing by Capt. Walker, 3rd Guards.

rapid fire: a feat probably beyond the limits of the physical endurance of both the gun and its crew, even in the unlikely event that the tactical situation demanded or allowed it. At the Battle of Waterloo, the most shots fired by any British artillery unit worked out at 183 rounds per gun, while the average across the Duke of Wellington's army that day was 129 rounds per gun, meaning that he could have fought a second battle of the same length and intensity without his cannon ammunition being replenished first. In the battles of Borodino and Leipzig, Napoleon's artillery fired 90,000 and 200,000 rounds respectively; assuming an average charge of 2½lb of powder per round, the Emperor's expectation that he would need 400,000 rounds for his 1814 campaign implied that the British peacetime powder stockpile could have sustained a quite intense eight-year land war even if all imports and domestic manufacturing of saltpetre had been halted.

Unfortunately for Napoleon, who lacked both domination of the world's sea-lanes and a petre-rich empire in India, his country was only able to come up with one-fourth of the gunpowder he wanted; and before the end of the year in question, his field artillery simply fell silent due to lack of ammunition – an event whose role in his first downfall and exile has often been overlooked.

But all that was far in the future during the invasion scares of the 1790s. Though Britain had the easiest access to petre and the most advanced techniques for converting it into gunpowder of any nation in the world at the time – 'British powder was considered by far the best'[10] – mixing saltpetre with its other two ingredients, sulphur and charcoal, remained a complex and hazardous undertaking. A 'steady supply of good-quality sulphur from Sicily' and experiments at Woolwich's Royal Laboratory led by Congreve, its tireless and polymathic comptroller, ensured that by the mid-1790s, British powder was more powerful by weight than either its French or Dutch counterparts, a fact that was confirmed empirically at Purfleet.[11]

Britain's government powder mills, supplying both land and sea forces, were located at Waltham Abbey in Essex ('the most important site for the history of explosives in Europe'[12]) and Faversham, Kent. Both were overseen by Congreve. A third, private, mill was opened at Ballincollig near Cork in 1794, and was nationalised not long afterwards.

Sir William Congreve the Elder, though best remembered for his improvements to gunpowder, also invented a lightweight and well-balanced block trail, deployed from 1792. This innovation 'probably made the British artillery more manoeuvrable than [that] of any other power' down to Waterloo, not least because it enabled the gun commander to aim the piece without anyone else's assistance.[13] Congreve's son and namesake (pictured) developed Indian rockets into an effective weapon for the British on land and sea beginning in 1804, in which year he also proposed an 'oar-powered, iron-armoured floating battery' that prefigured the warships of half a century later.[14]

A massive millstone at the Ballincollig Royal Gunpowder Mills, County Cork. Powder milling was by water or animal power in this period. Transformation of the raw powder into grains of the ideal size for combustion in a particular type of weapon, a process known as 'corning', relied on sieves made of hide or parchment.

Eighteenth-century artillery had many drawbacks, but sheer hitting power was not prominent among them. In an experiment conducted at Gibraltar in 1736, a shell from a 10-inch howitzer fired from a range of 150 yards 'pierced a target made of fir three feet thick and went five feet into the bank behind'.[15] Among guns *per se*, there was little difference in the damage caused by a 9-pounder and a 12-pounder, whose projectiles varied in diameter by less than 12 per cent; however, the latter's much louder bang and unearthly whistle gave it a distinct advantage as a weapon of psychological terror. A single well-aimed roundshot from either could be expected to cause seven or eight casualties to an enemy column at a moderate range, though one is recorded as having killed or wounded twenty-six men of the 40th Foot.[16] The Austrians estimated that redoubts of rammed earth seven feet thick could be penetrated by roundshot from their 6-pounders and 12-pounders at ranges of 600 to 650 yards.[17]

Roundshot – also known as shot, solid shot, cannonballs, balls, or (rarely) bullets – were of solid cast iron, but many other options were available to suit the situations gunners found themselves in. Langridge shot consisted of cast-iron bars in a tin case, and was found to be more effective against ships' sails and rigging than any of the other alternatives that were tried during this period, including various types using chains. Shells or common shells, as the name implied, were thin-walled metal spheres. Filled with explosives only, these would be ignited by a fuze that protruded through a small hole, and was lit – or so it was hoped – by the flaming gases produced by the firing of the gun. Upon detonation, fragments of the shell wall acted as an anti-personnel weapon, much as in a modern fragmentation grenade. Shells were effective at ranges of 700 to 1,200 yards, but 'comparatively feeble' despite the unusually high skill levels they demanded of

Austrian field gun firing, by Johann Baptist Seele, 1802.

Sketch of British artillerymen hauling a gun, 1800, by Benjamin West.

their users.[18] This was probably because they tended to break into a comparatively small number of large pieces, which were just as likely to fly uselessly skyward as downward onto the enemy. They also could not be used at all if the target was less than 650 yards away, since at that range the fuze was so short as to be flush with the surface of the projectile; cutting it any shorter 'would have left nothing outside the shell to be ignited by the flash of the discharge'.[19]

When fired from mortars, shells were normally referred to as 'bombs', though the relative weights of powder to metal cited by Ardesoif – e.g. 4lb to 36lb in the case of an 8-inch mortar bomb – may imply that mortar projectiles' cases were thicker than those of common shell. He also noted that bombs' fuzes were lit manually, rather than relying on the propellant.[20] Fuzes might be made of reed, linden wood, or seasoned beechwood. To ensure that they burned quickly enough, they were not filled with gunpowder only, but with a mixture of gunpowder with saltpetre and sulphur 'well pounded and sifted', usually in a ratio of 5:2:1 or 7:4:2, and sealed with wax at both ends if 'not intended for immediate service'.[21] Effectively, the resulting substance was a subtype of gunpowder with the proportion of charcoal, which might 'deaden' it, dramatically reduced. Ardesoif appeared to suggest, moreover, that fuzes could be made to burn underwater if the mixture were altered to 4:1:1.[22]

Canister, also known as case shot or just case, consisted of a tin cylinder – believed to have been painted red in the British forces – packed with metal balls which, just as in a modern shotgun, fanned out from the muzzle upon firing, to a width of around 11 per cent of the distance travelled. At 200 yards from the muzzle of the gun, for example, the balls would have spread out to a diameter of 64 feet. Because of this ever-increasing dispersal, canister had a distinct disadvantage in terms of effective range. In both British and French service, this was reckoned as one-half to two-thirds of the effective range of a roundshot of the same calibre. A British canister shot's balls ranged in weight from 1½ to 8oz each, and in number from as few as ten of 2oz each (in swivel guns) to as many as 258 of 2oz each (in certain howitzers). But by the end of the wars, considerable standardisation would occur, and a single canister shot for the 24-pounder, 18-pounder or 12-pounder in land service would contain exactly forty-six balls, respectively weighing 8, 6, or 4oz each.

Canister ammunition of the Georgian period has very often been referred to as 'grapeshot', but this is erroneous. The term grapeshot *was* used in the period, but to describe something quite different: many fewer, much larger balls – nine, in Royal Navy service, regardless of the gun's size – enclosed in a painted canvas bag, rather than a metal cylinder. This fixity of the number of 'grapes' in the 'bunch' meant that, in 12-pounders and smaller guns, the overall weight of shot was less than that of a round shot, e.g. 7lb 6oz in the case of a 9-pounder, and in larger pieces, it was up to 10 per cent heavier: e.g. 34lb 1oz for grape fired from a 32-pounder. However, such small variations in projectiles' weight did not usually cause any problems, and in desperate situations in close proximity to the enemy, gun crews would even 'double shot' their pieces, i.e. load them with two canisters, or two round shots, or one of each, with a smaller charge of powder to mitigate the risk of the gun bursting.[23]

Lt Shrapnel's eponymous invention, which was only used by Britain in this period – in the first instance, against the Dutch in Surinam in April 1804 – combined the killing power of canister with the long range of common shell.[24] In one action in Portugal, a single such round 'dropped every man and horse serving the first French gun to come into action'.[25] As finally adopted by the Ordnance, nineteen years after it had been perfected on what might be called a 'hobby' basis, it consisted of a shell filled partially with explosives and partially with standard musket balls. The usual name for it in Shrapnel's lifetime was, sensibly enough, 'spherical case', his surname being officially attached to it only from 1852.[26] These projectiles were said to be most effective if they exploded not much more or less than 50 yards from the target – meaning that they must have had roughly double the effective blast radius of common shell. Fuze-lengths had to be selected very carefully, albeit from among a range of pre-set lengths,[27] rather than being cut in the field.

A surprising array of ammunition of this period was more 'advanced' than one would be led to expect by historical television dramas. Hand grenades – essentially, tiny versions of common shell – had been in service in King Charles II's time, but in the 1770s, a cup attachment for the 'Brown Bess' musket was developed that could send a standard 3lb grenade 250 yards. Unlike with twentieth-century 'bullet-trap' and 'shoot-through' rifle grenades, six-drachm blanks rather than live rounds were used for this purpose. Another useful device, commonly issued to British vessels guarding river mouths, was ovoid 'light ball' ammunition for mortars and howitzers. Powered by linseed oil and resin and capable of floating on the surface of water, it was used to illuminate large areas for up to five minutes. 'Smoke balls' for the same two types of weapon were used for all their familiar modern concealment and deception purposes, but also to suffocate enemy personnel working underground.

Inspired by the Mysore campaigns of the preceding century, British forces used rockets against shore targets at Boulogne in November 1805 (abortively, due to weather) and again in October 1806, when they fired 200 'from eighteen boats in half an hour' and did considerable damage.[28] The following year, the Royal Navy fired 40,000 rockets into Copenhagen, substantially destroying it. This was mostly done from small sailing boats specially fitted out for the purpose, though larger vessels such as the ship-sloop HMS *Galgo* also had them, and 'all the gun brigs on the Boulogne station during Commodore Sir Edward Owen's command were fitted with rockets in frames'.[29] On one occasion, British soldiers armed with rockets destroyed three French gunboats on the River Adour, and forced a sloop to withdraw. While in the event, only the British made use of any rockets in Europe during the whole of the period covered by this book, it was far from certain that the French would *not* use them, as they were known to be conducting their own experiments; and a large quantity of British rockets was sold to then-neutral Austria in 1808.

The British Walcheren Island expedition of the following year employed clockwork-timed variants of the incendiary mortar and howitzer projectiles known as 'carcases',[30] which could be set to start burning up to 150 minutes after launch. Once triggered, a carcase would burn for three to twelve minutes, and was 'almost impossible to extinguish', due in part to the toxic fumes emitted by its mixture of antimony, turpentine, tar, pitch and other inflammables, which made it doubly hazardous to approach.[31] Some versions incorporated hand grenades and even 'pistol-barrels charged with powder and ball'.[32] The largest of Britain's

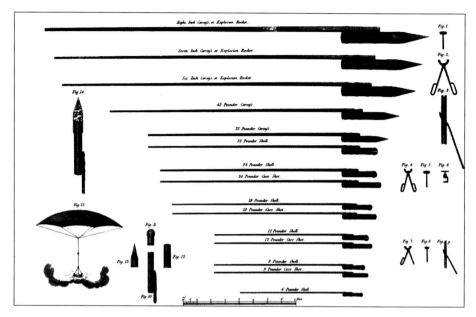

A selection of Congreve rockets and other advanced munitions.

'medium' rockets, the 42-pounder, carried carcases only. Smaller rockets down to 12-pounder size could carry common shells of half their own nominal weight. The 9-pounder rocket carried a single grenade, and the 6-pounder, a 3lb roundshot.[33]

As noted in previous chapters, the scope for aiming a gun in a shore fort with embrasures was strictly limited in both the horizontal and vertical planes, and the situation was similar for normal broadside-armed warships. Lt Ardesoif advised that the captain of a ship attacking a shore fort should first order a test shot to be fired from its lowest gun deck, and if, from the ship's current location, it 'cannot hit as high as the embrasures', then he has 'no business nearer; for in approaching nearer, your guns will require a greater elevation than the ports will admit of, and of course they will become useless'. Conversely, however, 'if the battery is so low that you can command it from the lower deck, the nearer you anchor your ship the better'. In terms of specific ranges, he warned that at three cables' distance (about 600 yards), damage to shore works would only be slight; and that beyond four cables (c. 800 yards) 'a ship should never attempt to engage a battery'.[34]

In field use, 'guns were rarely elevated more than one degree', since this meant the first 700 yards the ball travelled were above a man's height; whereas at a half, quarter, or zero-degree elevation, the projectile flew at head height or below throughout its (admittedly much shorter) journey.[35] Though due attention has been given above to their lack of vertical pointability, most guns of this period were quite accurate in the horizontal plane – to five yards either side of the intended target at a range of 600 yards, according to one test; and most targets, whether ships, forts, or bodies of troops, were more than 10 yards wide. As such, misses were generally down to elevation or loading problems. Experiments with 6-pounder canister rounds revealed that 41 per cent of their anti-personnel balls hit their targets at 400 yards, and that 23 per cent hit them at 600 yards. Unsurprisingly, the hit rate of 12-pounders fired from 600 yards (i.e. probably at 1 degree elevation) by British professional gunners against mock infantry lines was computed at 87 per cent. However, this fell to 40 per cent at 950 yards (i.e. 2 degrees elevation), and 17 per cent at an extreme range of 1,300 yards (4 degrees). Higher calibres equated to higher extreme ranges, so Koehler's naval guns above the Convention Redoubt in San Fiorenzo, Corsica in 1794 proved effective at 800 to 1,000 yards, even if their main impact was probably the psychological one of having appeared astonishingly on heights that appeared almost un-climbable by infantry, let alone artillery (see p. 85). Officers of the Royal Artillery were trained not to engage attacking cavalry and infantry at all if the range was more than 1,500 yards, and to use only shrapnel and common shell until the enemy had approached to within 650 yards. From that point, roundshot were to be used unless and until the attackers came within 350 yards, from which point, only canister was recommended.

All else being held equal, a longer barrel will result in higher velocity. As well as greater sheer hitting power, higher velocity translates into greater accuracy, because the projectile is more resistant both to 'drop', caused by gravity, and to being pushed about by the wind. However, presumably due to cost considerations as well as space restrictions both in garrisons and on warships, the barrel lengths of black-powder smoothbore artillery varied considerably, even across weapons of the same age, calibre and nationality. Britain's iron 32-pounders, for example, came in two barrel lengths, 9½ and 10 feet. The iron 24-pounder was the most popular fortress and shore-battery gun in Britain, Ireland, and Gibraltar as of the end of the eighteenth century,[36] and would be chosen as the sole artillery armament of the south coast's Martello towers.[37] It came in the same two lengths as its bigger brother, plus a third, 9 feet, though only 'long' ones are known to have been used in the Martello programme. The iron 18-pounder, an almost equally well-represented fortress gun with a similar extreme range, could be either 9 or 9½ feet long. And iron 12-pounders, which were used solely by British coastal artillery units from 1800 onwards, had barrels of 7½, 8½, 9, or 9½ feet – lengths that bore no resemblance to the those of the (more expensive) brass 12-pounders used by the field artillery, all of which were 6½ feet or shorter.[38] The non-cannon armament of British garrisons included 5½-inch howitzers of both brass and iron, both with barrels of 2 feet 9 inches,[39] and the 8-inch iron howitzer with a 4-foot barrel.

View from the roof of Martello No. 74, Seaford, East Sussex.

6

FROM MORTELLA TO MINORCA, 1794–98

While Toulon was still held by the allies, Pasquale Paoli's revolt against French rule in Corsica was in full cry. Having rejected, in part on republican grounds, the French Bourbon rule of the island that commenced in 1768, Paoli now rejected French republican rule on monarchist grounds, and offered his island to George III as a subsidiary realm on the pattern of the Kingdom of Ireland. Adm. Hood was prevailed upon to detach five ships under Cdre Robert Linzee to help the rebels by bombarding French forts; but Linzee 'withdrew with two ships very seriously damaged, the usual result of pitting wooden walls against masonry'.[1] Nevertheless, in the immediate aftermath of Toulon's fall, the Corsican situation would provide a further key moment in the evolution of British coastal defence. In January 1794, a small military mission was sent to assess the situation on the ground, and included John Moore, whom we last met at Majabigwaduce, and George Koehler of 'depressing carriage' fame. On the 24th, these officers rejoined the British fleet, now off the island of Elba, an important destination for anti-republican French exiles. Moore provided Hood with a positive, indeed over-optimistic, assessment of how easy the capture of Corsica would be, having underestimated the number of French defenders by some 2,000, a number equal to the entirety of the British land forces available for taking it. Worse,

> [t]he confusion of the retreat from Toulon had left to the British no artillery except four light howitzers and two mortars [...] and not one item of ordnance-stores had been received from England. Camp-equipment the troops had never had, and great part of their baggage had been lost, so that, as [Col] David Dundas said, they began the world naked and destitute. Yet again, the fleet was short of provisions; for, though the Admiralty had promised to send victualling ships in November 1793, none had arrived[.][2]

In spite of everything, Hood decided to seize Corsica's Gulf of San Fiorenzo, as it was then known, which was guarded by a new redoubt armed with twenty-one heavy guns; two shore batteries; and several stoutly built Genoese towers of the sixteenth or early seventeenth century, including two on the western shore, one at Mortella Point and another at Fornali,[3] two miles to the south. Some 1,500 British soldiers and sailors under Moore were landed in the hope of surprising the redoubt, and the Torra di Mortella was attacked directly by two warships. Unfortunately, Moore found that since his clandestine visit of the previous month, the redoubt's garrison had been augmented to 550 men, and was thus far too strong to take by any means available to him. The second prong of the attack, meanwhile, was a complete fiasco: both the thirty-two-gun HMS *Juno* and the seventy-four-gun HMS *Fortitude* 'were driven off with serious damage and a loss of over sixty killed and wounded, leaving the tower itself and its garrison of thirty-eight men wholly unhurt'.[4] Col Dundas of drill-manual fame was then put ashore, and erected a battery of four heavy naval guns just 150 yards from the tower. Still, it was only after two days' bombardment from both land and sea that it finally yielded. The redoubt, nearer Fornali and supported by its tower, was then taken by Moore, thanks in large measure to the 'plunging fire' of six more large naval guns, which – over an exhausting five days – had been manhandled to altitudes of up to 700 feet by a party led by Koehler.[5] The French at the redoubt lost 170 men killed, wounded and prisoners.

   The fall of Toulon had arguably been hastened by a rumour in November 1793 that England was about to be invaded by the French revolutionary army, an idea that kept 5,000 British troops aboard ship around the Isle of Wight and Southampton. There, 'overcrowded in the transports, [they] fell sick and died by scores of typhus-fever' before any were able to help the monarchist rebels, either around Nantes or on France's Mediterranean coast.[6] Clearly, if deemed credible, the *mere suggestion* that an invasion of one's enemy's homeland was in the offing

The French occupiers of the Torra di Mortella in northern Corsica, consisting of fewer than forty men with two 18-pounders and a 6-pounder, held out for two days against a British land force some forty times larger, including a siege battery of four 18-pounders, and inflicted sixty-two casualties on HMS *Fortitude* alone in February 1794. It was probably Lt-Col John Moore's mis-writing of its location that would eventually give Britain's Martello towers their name. The Mortella tower's walls were 15 feet thick, and prior to the battle it was 40 feet high and 45 feet in diameter at the base.

constituted a weapon of considerable power; but no propaganda weapon capable of defending against it had yet been developed, unless one counts the navy. In any case, when enemy landings or near-misses occurred, the British people were not hesitant about blaming their own navy's shortcomings, rather than the skill of its adversaries. As one ditty of the period put it,

> Now fair and strong the south-east blew,
> And high the billows rose;
> The French fleet bounded o'er the main,
> Freighted with Erin's foes.
> Oh! where was Hood, and where was Howe,
> And where Cornwallis[7] then;
> Where Colpoys, Bridport, or Pellew,
> And all their gallant men?[8]

After numerous twists and turns of fate, the hard fight at the Torra di Mortella would eventually provide a sort of solution.

A few words are in order about the general strategic position in the mid-1790s. First, it is important to remember that, in previous wars, French designs on England often focused on limited targets such as Portsmouth, to be held as prizes of war that would presumably, during subsequent peace-treaty negotiations, become the subject of complex horse-trading involving West Indian sugar islands and other far-flung assets. Even Dumouriez's remarkable Wight-Portsmouth plan of 1777, which envisaged depriving England 'for ever' of her 'greatest naval establishment', did not appear to contemplate the destruction of the British government or English society.[9] Now, however, having consolidated their grip on their own country, the French revolutionaries appeared to be seeking regime change in England as the best means of securing their own position.

> [T]o save themselves, [... France's] leaders seized on the idea of national expansion against the hostile royal powers surrounding it and sought to export its revolutionary creed [...]. When the success of Dumouriez's *levée en masse* became apparent, there seemed no limit to the possibilities of French domination of Europe. A new weapon, the mass popular army, was sure to defeat traditional aristocratic armies with their antiquated tactics and fighting seasons. From being an egalitarian revolution, it quickly became a nationalist one as well.[10]

As the above passage implies, our old antagonist Dumouriez had reinvented himself as a key supporter of the French Revolution, during its initial constitutional-monarchist phase. Indeed, he soon emerged as one of its greatest war heroes: blocking the Prussians who were advancing towards Paris in September 1792 at Valmy, crushing the Austrians at Jemappes that November, and then rapidly conquering the whole of the Austrian Netherlands, which occupied much of the territory of modern Belgium. Two months later, before war with Britain had even been declared, Dumouriez formed an 'Army of England', and began plotting to capture the Dutch fleet as the most straightforward means of carrying his troops across the water and into action.[11] Having been emboldened by the 'Miracle of Valmy' to abolish the monarchy (despite the action having been won largely by King Louis's artillerymen), the revolutionary National Convention embarked on an all-or-nothing programme of political murder at home and expansionism abroad. Tellingly, at the same moment Dumouriez was planning his latest invasion attempt, none of France's half a million citizen-soldiers were assigned to the defence of her own coasts.[12] As noted by an aristocratic Anglo-Irish officer who had commanded Hessian and American loyalist riflemen in the previous war, France was – even prior to its revolution – 'the most enterprizing nation on earth'. But in past ages, its common soldier

> did not feel that ardour which he now does, because he was a slave, badly paid and fed, worse treated, and fighting by compulsion for that phantom honour and glory: [but] make men enthusiastic in the cause of liberty or religion, or any thing else, it matters not what it is, so that they but feel it [...] and there is no undertaking, let it be ever so dangerous or arduous, they will not attempt.[13]

The British Ordnance's initial response to the outbreak of war was fairly sedate, and consisted of little more than augmenting the numbers of Royal Artillery gunners at the Landguard Fort by Felixstowe, which had been built in three stages in the Henrician, Jacobean, and Queen Anne periods, and at Bermuda, Guernsey, and Leith. The army *per se* had a tougher row to hoe. Given that Gibraltar, Canada, and the East and West Indies were deemed to require garrisons totalling 18,000 regulars, and Ireland nearly 10,000 more, the re-commencement of serious hostilities in early 1793 created an 'immediate requirement for tens of thousands of recruits',[14] amounting at worst to a new, untested army – for newcomers to the regulars, even in those days, were still 'raw' after six months' continuous training. Unsurprisingly, that new army experienced 'a long period of failure',[15] known to all subsequent generations of English schoolchildren via the song *The Grand Old Duke of York*. However, if it did not achieve any meaningful objectives in the early to mid-1790s, especially with the duke in the Low Countries, this was largely because it had not been set any. Its master, the British government, remained unsure whether it most wanted to take advantage of the post-revolutionary chaos to capture France's West Indian colonies; or to restore some claimant or other to the Bourbon throne by supporting the rural revolt in the west, or the urban revolt in the south; to take and keep Dunkirk; or simply to kill as many republicans as possible by seeking a 'general action'.[16] But the French, who had always had the upper hand in manpower, were now fighting the 'inside lines' in defence of their own country, directed largely by a polymathic engineer officer turned regicide, Lazare Carnot. Having worked tirelessly to transform his country's revolutionary hordes into an effective or at any rate controllable fighting force, and to supply them with gunpowder through the application of advanced chemistry, Carnot became known as 'The Organiser of Victory'. By the end of 1794, his efforts resulted in a reasonably capable army numbering more than a million men: a thing unprecedented in European history.

The Royal Navy fought its largest fleet action of the French Revolutionary War quite early, on and around 1 June 1794. Though this was claimed as a victory, it failed to achieve its main strategic aim: preventing the arrival in France of vital grain supplies from America, 'their sheet anchor against want'.[17] And, trapped in the ice at Den Helder, a major part of the Dutch fleet – as Dumouriez had prayed – was surprised and taken intact by invading French light cavalry with muffled hooves in January 1795. By that time, though the anti-regicide Dumouriez had long since defected to Austria,

> the Allies had been driven out of Belgium and across the Rhine [... and] the British Expeditionary Force, under the Duke of York, was retreating steadily through bitter winter weather [...]. By the beginning of February 1795 it had crossed the River Ems and, withdrawing into Hanoverian territory, was finally evacuated in April from Bremen to Britain, having suffered crippling losses from disease, cold, exhaustion, and undernourishment, and comparatively few from the enemy. Thus by the spring of 1795 Britain found herself opposed by a France which was holding the European coast-line from the Ems to the Pyrenees, with Antwerp like a loaded pistol pointed at her heart.[18]

In other words, a French or perhaps Franco-Dutch-Belgian invasion was suddenly likely rather than merely possible. As Maj. the Hon. George Hanger put it at the time, by 'the possession of Holland [... the French] have effectually turned the left flank of Britain'[19] and were now just as likely to strike England's east coast, which had always been the south coast's poor relation in terms of both the land and sea forces available to defend it.[20] In particular, Hanger argued that with Britain's main field army camped in Sussex,[21] a French force of just 10,000 or 20,000 men could land on the Essex side of the Thames between Mucking and East Tilbury, find 'neither troops, cannon, or works', brush aside the mere 4,000 troops camped at Warley, and seize the capital.[22] Tellingly, John Moore, by then a brigadier-general[23] and a rising star in the Army, conducted a survey of East Anglia's defensibility from seaborne attack in 1797;[24] and it was around that time that the lights at the North Foreland, Orford Ness, and Harwich were extinguished, and the Nore buoy sunk, 'to hinder enemy navigation'.[25] In short, it was universally recognised that 'French possession of the Dutch fleet and Dutch ports [...] gave the enemy the outstanding strategic advantage' of being able to strike Scotland and the north of Ireland as well as various points on the east coast of England.[26] Nevertheless, Adm. Adam Duncan, Commander-in-Chief North Sea, had

> a motley collection of ships of various rates and ages, comprising captured prizes, converted Indiamen and worn out war ships, numerically inadequate for the area he had to cover, from the far north of Scotland to the channel, and always being taken from him for other stations and duties.[27]

Estimates of the number of troops required for the defence of the British Isles in 1795 and 1796 ranged from 116,000 to 128,000, but unfortunately, in the latter year, the number actually available was not quite 80,000, even if raw recruits and volunteers were included.[28] The main reason was that – amid the cabinet-level dithering over war aims – the loss of Toulon and the ineffectiveness of the Duke of York's campaign in Flanders meant that a West Indian strategy had won out by default, despite that disease-wracked region's well-known status as a bottomless pit of British manpower. As of October 1795, the British regular army had been augmented to 105 infantry regiments worldwide, but of these, fifty-two were either in transit to the Caribbean or there already. In the eight years to 1801, a staggering 89,000 British enlisted men would go out to the West Indies, of whom half would die and thousands more desert. The 43,747 dead outnumbered, by 2,253, the whole of the army's personnel who had been stationed abroad as of 1794.[29]

In the two years after the fall of Toulon, Napoleon Bonaparte's star, though rising, cannot be said to have risen. Carnot appointed him head of the 'Army of Italy', but the string of victories there that would make him a household name would not commence until April 1796. With Dumouriez in self-imposed exile, and Carnot making policy at the highest level as one of the five directors of the remodelled French regime,[30] the Dumouriez-shaped hole in French public life that Bonaparte would eventually fill was, for the time being, occupied by Louis Lazare Hoche. Keenly intelligent and brutal, Hoche had been a corporal in Louis XVI's foot guards before the Revolution. First commissioned in 1792, at the age of 23 or 24, he was a major-general by the end of the following year, when he drove the Austrians and Prussians from Alsace. Starting in mid-1794, he pacified the whole of France's northwest; and when 6,000 French royalists landed from British ships were captured at the end of a dithering month-long sojourn on the Quiberon Peninsula in Brittany in 1795, and 'the Convention resolved to celebrate the occasion by a great massacre',[31] Hoche did nothing to stop it. A few months later, he did not even have to lift a finger to drive off the 3,000 British infantry and 2,000 cavalry who had occupied the royalist Île d'Yeu, between Saint-Nazaire and La Rochelle, as it had 'neither forage, nor pasture, nor sufficient corn to feed the [1,800 French] inhabitants, nor more than about forty oxen and a few miserable sheep'.[32] After they had been successfully extracted back to England, having achieved nothing whatsoever, news of these men and horses' suffering from hunger and exposure led some to wonder whether something akin to a scorched-earth policy should be pursued if the French got ashore in southeast England.[33]

In part because it had to compete for recruits with the land forces, especially the dozens of new fencible regiments of home-service regulars, the Royal Navy's operations 'during the first six months of 1795 [... were] of the feeblest description'.[34] Nevertheless, the senior service was responsible for a rare bright spot in that *annus horribilis*. In March, Capt. Sir Sidney Smith RN was given a flotilla of small estuarine craft to harass the shores of northern France. He had previously commanded the swarm of 'bomb ketches, galleys, and gunboats' that 'cleared the Russians from islands commanding the exit from the bay and enabled the Swedes to break out' in the run-up to the latter's victory in the Second Battle of Svensksund.[35] In July 1795, Smith's marines occupied the two uninhabited, one-acre islands known as East and West Saint-Marcouf, less than four miles from the east coast of the Cotentin Peninsula in Normandy, as he had recognised that they could be transformed into an ideal site from which to resupply the frigates blockading Le Havre and the Seine. Initially, two small vessels were dismantled to provide guns for each island and timber for huts. Capt. Hockings RE and twelve military artificers were then sent from England to construct permanent fortifications, comprising 'forts with blockhouses, ditches and stone revetments [...] on each island'.[36] By February 1796, these forts were completed, and East Saint-Marcouf occupied by forty-seven Invalid infantrymen, and West Saint-Marcouf by marines, while fourteen non-Invalid gunners from Portsmouth were divided across both. Eventually, with a garrison of more than 300, the islets would serve as a transit-point for French royalist refugees, supply vital information on enemy ship movements in and out of La Hougue, harass the coastal trade between Le Havre and Cherbourg, and generally make themselves 'an intolerable nuisance to the enemy'.[37]

It soon became known in Whitehall that Revolutionary France's successes on land had been assisted by the development of an important new communications technology, the optical-telegraph signal tower, a chain of which had connected Paris to Lille in 1794. The following year, John Gamble, a Cambridge mathematics graduate and future chaplain-general to the forces, published a pamphlet of his *Observations on Telegraphic Experiments [...] for the Purpose of Distant Communication*, which was well-received in British scientific circles and subsequently expanded into a book.[38] A similar proposal was also made by the Rev. Lord George Murray, archdeacon of Man, and in comparative tests of the two systems in the summer of 1795, Murray's 'proved superior'.[39] The first branch of a British optical-telegraph system based on Murray's work duly appeared in January 1796, and was praised to the skies by Lt-Col Alexander Dirom FRS, deputy quartermaster-general in Scotland and a well-known controversialist on defence matters who was steeped in North American operational lore of the 1770s and 1780s.[40] Though the British telegraph was '[d]esigned, built and manned by the navy', the rapidity of its construction was directly facilitated by the accuracy of the new Ordnance Survey mapping.[41]

The first two chains in England connected Portsmouth and Deal to the roof of the Admiralty, with Portsmouth-to-London messages arriving in just fifteen minutes. Powerful telescopes were fixed into position, trained on the next stations in the chain in either direction, and manned in shifts of just five minutes due to the immense visual concentration required to make out the positions of their six code-shutters. In contrast to the crude 'on/off' approach of

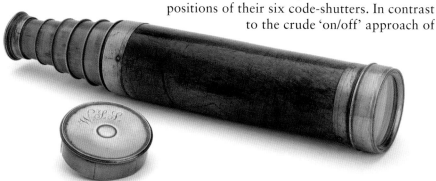

Capt. Sir Sidney Smith's personal telescope. Image copyright National Maritime Museum, Greenwich, London.

By 1800, France's optical-telegraph system for rapid, coded governmental communication extended from Paris northward to Lille, Dunkirk, Boulogne, and Brussels, westward to Brest, and southward and eastward to recent conquests in Italy and the Rhineland. This typical tower is between Metz and Strasbourg.

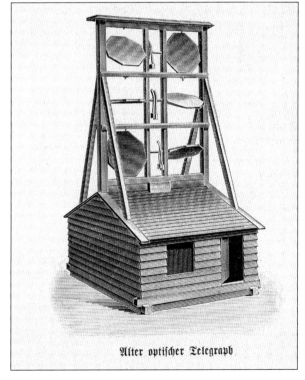

Alter optischer Telegraph

Optical shutter-telegraph tower of the type adopted in Britain.

the traditional signal fires that had been used to warn of raids and invasions since medieval times,[42] these shutters enabled the towers to send any message whatsoever.[43] Additionally, scores of crude timber signal stations, each equipped with a flagstaff for sending simple, pre-determined messages, were built an average of six miles apart along the entire south coast in 1794–97, and in three long sections of the east coast in 1798, when French privateer attacks seem to have reached an all-time peak.[44] Each of these stations was assigned two dragoons, who could carry important messages between the signallers and local unit commanders at the gallop.[45] By this point, messages sent from Yarmouth reached the Nore in five minutes. It was even briefly proposed that each optical-telegraph station be provided with two light guns 'in case of a landing in the vicinity', to be crewed by the signallers (usually a midshipman and two seamen, led by a lieutenant).[46] Thus, the British military establishment knew from experience by the mid-1790s that its three branches could work together effectively to design, acquire land for, and build large numbers of relatively inexpensive towers for counter-invasion purposes.

For Sheila Sutcliffe, whose *Martello Towers* (1972) was the first comprehensive work to include its subject's non-English dimensions, Martellos had an essentially 'amphibious nature', insofar as they were devised 'to be manned by the artillery in support of, or in place of, the navy'. She stated unequivocally that the first two were built in South Africa in 1796 or 'the very last weeks of 1795', at the behest of the colony's governor, Vice-Adm. George Elphinstone, who had been present during the Corsican expedition of 1794 and could have seen the Torra di Mortella's strong defensive performance with his own eyes.[47] However, Sutcliffe noted that the towers at the Cape of Good Hope and in Halifax, Nova Scotia were not built 'to recognised standards'.[48] This leads one to further question whether the Mortella episode truly inspired them, or if it merely spurred the continuation of existing ideas and programmes going back to at least the 1740s, when the British Caribbean island of Barbuda received a strong stone tower, now somewhat absurdly claimed by its tourist office as the world's first and oldest Martello. Sutcliffe conceded that the idea of coastal-defence towers 'was being gradually accepted' by the British civil and military authorities through the later eighteenth century, and began this story with the fortification of the Channel Islands in 1778. Circumstantial evidence favours this hypothesis. For instance, the distinction between Conway towers and true Martellos was rapidly forgotten: despite only three of the latter having been built on Jersey in the early nineteenth century, Sir John Le Couteur reported to the king in 1830 that the island had ten. To those with a keener architectural eye, however, the proto-Martellos in Jersey can be quickly distinguished from their successors by their far greater number of windows and gun-loops – no fewer than a dozen being visible on the landward side of the one at Le Hocq – and their four upper galleries, from which the defenders could fire small arms straight down onto anyone attempting to scale the tower or undermine its foundations. Possibly, the designers of the later, true Martellos felt that if enemy infantry or engineers were able to get that close to them, the game was probably up, in a grand-strategic as well as an immediate sense.[49]

Of the twenty-nine round coastal-defence towers approved for Jersey by Lt-Gen. Conway in 1778, twenty had been completed by 1794, and the remainder would all follow by 1801. Most had a height of 36 feet, a base diameter of 34 feet and a wall thickness of 8 feet in base and 6 at the top. The Guernsey towers were inferior to their Jersey counterparts in terms of the timeliness of their appearance, none having been begun until after the American War; their quantity, only fifteen; and their quality, being condemned as 'almost useless' in 1787 by Cols Robert Morse and Abraham D'Aubant, who were, nevertheless, at pains to clarify that they 'approve[d] of towers, but would recommend a different construction'.[50] Just 20 feet high with 4-foot-thick walls, the Guernsey examples had been intended to mount small mortars, but in the event were never provided with any.[51] The extant 1795 or 1796 gun tower overlooking False Bay in Simonstown, South Africa is of a more similar size to a true Martello, at 25 × 42 × 6 feet.

In July 1796, the foundation stone – 'cornerstone' seems un-apt – of the first proto-Martello in Halifax, Nova Scotia, known as Prince of Wales Tower, was laid by Prince Edward, namesake of Prince Edward Island (and, eventually, Queen Victoria's father). Just 28 feet high but 71 feet wide, it looks from a distance more like a crude-oil storage tank than a 'tower' in the general sense of that term. All three Halifax towers were designed by Capt. James Straton RE, and characterised by a hollow central pillar through which ammunition could be hoisted up to the gunners. By the subsequent standards of the home islands, the Canadian Martellos were extremely well manned and armed, with the Prince of Wales tower boasting two 68-pounder carronades and two 24-pounder cannon on the roof, as well as three 6-pounders on the floor below. It had space for 200 men, envisioned to include local volunteers as well as sailors in time of crisis. Similarly, the nearby Duke of Clarence's tower could house 164, and the Duke of York's, 100, reflecting their smaller diameters of no more than 50 feet.

Strategically speaking, however, these efforts in Nova Scotia and at the Cape were misdirected, for the main threat was much nearer to home. In 1796, France shelved Hoche's plans to seize Jersey and Guernsey, and instead authorised amphibious raids on 'Yarmouth and Newcastle [...] with the Humber as an alternative should it be more easy of access', by 5,000 troops in eight transports,

The 1796 proto-Martello tower in Simonstown, South Africa, reputedly the first British structure built in the Cape, may have been designed by Maj. William Kirstermann RE, whose plan of it (albeit with a date of 1798) survives in the National Archives of the UK.

TO THE IRISH NATION.

LIBERTY.   EQUALITY.

PEOPLE OF IRELAND,

'Let every Irish man rise spontaneously throughout this island [...] dare but look the enemy in the face, and victory is sure, complete, & allmost [sic] without a blow': Gen. Hoche's proclamation to the people of Ireland, which went un-delivered in 1796.

supported by twenty-two or twenty-four specially built gunboats.[52] Their leader was to be Lt A. M. Muskein: an Antwerper who, like Sidney Smith, was a veteran of the remarkable naval service of Sweden. Then, 5,000 'picked' troops with 10,000 spare muskets and uniforms were to be sent to aid any Irish rebels who could be collected in Connaught, followed up by 6,000 more troops from Brittany and the Netherlands.[53] This move against Ireland had been conceived as just one element of a three-pronged attack on British power worldwide, the other two being an invasion of the British mainland with 60,000 regulars, and an expedition to India in support of Tipu Sultan's anti-British resistance there.[54]

What emerged from all this planning in December 1796, following a shipboard mutiny by Muskein's troops en route to Newcastle in November, was from the British perspective 'the most dangerous single moment in the French Revolutionary War'.[55] On the 15th, a fleet of more than forty ships, including seventeen sail of the line and six to eight transports, broke out of Brest. Due to a clever disinformation campaign by the ever-victorious Gen. Hoche, the whole force was assumed by the British authorities to be headed for Portugal, but, in fact, it made for the southwest of Ireland. The senior British admiral in the vicinity, Sir John Colpoys, was not even 'aware that the expedition had sailed [from France] until the day after the majority of the ships had reached the mouth of Bantry Bay'.[56] The cabinet, meanwhile, 'hadn't the slightest idea what was happening' until eight days after the news had arrived in Cork:[57] a mediocre showing, in terms of news-transmission rates, even by the standards of Elizabethan and Jacobean times.[58] The French also came within a whisker of capturing Adm. Elphinstone's storm-damaged flagship HMS *Monarch*, struggling obliviously homeward from his successful conquest of the Cape Colony. Worst of all, the 15,000 troops the French ships were carrying[59] outnumbered by 5:2 all the British and Irish regulars then in Ireland, whose garrison had actually been reduced by 40 per cent since the immediate pre-war period; and the invaders had also brought enough small arms to equip 27,000 rebels.

Having befriended Hoche and reached an understanding with Lazare Carnot, the Irish republican leader Theobald Wolfe Tone by this time held the rank of adjutant-general in the French army, and was with the main invasion fleet, busily composing new proclamations of Irish independence to replace those that had gone astray when Hoche's ship was blown off-course. France, Tone believed,

> must send a large enough force to prevent a civil war. The object was to attain Irish independence, and the French general should issue a manifesto disavowing all idea of conquest, offering protection to property and religion, and inviting the people to establish a national convention which would then form a government. [...] [A]n Irish rising prior to a French invasion should be avoided.[60]

Hoche's proclamation to his own troops, which closely echoed these sentiments, also took pains to remind the invaders that only the 'perfidious English' were the enemy, and that the Irish – and especially the Irish women – must be treated with 'fraternity'.[61] But in the absence of Hoche and his storm-tossed division, the next most senior army commander quarrelled with the naval commander about whether to go looking for Hoche and the other ships, or to put a large body of troops ashore. In the end, as Hoche had not appeared and the weather continued to be awful beyond belief, the invaders sailed for home without having landed a man or fired a shot. But they had stayed for a week, faced comically by just 500 militia who had collected at Bantry town as the inefficient Irish regular forces trundled southward to meet them; and the blocking force of fewer than 2,000 men with just two field guns positioned between Bantry and Cork would not have very effectively blocked even those 6,400 French troops with four field guns who were safely anchored in the bay, and who intended (if Hoche ever arrived) to 'make a race for Cork, as if the devil were in our bodies'.[62] This brought the idea of a successful invasion into high relief for politicians and public alike. In England as in Ireland, 'the military measures taken for the defence of the kingdom […] cannot be regarded as adequate'.[63] The what-might-have-beens came thick and fast: Ireland's viceroy reporting to the British cabinet that 'had the enemy landed, their hope of assistance from the inhabitants would have been totally disappointed', and Bonaparte concluding that Hoche and his 'fine army' would have conquered Ireland if only they had landed.[64] On the face of it, these two assessments might appear contradictory; but given the paucity of government troops in Ireland on the date in question, Bonaparte could have meant that the French would have prevailed with or without local help. Indeed,

> [h]ad the weather been more moderate, or the French leadership more daring, Cork, with its sheltered harbour, would have been open to an attack, its defences neglected […]. Since winter was the season when the quays of the city were piled with thousands of barrels of newly slaughtered beef and pork, and plenty of biscuit awaiting distribution, Hoche's army would have needed no resupplying, and could have held out against any attempt to dislodge it. Such a turn of events would have dramatically altered the course of the war.[65]

But at least Cork was one of the just nine places in Ireland that had permanent coastal artillery positions, manned by regulars of the Royal Irish Artillery supplemented by local militia.[66] On the shores of Bantry Bay, the invasion's actual point of arrival, 'there were no coast-defences whatsoever'.[67]

In February, off Cape St Vincent, one of the largest fleet actions of the French Revolutionary War was fought between Britain and Spain, with the aim of preventing the Spanish fleet from joining those of Holland and France 'for the purpose of taking over a large army to England'.[68] And, lest any further proof were needed that the French Directory's invasion policy was alive and well, a cutter from St Ives on anti-smuggling patrol reported seeing a squadron of French warships near the north end of Lundy Island, beating eastward up the Bristol Channel.[69]

These ships contained a brigade-sized unit of infantry, officially the 2nd Legion of France, but known as the Black Legion from their brown-dyed British-made uniform coats. In their original colours, these garments had been taken from the French royalists captured at Quiberon in 1795. More than half of the Black Legion's members were recently released French convicts, with a leavening of French regulars and committed Irish republicans. Tone, who reviewed them before they sailed, described them as 'unmitigated blackguards'.[70] Their commander was Col William Tate, an American who had served in the rebel South Carolina Artillery during the previous war. Gen. Hoche's plan for this force, as he communicated it to the Directory, was that it should take Bristol by a 'surprise attack, which will be the easier because it is unfortified, and the troops are stationed some distance from it'.[71] Its strategic aims, as communicated to Tate, were 'to raise an insurrection in the country', 'to interrupt and embarrass [… its] commerce', and 'to prepare and facilitate a [general] descent, by distracting the attention of the English government'.[72] Tate's specific orders were to land at nightfall on the north bank of the Avon within five miles of the city, proceed to its windward side, and 'set fire to that quarter' with 'combustible matter' the troops were to carry with them. 'If the enterprize be conducted with dexterity, it cannot fail to produce the total ruin of the town, the port, the docks, and the vessels'. Horror at sharing Bristol's fate would then, Hoche supposed, compel Liverpool and other relatively defenceless west-coast ports to pay whatever amount of protection-money he demanded. In a sense, privateering had ceased to be a subsidiary strategy, and emerged as the French nation's strategy *tout court* – as Bonaparte would subsequently prove, by extracting the wealth of Italy on a previously unimaginable scale.

Further expansion of France's budding Continental empire at the end of the eighteenth century would have been impossible without the wealth of Italy, which Napoleon Bonaparte was chiefly responsible for purloining. Cartoons, like this one by Isaac Cruikshank from March 1797, were a vital source of news and news comment in this period, particularly to ordinary Londoners.

Next, Tate was to re-embark, land to the west of Cardiff, and proceed directly to Chester and Liverpool, which were to share the same fate as Bristol, with the addition that their waterways would be filled in to prevent their further use as ports – though by whose labour, and with what material, was left to his imagination. Along the way, he was to recruit from among the Welsh poor, and lead them in stealing everything from the houses and land of officers ('especially of the militia'), peers, and the clergy, but spare the goods of mere country gentlemen who had only a 'civil function'. The list of economic targets the Legion was to destroy included even mail coaches, private carriages, canal boats, bridges, causeways, and rope-walks, 'as by these means a crowd of artizans will be thrown out of employment' and thus, newly poor, made susceptible to the charms of the revolution.[73] Entrenched British positions, 'especially with cannon', were simply to be bypassed. And if superior forces pushed the Legion inland from the west coast, it was to link up with 'two French parties sent into the counties of York, Durham and Northumberland':[74] possibly a reference to a reanimated version of the previous year's abortive attack on Newcastle by Muskein. Clearly, Hoche had never changed his opinion, first expressed in October 1793, that '[d]ash and love of liberty is all that is necessary to overthrow Pitt'.[75]

In the event, contrary winds having made a landing near Bristol impossible, Tate's force made its way by sea to Carreg Wastad Point, three miles northwest of Fishguard on the northern side of Pembrokeshire, where it disembarked over

French troops, having placed a liberty cap over the king's arms in the House of Commons, burn the Magna Carta and prepare to exile the MPs to Australia. Cartoon by James Gillray, 1 March 1798, with later colour.

a period of nine hours in unseasonable, 'spring-like' weather, 'perfect […] for an invasion'.[76] During that whole time, as one of the French sea officers noted, '[n]o kind of resistance was offered'.[77] As the local militia commander Lord Cawdor put it afterwards, 'it was obvious that the Fishguard Battery was as useless for land operation as it had been to impede the disembarkation'.[78]

The planned Bristol raid was an almost exact re-run of Carrickfergus in 1760, in the sense that it had originally been meant as a distraction from a main invasion attempt that, itself, failed to take place. In the Carrickfergus case, the principal thrusts would have been at Glasgow (from Brest) and Essex (from Ostend);[79] whereas the Bristol one had been planned as a diversion from the abortive Bantry Bay landing described above.[80] This time, the Royal Pembrokeshire Militia, though 'formed to cope with such an emergency', were serving the guns of the Landguard Fort, literally on the opposite side of the country; and the only regular forces near enough to offer battle to the Black Legion consisted of three Royal Artillery Invalids and a few hundred fencibles.[81] Nevertheless, Tate's landing would be 'the greatest fiasco in the entire history of projected invasions against the British Isles'.[82] Having been specially selected for their bad character, given almost no training, refused even such artillery as might have been spared by the frigates,[83] unsure of the value of their mission to themselves or anyone else, and fearful of a brutal counterstroke by the British Army, the Black Legion surrendered as a body to Lord Cawdor's smaller and scarcely more professional force, after just two days of malingering and desultory looting of isolated farmhouses on the Llanwnda Peninsula.

As well as a brief run on the banks,[84] the Fishguard campaign would indeed spark 'a revolution – albeit not […] the one that Hoche and Tate had hoped for', but rather in favour of mass-participation national defence: lead even being taken from the roof of St David's Cathedral to be cast into bullets to resist the invasion.[85] This new spirit was made especially evident by an incident before the surrender was agreed.

> [A]n engineer from Liverpool who was directing the building of a lighthouse in the area […] led his men with such determination against the enemy holding Carngowil Farm that the French were routed, leaving two men severely wounded and one dead. Tate […] remarked that if this was how undisciplined English civilians behaved under fire he dared not contemplate what his men could expect from real British soldiers.[86]

A Fishguard shoemaker named Jemima Nicholas, armed only with a pitchfork, was said to have singlehandedly taken twelve French prisoners; Englishmen flocked to join whatever home-defence units they could; and a whip-round for provisions for the City Volunteers on Bristol's College Green raised £94 10s. 'in a few minutes'.[87] Eagerness in defence of the realm could, of course, be taken too far. William Wordsworth and Samuel Taylor Coleridge, walking on the coast of Somerset, were reported to the authorities for their dealings with 'spy Noza' – in fact, the peaceable Dutch philosopher Baruch Spinoza, who had been dead for 120 years.[88]

The dozens of Martello towers built in Ireland differed from their English counterparts in various ways, most notably in the use of stone blocks rather than brickwork, and a greater provision of musket-loops and other features for defence against invaders on foot. Like those built much later on the east coast of England, each could mount up to three artillery pieces including howitzers and carronades, though unlike in England, a carronade-only arrangement was fairly common. This restored one, at Killiney Bay, County Dublin, mounts a Blomefield 18-pounder – the muzzle of which is just visible here – on a traversing carriage on the roof.

A rare 'cutaway view' illustrative of the sheer mass of the stone-built Martellos of Ireland and the New World. This is Quebec City Martello No. 3 during its demolition in 1904.

Ireland was, of course, another matter. In the summer, another force of around 21,000 men, 15,000 of them Dutch and the remainder, French, were to head from the Texel to the north of Ireland: at that time, the part of the island most strongly disaffected to British rule.[89] Meanwhile, from Brest, Hoche would take between 6,000 and 8,000 troops to the south or west of Ireland.[90] Certainly, even if Tone's predominately Dutch force never effected a link-up with Hoche's troops, the Bantry Bay escapade suggested that – provided it could evade the Royal Navy and the worst of the weather – it was big enough by itself to have a good chance of defeating whatever pro-government Irish land forces came out of the woodwork.

The result, however, was France's greatest missed opportunity of the war. Despite favourable winds, and a month-long mutiny over pay and conditions in the British fleet (of which the would-be invaders were totally unaware), Tone's expedition did not sail in May or June. The mediocre Dutch admiral and pro-French fanatic Jan de Winter had been hoodwinked by the farrago of false signals sent by giant and cunning Adm. Duncan – whose career stretched back to the War of the Austrian Succession in the 1740s – into believing that the latter's command was at full strength, when, in fact, all but a handful of British crews were on strike. When the Dutch fleet finally did venture out in October, *sans* the troops, who had 'eaten up all the provisions intended to sustain them at sea',[91] the strike was over and Duncan pursued them. In a confused and harrowing fight in heavy seas and rain, which would become known as the Battle of Camperdown after the nearby coastal village of Camperduin, Duncan captured eleven Dutch ships, of which nine were (with great difficulty) brought safely back to England. It was the most decisive victory of a British fleet over an enemy one of equal size to have occurred down to that point in history, and also one of the largest naval engagements of the French Revolutionary War: a fact intimately related to the Dutch fleet's concentration as a would-be invasion force.

But, as was usually the case in the immediate wake of spectacular, headline-grabbing naval victories, the country was hardly safer than before. On 19 September, aged 29, Hoche died of 'bronchial troubles probably brought on by his futile voyage to Bantry Bay',[92] and on 26 October the French 'Army of England' acquired a new commander: Napoleon Bonaparte, 'with the laurels of his great victories in Italy fresh upon his brow'.[93] Bonaparte soon ordered 'Corsairs, with engineers on board [...] to reconnoitre the English coast from Folkestone to Rye, and to find out what batteries would have to be taken or silenced by a landing expedition'.[94] In early February, he followed this up with a thorough inspection of his own invasion ports, seeking data 'from all and sundry' and often discussing aspects of the attack 'with smugglers and other seafaring men long after his subordinates had retired to rest'.[95] The same week, an English spy observed on the road to Lille 'every useful tree cut down', sawyers furiously at work, and carts hauling wood to the coast 'in great numbers'. Some of the boats 'without number' that the same individual saw under construction had, like those of the Swedish Arméns Flotta, masts one could 'lay down when needful' and 'a number of oars'. He or she also estimated that there were 25,000 troops including 3,000 dismounted cavalry ready for the invasion at Rouen, another 21,000 at Le Havre, 5,000 at Évreux, and 4,000 (Dutch) at Lille, as well as ninety-one pieces of field artillery in a churchyard in Douai.[96] The spy also imagined that many tens of thousands more enemy troops were within a day's march of the coast, but French figures confirm the accuracy of the specific observations made: i.e. that the 'Army of England' numbered 56,424 men.[97]

In April, after a three-month whirlwind of preparations, Bonaparte made clear his views – closely echoing those published in the previous year by Scotland's deputy quartermaster-general[98] – that, while an invasion could succeed under the right circumstances, *threatening* invasion had a separate status as a war-fighting and potentially war-winning weapon:[99]

> In our position we ought to fight England with success, and we can do so. Whether we have peace or war, we ought to spend forty or fifty millions in re-organising our navy. Our land army will be neither more nor less powerful in consequence; but, on the other hand, war will force England to make immense preparations which will ruin her finances, destroy her commercial spirit, and completely change the constitution and manners of her people. We ought to spend the whole summer in getting ready our Brest fleet, in exercising our seamen in the roadstead, and in finishing the vessels which are under construction at Rochefort, Lorient, and Brest. [...] Towards the end of this month we shall have in the various ports of the Channel nearly two hundred gunboats. These should be stationed at Cherbourg, Le Havre, Boulogne, Dunquerque, and Ostend, and should be utilised throughout the summer for training our soldiers. [And for ...] 300,000 francs every ten days, we can effect the construction of two hundred other boats, larger in size, and fit for the transport of horses. Thus we should have in September four hundred gunboats at Boulogne [... and in] the course of October or November, we should have at Brest fifty men of war and nearly as many frigates. It would then be possible to transport to any desired spot in England 40,000 men, without even fighting a naval action if the enemy should be in stronger force; for, while 40,000 men would threaten to cross in the four hundred gunboats and in as many Boulogne fishing-boats, the Dutch squadron, with 10,000 men on board, would threaten to land in Scotland. An invasion [...] carried out in that way, and in the month of November or December, would be almost certainly successful. England would exhaust herself by an effort which, though immense, would not protect her[.][100]

Thus, though the types of boats to be used and the number of French troops per boat had scarcely changed since the Dumouriez scheme of 1777 (p. 118), Bonaparte's approach – far from keeping his invasion preparations the deepest, darkest secret of the French state – was to ensure that they were 'much advertised'.[101] Such advertising, of course, also helped him to mask the fact that he had changed his mind about England, for the time being. His next strategic target was, in fact, Egypt, as a prelude to the conquest of India: an expedition whose very existence would take the British entirely by surprise, and cost Bonaparte himself 'the greatest opportunity of his life'.[102]

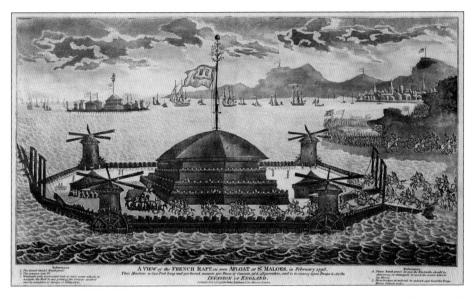

Beginning in 1797, the French public were told that the invasion of England would proceed via vast, town-sized rafts, each weighing 44,500 tons (four times more than a County-class heavy cruiser of the Second World War) and capable of carrying 18,000 soldiers and 2,000 horses.

The 1790s saw 'radical' modernisation of the outer defences of Dover Castle, 'heart of the coastal defence system', by Lt-Col William Twiss RE. Being highly visible, these works on *trace italienne* principles were also a propaganda weapon of considerable value, and may even have prompted France 'to look instead toward a "softer" target, Ireland'.[103]

It is not necessary to accept my hypothesis that the two square gun towers at Old Fort Niagara, dating from 1770–71 during the first phase of British occupation of that site, could have helped inspire the Conway towers,[104] since Martellos had numerous and ancient Western Mediterranean antecedents. Some of these have been termed 'corsair towers', as their primary purpose was as signal towers to warn of North African maritime slave-raids of the type that so afflicted the southwest of England in Stuart times. Interestingly, in terms of these towers' effectiveness in their ostensible role, Pasquale Paoli's father Giacinto Paoli revolted against Genoese rule in the 1720s in part because he felt Genoa provided Corsica with insufficient protection against the corsairs, eighty-five towers notwithstanding.[105] I. H. Glendinning's study of Martellos claimed that examples built along the coast of Genoa in the sixteenth-century heyday of the Spanish empire could, in turn, have been inspired by the even earlier Nuraghe sentinel towers of Sardinia.[106]

In any case, as of 1797, when French invasion planning was at fever pitch, 'no design was entirely satisfactory'; and a clear need had emerged

> not for one or two towers only but for mass production, and not at local command level in some far corner of the empire but at headquarters, as a concerted effort by the best military architects and with the blessing of the Board of Ordnance.[107]

In 1782, the Spanish conquerors of Minorca had 'razed and blown up'[108] Fort St Philip and sent its 'surplus' artillery to Barcelona. Thus, when the British re-took the island – acquiring its new naval shipyard – in November 1798, it had just 116 guns 'dispersed about the island in twenty-four coastal defence batteries'.[109] As the capture of the island would evidently 'pose fewer problems than its subsequent retention',[110] new strong points were needed, and the building of eleven or twelve round towers[111] for Minorca's coastal defence was entrusted to Capt. Robert D'Arcy RE, a veteran of the Siege of Fort St Philip in 1781–82. This work was 'undertaken at a feverish pace' so that the British defenders 'would be in a position to contain any Spanish attack' until the over-stretched British Mediterranean fleet arrived to help.[112] Up to 55 feet in diameter and 36 feet high, each mounted one gun, usually a 24-pounder, plus one carronade or howitzer, both on the flat roof; and their complement of men, according to historian D. W. Donaldson, ranged from thirteen led by a sergeant, to twenty-one led by a lieutenant, 'with enough provisions and ammunition to last for ten days in the event of an attack'.[113] However, a *Journal of the Late Campaign in Egypt* published by Capt. Thomas Walsh of the 93rd Foot in London in 1803, which contained clear engravings of D'Arcy's tower at 'Adaya' (Addaia) that probably influenced subsequent English Martello design, noted that at least one Minorcan tower's garrison was of eighteen men with provisions for a month.[114] According to Sutcliffe, D'Arcy 'may' have been assisted in his work by Capt. W. H. Ford RE, who would later receive the credit for key aspects of English Martello towers' standardised design.[115] But on balance, propagation of such a design via observation of D'Arcy's towers after they were finished – e.g. by Walsh – seems a more likely scenario. In any case, '[t]he likenesses between these [Minorcan] towers and the English Martello towers are startling'.[116]

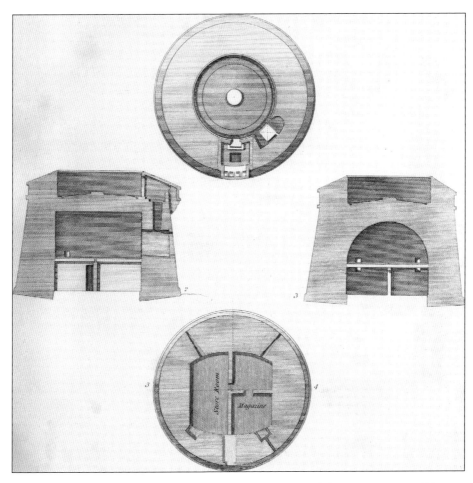

An 1803 engraving of one of Capt. Robert D'Arcy's 1798 defensive towers on Minorca, based on a drawing made by Capt. Thomas Walsh in the autumn of 1800.

The mortar used to build the Martellos of England was developed by the Royal Engineers at Woolwich, via experiments that revealed that 'hot' lime mortar – consisting of lime, ash, and hot tallow – 'set as hard as iron', and cannonballs literally bounced off it.[117] But nothing, not even Martello no. 19 at Hythe, can resist the awe-inspiring power of the sea.

7

LOW TREASON

When a brigade of French infantry, led by an American and officered in part by Irish republicans, landed in Wales in 1797, they fully expected that the 'oppressed' Welsh would rise up and materially assist them in burning Chester and Liverpool to the ground. The invaders 'did not see […] that the Dissenters in Wales were consoled by their faith, not revolutionised by it. […] If anything, there was a strong anti-revolutionary lobby among the ordinary men and women of Wales'.[1] Thus, far from assisting or even passively accepting the invaders, the Welsh of both sexes and every social type rushed to the scene, with the professed intention of driving the Directory's 'Black Legion' back into the sea. Its commander and his political masters in Paris had fatally failed to comprehend that not only Wales, but the whole of Britain, had just undergone a revolution of its own.

Non-violent though it was, this British revolution's effects were, nonetheless, profound: amounting to a massive transfer of public affection, and therefore power, away from the Whig aristocracy – French in manners, lukewarm in religion, and pro-American in political sentiment[2] – and toward what would nowadays be termed the upper-middle class, with its indisputably, unabashedly British, pro-British, and Christian outlook. It was thus unsurprising to those with a clearer understanding of the local scene that French calls to overthrow the nobility met not so much with opposition as incomprehension. The not-very-aristocratic Tory government of William Pitt the Younger, in place since 1784 and epitomised by the all-seeing, all-knowing Evan Nepean, son of a Cornish innkeeper, was living proof that the ship of that particular revolution had already sailed. Moreover, having commenced sooner, during and because of the doomed final phase of the American War of Independence, this British revolution had 'bedded in' in a way that the French one had not; and among other things, it had led to root-and-branch reform of the British armed forces.

Regiments, hitherto considered their colonels' personal property and named 'Babington's', 'Jacob's' and so forth for that reason, were in 1782 at last given the county designations that would last into the twentieth century, and with this change, longstanding popular objections to a 'standing army' began rapidly to disappear. By the 1790s, the Royal Navy's 'administrative structure of offices, dockyards, stores, foundries and factories constituted the largest and most technologically advanced industrial system in the Western world'.[3] The officers of the reformed Royal Navy of the era of Adm. Nelson, grammar school-educated sixth child of a rural clergyman, embodied 'a new gentility of behaviour rather than property or family'.[4] Where the French revolutionary navy disdained even such training as its former aristocratic officers had deigned to engage in, British naval officers 'had always adhered to […] bourgeois standards of professional skill and devotion to duty, which were now coming to be regarded as national

Dating from shortly after the Bantry Bay expedition, this James Gillray cartoon depicts Prime Minister Pitt (upper left) as leader of the ferocious winds, and Whig statesman Charles James Fox (centre) as the figurehead of the storm-tossed French ship. Though not a shot was fired on land, Louis Lazare Hoche's armada lost ten ships and around 4,000 men, mostly due to the weather.

Whig creatures, led by John Russell MP (future 6th Duke of Bedford) as a vast sea-monster, flocking to hear an anti-Christian speech by leading French revolutionary politician L.-M. la Révellière-Lépaux. By Gillray for the *Anti-Jacobin Magazine & Review*, 1 August 1798.

Mockery of religion clearly cut both ways for Gillray, who created this Apotheosis of Hoche in the same year.

and patriotic qualities transcending birth'.[5] Not, perhaps, until the parliamentary, judicial and civil-service crisis of 2018–19 would the public again be treated to any equivalent of 'Whig peers openly rejoicing at British naval defeats [...,] Whig admirals refusing to fight',[6] and Whig MPs referring to British Army victories as 'terrible news'.[7]

Its unambiguously patriotic attitude of mind often stood the new officer subset of the rising middle class in opposition to its mercantile counterpart. Down to the 1760s, a host of Britons who made their living from trade were very happy to throw in their lot with Jacobite rebels and schemers, but with the burial of the Stuart cause by the Pope and French king in 1766,[8] many traders' minds turned to the burgeoning ultra-Whig revolt of the New England colonies. Mountains of evidence indicate that the New England patriot faction saw themselves as spiritual and, in many cases, biological descendants of Oliver Cromwell's army.[9] So, too, did many of the Whig politicians of England, whose 1770s incarnation Fortescue described as a 'far more dangerous and unscrupulous enemy' than the American revolutionaries themselves.[10]

From the outset of the American War of Independence, merchants on the Dutch West Indian island of Sint Eustatius were accused of furnishing 'all Sorts of Provisions and warlike Stores [...] almost daily & publickly' to the rebels.[11] When a British fleet seized the place in early 1781, even the British subjects there had their goods, money, and account books confiscated. Because they had put 'personal profit before the duty owed to their King and country', Vice-Adm. Rodney considered them 'guilty of treason' and treated them even worse than their French counterparts – though his personal antisemitism and greed both also played a role.[12]

Bizarrely, then, a Whig ideology conceived in the anti-Catholic and broadly anti-monarchist fight for survival of the North Netherlands that began in the 1560s, and which was imported into England chiefly via a Dutch-led, anti-Catholic and anti-French military coup in 1688, spread to America, whose revolt was materially helped by France's Most Catholic Monarch, and therefore became pro-French – though in some quarters, its anti-Catholicism remained adamantine. In Scotland,

> [g]reat numbers of the clergy of all [Protestant] denominations were avowed Americans and Republicans, and, exasperated by the repeal of the penal laws against Roman Catholics, had been inflaming the minds of the populace with the cry of No Popery.[13]

It is also interesting to note that in the case of the Irish rebel leader, Tone, 'the militant republicanism for which he is best known was something of an accident of timing'. A privately educated Protestant barrister, who did not share the anti-Catholic views of his Scottish counterparts, he was in many respects simply a rigid Whig, driven to extreme courses of action because 'the French revolutionary wars had made treasonable ideas which would not have been considered so a few years earlier'.[14] British writers who look at those wars in isolation, and speak with some bafflement of republicanism as an 'infection' or 'contagion',[15] would do well to look in their rear-view mirrors for a line of the infected stretching back to Algernon Sidney and beyond.

Many of the Whigs of England expected during the earlier years of the French Revolution that it would, like American independence and their own so-called Revolution of a hundred years earlier, produce aristocratic-oligarchic political arrangements roughly akin to those of the Dutch Republic. Yet, even after it degenerated into an orgy of beheading, not all the Whigs were prepared to condemn it; and their parliamentary leader Fox would subsequently latch onto the dictator Napoleon Bonaparte as a sort of second coming of William of Orange, sadly delayed (much as Fox's political descendant David Lloyd George would praise Adolf Hitler as 'the George Washington of Germany' in 1936).[16]

All of this meant that Britain's defences were vulnerable to sabotage – whether crude and direct, or sophisticated and bureaucratic – long before 'Jacobin' was even a word. As early as 1776, a major fire at Portsmouth Naval Dockyard was started by 'an American rebel sympathiser, "Jack the Painter"'.[17] 'Jack' was, in fact, James Aitken, a robber and rapist from Edinburgh who had imbibed radical Whig ideas while seeking to escape punishment for his crimes in no fewer than six of the Thirteen Colonies, and who had also attacked British commercial shipping at anchor in Bristol, albeit less successfully.[18] Espionage was rife, but not always necessary, as there was no shortage of Georgian British businessmen who were willing to sell their industrial secrets to the highest bidder, even if that bidder was an enemy in wartime. For example, the ironmaster William Wilkinson 'set up the large cannon foundry at Nantes and [...] the great coke-iron making plant at Le Creusot' in 1777 and 1781–84, respectively, with the full knowledge and permission of his more famous half-brother, John.[19]

A measure of fear can be discerned alongside disgust in this extraordinarily complex and detailed James Gillray image of the Whigs as Jacobins, dating from October 1796.

For setting a fire that destroyed the Portsmouth rope-walk, pro-American arsonist James Aitken, better known as 'Jack the Painter', was hanged from the mizzenmast of HMS *Arethusa* in March 1777 and his rotting body displayed in chains at Fort Blockhouse for another four years. Execution remained the penalty for arson in the Royal Naval Dockyards until 1971, two years after the abolition of the death penalty for murder.

It did not help that a rapidly urbanising and industrialising Britain was already less than self-sufficient in food. A London bread riot on 13 July 1795 saw the prime minister's windows broken and two of the estimated 12,000 rioters trampled to death by the cavalry. In the same year, militiamen participated on the side of the food rioters in sixteen different incidents around the country, and at least five were hanged for it.[20]

The choice of Bantry Bay as an ideal landing site for taking the vital port of Cork from the landward side in 1796 was made on the advice of a Dublin solicitors' clerk, E. J. Lewins, who sent his assessment that it had 'not a gun, not a fort, no military force' straight to the French Directory.[21] The revolt of Ireland that the British and French governments had both, for different reasons, been striving for years to forestall finally burst forth in May 1798. Due to a shortage of regular troops, it emerged as 'one of the most unsavoury episodes in Irish history, in which sporadic fighting and bloodthirsty outrages on both sides marked an unpredictable contest between disorganized rebels and an almost equally disorderly force of loyalists and semi-professional soldiers'.[22] For our purposes, the story begins after the main rebellion had already been defeated: with the departure from Rochefort, on 6 August, of slightly more than a thousand French troops under Gen. Jean Joseph Humbert, who had previously served in the Bantry Bay expedition of 1796. Mostly infantry, Humbert's force also included some hussars, and artillerymen with four field guns, as well as '5,500 stand of arms, 1,000 French uniforms [...,] several hundred barrels of gunpowder', 200,000 musket cartridges, and 400 swords for the use of the rebels.[23] Unmolested while at sea, they arrived in Killala Bay in the northwest of Ireland on the 22nd, and disembarked in the face of 'very feeble resistance' at Kilcummin, County Mayo, where – again – there were no shore batteries.[24] Feeble though its resistance may have been, Humbert also found 'little enthusiasm for the French Revolution' in Mayo, so headed inland to seek out the disaffected, but not before writing to the Directory 'that, if he were reinforced by two thousand men, Ireland would be free'.[25] At Castlebar, with the uncertain help of a thousand Irish volunteers, the French routed the Kilkenny and Longford militia, some of whom deserted and joined them; and also put to flight a regular cavalry regiment and a Galway volunteer unit. (Another regiment of regular cavalry, the 5th Dragoons, was later found to have been so thoroughly penetrated by rebel sympathisers that it was simply dissolved.) And Humbert's initial crop of Irish volunteers had grown to 1,600. Nevertheless, he 'very soon found that all hopes of real help from the Irish were groundless'.[26]

The following month, not realising that Humbert's whole force had already been captured at Ballinamuck, County Longford, the French acceded to his request, and sought to reinforce him with 3,000 men, siege guns, and a 'vast' supply of equipment for the rebel army, carried by nine frigates and a seventy-four-gun ship of the line, named after Hoche and carrying Tone.[27] This time, unlike in Humbert's case, the naval squadron that had brought them over was observed by the Royal Navy, and pursued to Tory Island off County Donegal. In a long, confused series of fights at sea over a period of nine days, seven of the French ships were seized, including the *Hoche*, and more than 400 French killed and wounded. Taken alive, Tone cheated the hangman by cutting his own throat with a razor. Further Irish resistance to British rule, including an open rebellion led by Robert Emmet, would occur during the remainder of the war years; and Bonaparte seems to have

Pitt steering Britannia to happiness, represented by a small castle on a small island, between the Scylla of Democracy and the Charybdis of Arbitrary Power, April 1793.

used 'the implied threat of another French invasion of Ireland to strengthen his hand in peace negotiations with Britain' in 1801–02.[28] But the French would never again support Irish independence or an Irish republic with their own troops.

During the war years, strikes were frequent, and food-price-related civil unrest peaked again in 1800–01. Opposition to the navy's press gangs 'led to violence in all the major seaports of the country' at one time or another, with 11 per cent of such incidents resulting in casualties.[29] On at least one occasion, the volunteers fought a naval press gang that had 'pressed' one of their members; and in October 1800, a peer expressed his concern that town- and city-based English volunteer cavalry units would soon be fanning out to attack farmers due to high bread prices, and thus potentially fighting their rural volunteer-cavalry counterparts.[30] If this was an accurate reflection of food shortage-induced paranoia, it was hardly a fair assessment of the volunteers' actual or probable behaviour. Nonetheless, others also entertained 'exaggerated' fears that volunteer units' relatively democratic internal structures would be a Trojan horse for democracy[31] – then widely considered one of two extreme ideologies, the other being authoritarianism, between which the ship of state had constantly to be steered (see illustration above). William Windham MP, disastrous Whig secretary of state for war in 1806–07 and by modern standards probably a traitor, described the volunteers in such offensive terms in the House that 11,000 of them 'resigned immediately', leaving the hitherto 'reasonably efficient' force 'virtually destroyed'.[32]

INVASION AND COUNTER-INVASION CRAFT
OF THE 1790s

Formed in 1756, Sweden's Arméns Flotta was, at the time of the Second Battle of
Svensksund in 1790, equipped with more than 200 vessels designed for fighting
in shallow water. They had a bewildering array of names and characteristics,
including twenty-four-gun frigates with shallow draughts and fourteen oars,
known as *prams*; 'gun sloops' armed with heavy cannon pointing fore and aft, two
masts that could both be lowered, and up to twenty-four oars; gun yawls, which
were essentially similar but with the cannon pointing only backwards, and no
more than twenty oars; sixteen-oared longboats, with one heavy or medium gun
in the bow, and sides bristling with swivel-guns; and fourteen-oared longboats,
each carrying a single 8-inch mortar. The most remarkable were the three *udemas*,
designed by Fredrik af Chapman between 1760 and 1776, which were similar
to British ship-sloops and brig-sloops in size and sail configuration, but each
mounting a single row of eight to thirteen 12-pounders along its centre line, on
platforms that allowed them to be pointed in any direction: a prefiguration of
modern warships' gun turrets. Much of the unique and highly successful Arméns
Flotta's doctrine would pass directly to Revolutionary France via the Flemish
soldier of fortune A. M. Muskein. Indeed, the many hundreds of flat-bottomed
invasion boats that were built on the Channel coast of France 'were popularly
known as "bateaux a la Muskein"', since that officer 'had introduced the plans
of them to France'; but 'the plans themselves seem to have been the work of the
Swedish naval architect Chapman'.[1]

   As we have seen, Britain's master-general of the Ordnance was personally
in command of all barrack- and fortification-building projects and military
mapmaking endeavours. It was remembered that 'competition in the market
between the navy, Ordnance and army [...] had bedevilled transport operations in
the American Revolutionary War', so a specialist Transport Board, answerable to
the Treasury, was set up in 1794 and generally proved effective, within the limits
I have already discussed.[2] However, the British government at that date either
anticipated making few opposed landings, or felt that, for those they would
make, normal troop transports and landing boats of the sort used in the Cherbourg
and Saint-Malo campaigns of the 1750s would still suffice. Thus, virtually all British
innovation in the design, arming, and manning of boats was focused on inshore
defence, at least until the brilliant offensive showing of Capt. Sir Home Popham
RN's gunboat flotilla in the opposed landing at Callantsoog in 1799 (pp. 137-38),
and the development of rocket-bombardment technology by Congreve the Younger
early in the new century. As of 1797, certainly, British gun-brigs were held to be

   useful against the enemy, were they to send over troops in boats, and to
   attempt a descent, unprotected by ships of war; but their chief use would

A 1:24 scale model of a Swedish naval galley of the mid-eighteenth century.

Built in 1776, the *Ingeborg* had a centre line of 12-pounders on pivots, flanked by three-man rowing benches, and two 18-pounders in the bow. Its shallow draught is clearly visible in this 1:16 scale model.

be probably in obstructing the supplies of an enemy from being brought by water carriage up friths [sic] or rivers, or across lakes, and thus acting upon his line of operation, after he had landed; or by flanking his line of march whenever it might approach within their reach.[3]

The earliest type of purpose-built British gun-brig was the *Conquest* class, all twelve members of which were launched between May and July 1794 from various yards in London and Kent. Each mounted two 24-pounder guns facing forward in the bow, and five 18-pounder carronades per side. Their names, including *Aimwell*, *Borer*, and *Piercer*, imply that the 24-pounders were seen as their key feature, and intended as precision instruments for sinking enemy vessels. Indeed, events would later show that two or three dozen similar gunboats could, sequentially, deliver the equivalent shot weight of a third-rate's broadside into an enemy ship of the line's bow- or stern-quarters alone, while remaining relatively safe from any broadsides offered in reply. Flat-bottomed, they had eighteen oars, which – as much as for propulsion – were essential to reorienting the vessel, as a means of aiming its bow guns. As such, gun-brigs of the *Conquest* type would have been quite at home in the eastern Baltic, though small galleys were also used to great effect in this period both by southeastern English smugglers and by King George's spies – often, be it said, the same individuals. Also in 1794, *Conquest*-class architect Sir John Henslow designed two floating batteries, one of which went on to form part of the defences of Jersey, the Franco-Spanish failure at Gibraltar in the previous war notwithstanding. In the following year, Capt. Smith, whose Inshore Squadron had been given the *Conquest* class of gun-brigs *en bloc*, took delivery of a further two floating batteries he had designed himself. Boasting three drop-keels, and armed with two 24-pounder guns and two giant 68-pounder carronades, both were earmarked for the defence of Normandy's Îles Saint-Marcouf, which – as we have seen – British Army, Navy and Ordnance personnel occupied and fortified beginning in the summer of 1795.

The fifteen Henslow-designed *Acute*-class gun-brigs, all launched in April 1797, were fractionally larger than their predecessors and fitted with retractable keels, but were otherwise quite similar to them. So were Sir William Rule's *Courser* class. In all, at least eighty-seven of these curious vessels were built in England, and another fifty or so converted from prizes. Some British gun-brigs, in place of the two large forward-mounted guns, had one 18-pounder mounted centrally in the bow and a second in the stern, both on pivots; and again, Swedish precedents can be cited for both the pivots and for the overall configuration (though not both together). However, the directionality of Swedish influence is unclear, since af Chapman's father had served in the British navy, and he himself had spent years studying science, mathematics, and ship design in London, Woolwich, Chatham, and Deptford, among other places, during which period he was even placed under house arrest for suspected spying.

Over the course of the French Revolutionary and Napoleonic wars, the Royal Navy would order no fewer than 174 two-masted brig sloops, around 80 feet in length, usually armed with sixteen guns and crewed by 120 men.[4] Though markedly smaller than brig sloops, gun-brigs seem to have had crews roughly the same size, since when three of the latter sank with all hands in the Channel in June 1805, 350 lives were lost.[5]

Design model for a British cutter of 1790,
showing its three Schank drop-keels.
Image copyright the National Maritime
Museum, Greenwich, London.

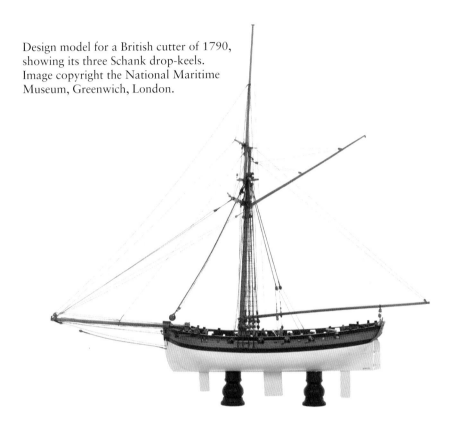

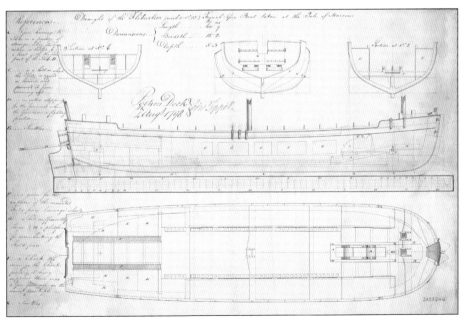

British measured drawing of a French invasion boat captured at Saint-Marcouf, 1798.
Image copyright National Maritime Museum, Greenwich, London.

The French approach was the reverse, with nearly all novelty in ship and boat design being devoted to cross-Channel attack. They had form for this. Adm. d'Annebault's assault on Portsmouth back in the mid-1540s had been led by two dozen galleys, 'each with a single gun mounted in the bow':[6] distant ancestors of the Pitt government's beloved first-generation gun-brigs, as well as the Spanish vessels that had bashed the town of Gibraltar into ruins in the previous war. And in 1777, Dumouriez had proposed seizing the Isle of Wight with 12,000 men, hidden in the holds of 200 oyster-boats, of which thirty would have 24-pounder guns mounted in their bows.[7] Having taken the island, which was rich in everything including timber, they would be joined by 'a number of shipwrights, caulkers, sailmakers and six hundred seamen' who would build scores of gun-sloops and bomb-ketches for the further assault on the mainland. It is hardly surprising, then, that in 1797–98, in the wake of Britain's naval mutinies,

> [e]xaggerated tales of vast invasion craft spread across the nation, fanned by uncertainty and rumour. Prints were published with absurdist configurations of windmills, paddle wheels, citadels and armaments, as artists attempted to convey the imagined, unquantifiable threat from across the Channel.[8]

By April 1798, Muskein had been promoted to captain, and despite harassment by three British frigates, managed to bring a total of seventy-three invasion boats full of troops, plus at least seven gun-brigs, out of Cherbourg and Le Havre and assemble them in good order at La Hougue, 'where he lay, awaiting neap tides and calm weather, in order to attack Lieutenant [Charles Papps] Price' on Saint-Marcouf.[9]

On the windless night of 6 May, with no British frigates able to sail to the islands' relief, Muskein led fifty or fifty-one[10] of his boats, carrying between 5,000 and 6,000 soldiers in all, to take them by storm. Fortunately, a tiny 'Guard Boat' containing Midn Moore of HMS *Eurydice* was able to signal the islands that Muskein's flotilla was on the move, having 'clearly heard the Enemy talk'; so the garrison was well prepared for an attack.[11]

Arriving at daybreak on the 7th, the French boats were sighted 300–400 yards from the southwest shore of West Marcouf. When the British defenders began firing roundshot, grape and case from six 24-pounders, two 32-pounder carronades, three 24-pounder carronades, and six lighter pieces, '[t]he French replied vigorously' with 'upwards of 80 guns'.

> [T]heir flats advanced with great determination [...] to land their men, but, when six or seven flats had been sunk, the rest were glad to retire. The loss of the attacking force was never officially announced; but one French authority has put it at upwards of 1,200 killed, drowned and wounded.[12]

Before the end of the action, which lasted more than two hours, at least two 68-pounder carronades on East Marcouf were able to fire 'Shells [...] over the Length of the West Island' and into the enemy formation. Price also reported capturing one French flat-boat carrying 129 men of the Boulogne Marine Battalion. As Tone noted sourly afterwards, 'What! [...] you are going to conquer England, and you cannot conquer the Isles Marcouf!'[13]

Thomas Rowlandson's 'semi-caricature' of the repulse of the French at Saint-Marcouf, 7 May 1798.

The British losses were one marine, Thomas Hall, killed; three marines wounded; one sailor wounded; and four guns dismounted.[14] With the element of surprise lost, a superiority of 4:1 in artillery and 15:1 in manpower had availed the attackers nothing but pain and death. At a strategic level, too, it is therefore worth wondering if the very publicity that made threats of invasion such a potent economic and terror weapon made actual invasion more difficult.

Curiously, the most promising French terror weapon of the seas was barely publicised at all. Designed by a Pennsylvanian named Robert Fulton, the *Nautilus* was the world's first practical submarine, armed with waterproof carcases that were probably the first useful sea-mines. It would be launched twice against Saint-Marcouf from Isigny-sur-Mer, but on both occasions, the British sloops it was targeting sailed off before it could get close enough to do them any damage.[15]

In 1798,

[t]here had recently been completed, at a cost of five millions sterling, a canal from Bruges to Ostend, fourteen miles long, one hundred yards broad, and thirteen feet deep, extremely convenient for the transport of men, stores, and even gunboats to Ostend, for a descent upon the British Isles. [...] [I]f the lock of this canal at Saas, a mile from Ostend, were blown up, much damage would be done to the port itself, while the principal internal communication between Holland and West Flanders would be destroyed, and the hostile coast [...] at any rate alarmed.[16]

Moreover, rumour had it that transports, destined for the invasion of Britain, would be moving through the canal imminently.

Unfortunately, the British attempt to take advantage of this opportunity was hampered by having very few specialist vessels for the attack.[17] Indeed, in the absence of Smith – who had been held prisoner in Paris since April 1796 and only just escaped – the Army and Royal Navy alike seemed to be sticking with a theory and practice of 'descents' that had not materially altered since the Saint-Cast disaster of the 1750s. Thus, around 1,200 men drawn from the Foot Guards, Royal Artillery, and three line regiments, with a handful of light dragoons, 'were thrown ashore forthwith without respect to the prearranged order of disembarkation'. HMS *Wolverine* (14) and HMS *Asp* (12) were so badly damaged by shore batteries that they had to withdraw; and when the troops had accomplished their mission, on the late morning of 19 May 1798, 'the wind and surf had increased to a height that forbade re-embarkation'. Having spent the night 'entrenched [...] among the sandhills', the soldiers were attacked by 'two strong columns of French', losing sixty-five killed and the rest captured.[18]

The British Ostend operation did, however, include at least three specialist vessels. One was *Wolverine*, which was configured essentially as a Swedish *udema*, with a centre line of guns that could be fired in either direction. But like af Chapman's *udemas*, it was never successful in battle.[19] Its designer was the ever-inventive Capt. John Schank RN, best known for devising the drop keel, but who would later superintend coastal defences.[20] The other two were sloops specially equipped with mortars, known as 'bomb vessels' or sometimes just 'bombs'. These were first used in early modern times by the French, when

> [i]t was discovered that a ship with conventional armament could not get close enough to a fort on shore for its guns to have any effect and that the fort's guns were capable of pulverising any ship audacious enough to come in too close.[21]

By the first decade of the eighteenth century in British service, bomb vessels had shallow draughts and specially positioned masts to avoid their own projectiles hitting the rigging, and were more stoutly constructed than other vessels of the same size. Their mortars, too, 'were considerably larger than their land counterparts of the same calibres', normally 10 and 13 inches, due to the requirement that they fire from much longer ranges, i.e. from beyond the effective range of the enemy's fortress guns.[22] Because mortars of this period fired at a fixed elevation of forty-five degrees, the only way to alter their range was through varying the amount of propellant.[23] In the case of the 13-inch mortar, ranges could be as short as 690 yards (2lb powder) to as much as 4,200 yards (20lb powder); and the 10-inch variant could achieve roughly the same ranges with roughly half the charges, the only trade-off being that the projectile was smaller. Firing from a range of 2,500 yards – achievable with 8lb of powder in the larger mortars, and 4lb in the smaller – would place a bomb-vessel effectively beyond the reach of shore-based 24-pounders.

A British bomb vessel carried 24,000lb of powder, 5,000 1-pounder balls (which were fired in batches of varying sizes), 400 shells, and 180 incendiary carcases.

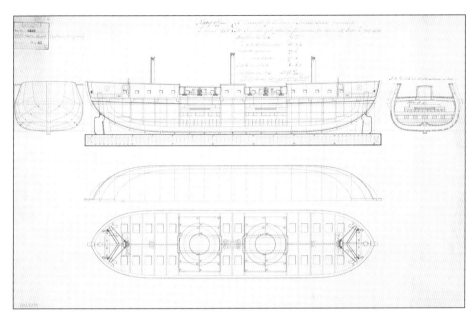

A William Congreve the Younger design for a British two-mortar bomb vessel, 1805. Image copyright National Maritime Museum, Greenwich, London.

Model for a Cruizer-class brig-sloop, c.1810. With more than a hundred examples completed between 1802 and 1813, this was the most numerous class of British naval vessel of the Napoleonic War. When armed with 32-pounder carronades, such a vessel's broadside would nearly equal that of a thirty-six-gun frigate armed with 18-pounders in shot-weight (though not in range), and with less than half the manning requirement.

The members of a gun crew on the roof of a Martello, Conway, or other such tower were very well protected from small-arms fire and flat-trajectory artillery. However, they would have had no defence against a deadly rain of 'pound shot' from a French or Dutch bomb vessel, other than dashing down the stairs in single file, hardly an easy operation. Indeed, the best that can be said about such a situation, from the British defenders' point of view, is that any particular tower would have been quite difficult to hit from an inherently unstable platform three quarters of mile out at sea.[24] Nevertheless, one must rate French bomb vessels among the Martellos' most dangerous potential adversaries.

Of even more concern to three eventual supporters of the Martello programme was the bringing of enemy mortars onto the land. This, they said, 'might in a short time destroy the carriages of the guns on the platform or top of the tower and thereby render its effect as a sea-battery useless'.[25]

'MY TROOPS AND MY OTHER ARMED SUBJECTS'[1]

Apart from the completion of Twiss's modernisation of the Dover Castle complex, the building of D'Arcy's towers on Minorca, and a few other scattered projects, British coastal defence during the final phase of the French Revolutionary War (i.e. beginning with Bonaparte's departure from the Channel coast to Egypt in 1798, and ending with the Peace of Amiens in 1802) revolved around finding, equipping, and training home-defence personnel. The original 1793–94 volunteers 'were intended as static defensive forces [...] to man coastal batteries and defend the principal coastal towns against raiding or invasion attempts',[2] as the nation's sparse chain of coastal forts, fortresses and batteries from the Scilly Isles to Berwick was 'almost unmanned' at that date.[3] As of April 1797, offers to raise new infantry volunteers in rural inland areas were being rejected out of hand, but those from 'ports [... and] the principal coastal towns' were still encouraged.[4] Some of the new companies raised starting in 1798 would thus be garrison artillerymen right from the start,[5] and some others, inshore marines on the rough pattern of the Provincial Marine of the Canadas. But it was chiefly infantry and cavalry that were now sought. This was because, from the king downward, it was agreed that cooperation between regular and irregular forces, operating not in fixed fortifications but in the woods and fields, would be the key to counter-invasion success. Some observers took this view almost so far as to reject coastal defence as a concept. Maj. Hanger, author of *Military Reflections on the Attack and Defence of the City of London*, sneered in March 1795 that the French laying waste to any coastal town in Sussex was 'of no more detriment to the state at large' than one alderman eating himself to death at a turtle-feast was a threat to the wealth of London.[6]

Moreover, empirical support for the great value of mobile forces, and the relative uselessness of traditional shore batteries, had been provided by the Black Legion's 1797 landing at Fishguard:

a massive test, under realistic conditions, of Pitt's home defence measures [... of which] the results were highly reassuring. There had been an effective 'closing up' of forces from as far away as Hereford and Gloucester, and some impressive performances by individual units. The New Romney Fencible Cavalry covered 61 miles from Worcester to Brecon in 5 hours, [and] the Brecon Volunteers marched 20 miles to Llandovery in four, double the [expected] official rate of three miles in an hour and a quarter. The speed of communications, too, exceeded expectations.[7]

Lord Cornwallis, based on his experience of combating the American and Irish risings, worried that the government might lack 'sufficient force both to hold the coast and maintain civil order, and began planning a "system of internal fortification" on which defence and counter-attack could be based however large the loss of territorial control'.[8] Likewise, the commanding general of the Western

Military District – perhaps spooked by the writings of the battery-sceptic Dirom[9] – thought open coastal batteries so useless that he wanted them replaced, either by field artillery or by 'strong redoubts defended by at least 200 infantry'.[10] Dirom also advocated a minimalistic approach to coastal fortresses, on the grounds that if seized by the enemy they could be resupplied by sea indefinitely, and instead favoured 'forts of considerable strength [...] situated in the interior part of the country, between the coast and the capital'.[11]

But Lord Melville expressed the traditional majority view: that it was irrational to build forts deep in the interior of England, or even in inland parts of coastal counties like Kent and Essex, when one could instead 'meet the invader on or as near to the beaches as possible with "torrents of armed men"'.[12] As in 1547, it was 'not England's profession to trust in lime and stone'.[13] In any defensive war, as Dirom himself noted in 1797,

> a regularly disciplined army, equal to that of the enemy, is not so necessary as a *numerous* irregular, but *active* force, which may circumscribe his position, [and] obstruct and harass his movements [... Thus,] the most effectual means of augmenting our military forces, for the purpose of repelling invasion, are by arming a considerable proportion of the resident inhabitants of the country.[14]

In a synthesis of the above ideas, the 'armed citizens' also figured heavily in manning the new fortifications on the inland approaches to London that were proposed by Maj. Hanger, citing the precedent of the spirited defence of Breed's Hill by untrained Americans with 'some few unwieldy old Queen Anne's muskets, and [...] duck guns'.[15] A seldom-sung couplet from *Heart of Oak*, penned by actor David Garrick following a thwarted invasion attempt in 1759, provides further evidence of this perennial attitude of mind:

> But should their flat-bottoms in darkness get o'er
> Stout Britons they'll find to defeat them on shore.[16]

Actually finding, arming and training Melville's 'torrents of men' was, of course, easier said than done. The problem was compounded by the 'lamentable lack of system' in matters pertaining to internal defence that prevailed at both the War Office and the Home Office throughout the French Revolutionary War.[17] Britain and Ireland were regularly denuded of regular soldiers in pursuit of the conquest, re-conquest, and/or pacification of Tobago, Martinique, Guadeloupe, St Lucia, Saint-Domingue (now Haiti), Puerto Rico, Grenada, and Trinidad, among other places. This meant that the troops who would face any invaders of the home islands would include a very high proportion of part-timers. This was the case even after the Army created eight new West India Regiments in 1795, and started buying slaves in enormous numbers to fill their ranks, giving them an enhanced status – though not their freedom, unlike in the American War.[18] Many excellent British non-commissioned officers, and a few terrible ones, were also lost to those new units through the lure of commissions, which in British or Irish regiments they

Camps of the West Suffolk, Derbyshire and Montgomeryshire regiments of militia and the Cornish Fencible Cavalry at Eastbourne in 1796.

would not have been able to afford.[19] More importantly, however, the bigger the various home-defence forces became, the more competition there was among them for a dwindling pool of potential recruits.

Dirom advocated merging the army and marines as a means of giving the former more sea experience ('training [… them] to endure hardship, and to face danger'[20]), apparently unaware that thousands of soldiers were serving afloat on a stop-gap basis, due to the general recruiting melee, which was leading to inflation in the already sizeable lump-sum payments made to new members of the regular forces on enlistment. Naval matters aside, the core of Pitt's home-defence measures alluded to above was the creation of the 60,000-man Supplementary Reserve of Militia in 1796, which operated relative to England's sixty-nine regiments of

Supplementary-Militia, turning out for Twenty-Days Amusement; _'The French Invade us, hey'—damme, where afraid?'

Gillray's response to Pitt's supplementary militia plan of 1796, including a depiction of the artist's colleague John Hoppner.

traditional militia, collectively 45,000 strong, much in the same way as reservists do vis-à-vis the regular army today. That is, unlike the 'embodied' militia, they were not 'immediately called out', but 'enrolled, officered, and gradually trained so as to be fit for service at a time of danger'.[21]

Unlike in the regular army or the Irish militia, which were both voluntary, service in England's embodied militia or supplementary militia was – while not universal – compulsory: operating by a lottery system known as 'balloting', with those selected serving for five years.[22] Yet, it was perfectly legal for a man called into the militia by the ballot to pay someone else to serve in his place, even using the proceeds of an insurance policy he had bought against this very eventuality. And the precise sorts of 'idlers and vagabonds' who were most sought-after as recruits to the regulars were naturally eager to serve as paid militia substitutes, perceiving correctly that the danger to their lives was much lower.[23] The government would cut this gordian knot beginning in 1799 by authorising militiamen who enjoyed serving to transfer into the Army, and later, by 'balloting' men directly into home-service-only battalions of existing regular regiments for the duration of the war plus six months, or for five years, whichever was longer. In practice, these measures resulted in tens of thousands of 'balloted' men voluntarily transferring to first-line battalions that could be sent anywhere in the world.[24] This seemingly ingenious two-stage process of quasi-conscription, though arrived at more or less by accident, would eventually result in a British Army of unprecedented size and commitment.

The volunteer movement was provided with a new statutory basis in the spring of 1798, via a bill – passed unopposed – that went further than the Volunteer Act 1794 by promising compensation to those whose property was destroyed 'to prevent it from falling into the hands of the enemy'.[25] This was a sign of the growing integration, in the official mind, of irregular infantry and cavalry warfare with a policy of 'driving the country', which had been advocated as 'a measure of the greatest importance' by Dirom in a book dedicated to the Duke of York in 1797. As well as the removal of people and animals from the path of the invaders, mills should be disabled, and surplus fodder and anything else of use to them 'set fire to and destroyed without compunction'.[26] At the start of 1798, the number of unmounted volunteers stood at 51,000, but by the end of the summer, this figure had more than doubled. Some 40 per cent of all the new volunteer units raised in the calendar year 1798 were from the south coast, Essex, and Suffolk.[27] From May to August alone,

> probably 264 volunteer infantry corps, 80 yeomanry cavalry troops, and 275 armed associations were approved by the crown [... as] part of wider plans for enlisting civilian help against an invasion. Lords lieutenant were authorised to order the removal of boats, waggons, horses and provisions in the event of an invasion, and the destruction of anything which might be an advantage to the enemy. Labourers were to act as pioneers to destroy roads and bridges [...] to impede the enemy, and to help remove food and drive livestock from the coasts.[28]

The case for assigning these draconian powers to the lords lieutenant in particular was bolstered by an official inquiry into 'the Arrangements which were made, for the internal defence of these Kingdoms, when Spain, by its Armada, projected the Invasion and Conquest of England' in 1588,[29] and subsequently enshrined in the Defence of the Realm Act 1798. The main foe of these scorched-earth tactics was the Duke of Richmond, no longer master-general of the Ordnance,[30] but nevertheless – as lord-lieutenant of Sussex – responsible for carrying them out, in one of the three counties most likely to be actually invaded.

Unsurprisingly, in light of the vast increase in volunteer numbers, the King's Birthday review of sixty-five units in Hyde Park on 4 June 1799 was a 'sensation' and the largest such event up to that time, attended by 150,000 spectators.[31] Though drawn exclusively from London and Westminster, the volunteers being reviewed numbered 12,208 on paper and more than 8,000 on the day.[32] Indeed, British volunteering was 'one of the largest movements of any sort during the eighteenth century'.[33] Contrary to stereotype, however, its members were motivated overwhelmingly by 'the apparent threat of invasion and the compulsory measures taken to raise men to face it' – i.e. balloting, from which volunteers were exempt – and not 'fears of political subversion'.[34] Indeed, a government spokesman was at pains to reassure the House on 6 May 1798 that the issue of military-grade weapons to the general populace would not directly facilitate pro-French revolutionary activity:[35] a statement he would hardly have needed to make if the British volunteers had been a primarily political, conservative force like the American loyalists of the generation before.

In 'the counties with the greatest threat of invasion' and Scotland, membership of the volunteers eventually approached 'a third of the adult males', as against a Britain-wide participation rate that never exceeded 18 per cent.[36] By 1798, the best-trained volunteer units were joining in the regular army's anti-invasion manoeuvres.[37] Though answerable to the county lieutenancy, they were – with some local exceptions – clothed at the expense of the Home Office, armed by the Board of Ordnance, and paid by the War Office for two six-hour days of training per week.[38] Unlike the militia, who were often derided in this period for their poor turnout, lack of martial spirit, and even (when sent over to Ireland) cruelty,[39] the volunteers were generally well respected by both non-uniformed civilians and by the armed forces proper.

The strength of the Royal Artillery at the start of 1798 was 117 companies. In theory, these were far larger than the Army's infantry companies, and even in practice mustered around 120 men on average. Once fully equipped with five guns and a howitzer, eight ammunition waggons, two or three baggage waggons, a spare-wheel waggon, a field forge, all necessary draught animals and around a hundred attached personnel from the separate Corps of Artillery Drivers, a company in the field became known as a 'brigade'; the current term 'battery' for this level of organisation was not yet in use. Royal Horse Artillery troops, of which there four at the end of 1793 and seven by 1801, had the same number and calibre of main armament as a Royal Artillery brigade,[40] but were leaner: with a maximum strength in men of 106 gunners and sixty drivers, and only six ammunition waggons. Instigated by the Duke of Richmond, their main role was to provide artillery support to the cavalry during land battles, and not – as in France – to continuously patrol the coastline and exchange fire with any enemy ships that came close enough.[41]

Not having reached puberty was no obstacle to obtaining a commission, as indicated by this portrait from life of Ens. M'Dougal of the Hopetoun Fencibles.

When arrayed for battle, the even-numbered pieces in each field-artillery brigade formed the left division, and the odd-numbered ones the right division, with no. 3 gun (i.e. the second from the right) being the 'gun of direction' from which the other five were expected to copy their aim, rate, and type of fire, in the absence of any orders to the contrary. As it was widely assumed that the French forces invading England would be accompanied by many fewer draught animals, and fewer and much smaller field-artillery pieces, than would be the case in their invasions of their neighbours by land, measures to bolster the mobility of Britain's field artillery were considered of potentially decisive importance in repelling them.[42] Nevertheless, six precious 'Marching Companies' of the Royal Artillery, as distinct from its Invalids, were serving in fixed positions at Plymouth, Portsmouth, Tynemouth, and Leith Fort in 1798, and the same number of companies three years later, albeit spread more thinly: i.e. across the same four places plus Dover.[43]

As of new year's day 1798, the number of volunteer units that had either been raised as, or converted to, a coastal-artillery role was thirty-five, covering forty-three coastal towns and the Isle of Wight. By 1801, the number of such units had grown to fifty-four, in all the same places plus twenty-one others.[44] They were clearly not all bad shots, nor lacking in initiative: on one occasion, the Gravesend Volunteer Artillery managed to force the surrender of a ship of the line that had been taken over by mutineers.[45] In fixed fortifications, with a typical crew of six and a 'traversing' garrison platform that pivoted at the front, the artillerymen numbered 2, 4, 5, and 6 would run the gun out, 3 and 4 would elevate it, and 5 and 6 would traverse it. That type of carriage was intended to be fired in a narrow arc through a particular embrasure, or in an arc of up to 160 degrees over a low parapet if there were no embrasures. It had been invented by Lt John Rutherford RE in the Scilly Isles in 1793, and soon thereafter adopted in Nova Scotia.[46] If the pivot was at the back (as in the later Martello towers) to allow up to a 360-degree arc of fire, gunners 5 and 6 elevated and 3 and 4 traversed. Once it had been aimed, number 6 would climb up onto the platform to apply the portfire. In the case of a five-man shore-based carronade crew, number 4 fired and shared the traversing duty with number 3. In all cases,

Pioneering balloonist James Sadler unveiled his 'War Chariot', armed with two 3-pounder cannon, in June 1798.

number 1 was the sponger and number 2 the loader, while the highest-numbered man available acted as the gun's commander/aimer. Throughout this period, each gunner below the rank of sergeant was equipped with a .65 calibre flintlock carbine with a 37-inch barrel and a 13-inch bayonet, as well as a short, curved, brass-hilted sword known as a 'hanger', and each sergeant carried a shortened pike or spontoon.

The fencibles, technically regulars, were criticised by Dirom in 1797 as a drain on recruiting for those regular units that could be sent abroad, as well as on the civilian labour force.[47] There were just over 11,000 fencible infantry at the beginning of the following year. Fortescue, the implacable Edwardian critic of Pitt and all his works, was characteristically scathing about the fencibles: 'in spite of all the levying [...] to release the regular Army for foreign service, it was actually found impossible to make an end of one thousand French troops [i.e. Gen. Humbert's expedition] without throwing Ireland on the mercy of the British Militia', fourteen regiments of which were sent across the Irish Sea between June and September 1798, thus 'denuding England of the territorial garrison which strictly and legally belonged to it'.[48] Though Fortescue no doubt used the term 'fencibles' in its correct technical sense, we should remember when interpreting contemporary accounts of the doings of fencibles that the term was 'commonly applied [...] to unpaid part-timers', presumably by civilians unfamiliar with units from outside their local area.[49] True fencible units could be found everywhere in the British Isles, and were especially important in plans for the defence of Scotland, which had no militia until 1797. However, 'not being levied by ballot', the Scottish fencibles could not 'with certainty' be augmented in numbers during emergencies, as a true militia could.[50]

Sir Home Popham.

Back in 1793, then-Lt Home Popham RN had organised the anti-French fishermen in British-held parts of Flanders to help defend their own villages and towns using heavily armed inshore craft, and he is believed to have coined the term 'Sea Fencibles' to describe these Flemish units. They particularly distinguished themselves in the Siege of Nieuwpoort, but the scheme thereafter seems to have been forgotten until 1797, when Alexander Dirom recommended that in Britain, too, 'ferrymen, fishermen, and resident seafaring people in the neighbourhood' be 'taught the gun exercise' and enrolled on a part-time basis to man gunboats and floating batteries for home defence.[51] Again at the instigation of now-Capt. Popham, the idea was duly revived, and the name 'Corps of Sea Fencibles' made official in March 1798. Within two months they were also being called upon to man shore batteries, and at least four companies were assigned this role on the Isle of Wight alone.[52] For attending their one weekly assembly day, the men were paid one shilling plus provisions, or if no food or drink were given, two shillings.[53] Much as with the drain of potential regular soldiers into the militia, the negative impact of the Sea Fencibles' existence on Royal Navy recruitment and impressment was complained of at the highest levels; but their combat performance was not to be sneezed at. In Weymouth Bay in 1799, some Sea Fencibles and an under-strength company of the Weymouth and Wyke Volunteers, 'armed only with muskets and bayonets', put to sea to attack a French privateer and succeeded in retaking her British prize, the civilian brig *Somerset*, which had just been captured en route to Bristol from Poole.[54] Sea Fencibles were eligible for prize money, and this undoubtedly played a part in such madcap episodes, which were fairly common. Indeed, these units were probably the best deterrent to privateer raids on coastal towns that the country had ever had. How they would have fared against a massive invasion flotilla remains an open question.[55] Initially, there were five Sea Fencibles districts, extending from Hampshire's border with Sussex to Great Yarmouth, each commanded by a Royal Navy post captain. Before the end of 1798, the system was extended west to Land's End and north to Flamborough Head via the addition of six districts. Quite a few of the district captains were elderly and semi-retired, but some were in the prime of their careers, including Popham himself, and Jane Austen's brother Francis, a distinguished sea-officer and future admiral.[56]

Confusingly, four classes of home-service cavalry – two of them fairly indistinct from each other – were in existence at this time. These were the yeomanry, comprising 'farmers, and other persons [...] who can mount themselves on good horses' in rural regions; volunteer cavalry, initially 'consisting of gentlemen who keep horses', usually from major cities, supplemented by 'their servants, who are trust-worthy';[57] fencible cavalry; and provisional cavalry. Modern observers lump together the first two of these groups under the term 'yeomanry', as indeed contemporaries increasingly did as the wars dragged on, despite its clear rural connotations. The provisional cavalry, which existed from 1796 to 1800 and remained on the statute book until 1805, was conceived as a punishment levied against counties that did not produce enough yeomanry: consisting of an arguably feudal tax of one man and one horse from among each group of ten 'horses kept for pleasure in England and Wales'.[58] Men who owned fewer than ten horses were grouped together into syndicates, each of which had to nominate a particular horse and rider to serve, unless they joined the yeomanry or a volunteer infantry unit, at which point they became exempt.

In January 1798, the yeomanry numbered between 10,000 and 15,000, and the fencible cavalry, 13,000.[59] Over the first six months of that year, the size of the yeomanry approximately doubled, and it showed itself to be more efficient than the provisionals, for whom government demands then largely ceased. All mounted troops were considered particularly useful for internal policing: Dirom remarking in 1797 that a hundred of them would have 'more effect than a thousand [infantry] soldiers' in quelling riots.[60] In reality, however,

[m]any incidents indicated that volunteers could not be trusted unconditionally to carry out peace-keeping or police duties. [… They] saw themselves as 'citizen soldiers' who had associated to defend their localities against invasion and consequent disorder, but did not thereby become military men or renounce their rights as civilians. They retained strong local loyalties and commitments, and were ready to put them first when they conflicted with their obligations to their corps.[61]

Lastly, mention should be made of Pitt's plan to declare the nation's 7,000 licensed gamekeepers a corps of reservist sharpshooters, which historian Norman Longmate dismissed as an absurdity.[62] Presumably, what Pitt had in mind was the Hesse-Kassel Field Jäger Corps, comprising five foot companies and a mounted squadron. Armed with short-barrelled rifles, 'very often personally owned weapons which the men had used in the woods of their homeland', they 'saw action in all the major campaigns' of the American War of Independence, and were absolutely deadly in battle: becoming revered as 'the élite marksmen of the British armies'.[63] Maj. Hanger, who had served with both the Hessian Jägers and with rifle innovator Maj. Patrick Ferguson's American loyalist unit during that previous war, was an eloquent public advocate of a British jäger corps for home defence, and presumably his writings[64] played some role in Pitt's thinking on this topic.

Disappointed in his Indian ambitions, Bonaparte left his expeditionary force to its own devices in Egypt, arriving back in France on 8 October 1799. He overthrew the Directory in a coup one month later, making himself First Consul for ten years 'with almost unlimited powers' in a new government known as the Consulate.[65] However, he did not immediately revive his cross-Channel invasion plans, being fully occupied with defeating Austria, notably at the Battle of Marengo. By December 1800, Austria had been knocked out of the war.

English militia types returning home after an invasion false alarm, 1799. Etching by Isaac Cruikshank after a drawing by George Moutard Woodward.

Guided by the angel of Fame and a heavenly vision of future imperial glory, Bonaparte abandons his troops in Egypt to their fate.

Worse, Britain and her only other European ally, Russia, had drifted apart since the failure of their joint invasion of Holland (see pp. 137-38); and their relations had become positively strained since Lord Nelson's refusal to return Malta to the Knights of St John, of which Tsar Paul I was styled a Protector. These and other problems led to a second League of Armed Neutrality, patterned on that of 1780, being formed by Russia, Denmark–Norway, Sweden and Prussia before the end of the year. The Baltic was closed to British commerce – including imports of vital masting timber – and British ships in Russian ports were seized. Bonaparte and his new friend the tsar also began planning a 70,000-man joint expedition to conquer British India. So, whether in spite of or because of Britain's new-found isolation, and this new flare-up of his own Indian desires, Bonaparte might well have shelved his cross-Channel invasion plans indefinitely.

But then, on 8 March 1801, came Sir Ralph Abercromby's successful amphibious assault on Egypt. Suddenly, knocking Britain completely out of the war via the capture of London seemed both necessary and possible.[66] Almost at the same moment, Pitt – for reasons only tangentially related to the war – resigned as prime minister, to be replaced by the weaker character Henry Addington. And Neutrality League member Prussia, with the tacit support of both Russia and France, completed her mobilisation for an invasion of King George III's ancestral homeland, Hanover.

Though both had probably been planned far in advance, the two British counter-moves were astonishing in their swiftness and ferocity. First, on 23 March, Levin von Bennigsen, an anglophile Hanoverian officer in Russian service, led a gang of assassins that stomped Tsar Paul to death in his own bedroom, 'an act widely attributed to the British secret service'.[67] Eight days later, 20,000 Prussian troops crossed the Hanoverian border; and one day after that, without war even being declared, Nelson sailed nineteen ships through a dangerously narrow channel into Copenhagen Harbour and basically blew it to bits.[68] After 'a brutal war of attrition between the British fleet and the

Tsar Paul I, in fury over Malta, which had become a British protectorate at its own request in September 1800, tramples on his friendship with King George in this print published by Hannah Humphrey in January 1801. The following month, the tsar would be caricatured as Bonaparte's pet bear.

The Magnanimous Ally — Painted at Petersburg

shore defences of the city' lasting 'four terrible hours', Nelson secured a truce by threatening to burn the crews of its defensive floating batteries alive.[69] The Danes had no reason to disbelieve him; it was well known by this time that in Naples, Nelson had stood happily by as the local royalists rounded up the Jacobins, roasted, and indeed ate some of them.[70] Of the Dano-Norwegian naval vessels present that did not sink, one was blown up, eleven were captured and intentionally burnt, and one was captured and preserved so that it could be sailed back to England with the hundreds of British wounded aboard. Nelson then brought up his half-dozen bomb-vessels and threatened to destroy the whole wooden-built city with carcase rounds unless Denmark quit the League. This had the desired effect, not only on the Danes but on the Russians, who reopened the Baltic to British merchant ships and released the ones they had previously arrested. Britain had shocked the civilised world with a demonstration of how much life and property – its own, as well as other people's, combatants or otherwise – it would willingly destroy in pursuit of a marginal advantage in northern European waters.[71]

The killing of the tsar, in particular, had 'dramatically altered the drift of events in Europe', not least by forcing Bonaparte 'to shelve his eastern ambitions'.[72] This, of course, meant that Britain itself was firmly back on his menu, and 30,000 troops and 276 invasion craft were assembled 'between Flushing [Vlissingen] in Flanders and the Morbihan in Brittany'.[73] These were then steadily concentrated at Boulogne, which at enormous expense was dredged for the purpose, and had its jetties and quays improved.[74]

Danish print of the First Battle of Copenhagen, 1801, by J. F. Clemens after C. A. Lorentzen.

In part to reassure the public, Nelson – who believed that 40,000 French troops would soon land in equal numbers in two places, one on either side of Dover – was placed in charge of the coastal defence of Kent and Essex, and began gleefully plotting a cataclysmic gunboat-vs.-gunboat battle near the British shore.[75] '[T]he moment the enemy touch our coast', he wrote to the Admiralty in July 1801, 'be it where it may, they are to be attacked by every man afloat and on shore: this must be perfectly understood. *Never fear the event*'.[76] But in August, no doubt tired of waiting for the French to oblige him, he went on the offensive against the 'lately strengthened' harbour of Boulogne with five bomb vessels and twenty-eight gunboats, supported by one frigate.[77] Attacking a roughly equal number of armed French invasion craft with more than 750 rounds of common shell over a period of sixteen hours, he claimed that his flotilla 'entirely disabled ten of them', though the French said it was only four; in any case, the outcome was immediately perceived on the British side as disappointing, relative to the effort and ammunition expended.[78] Later the same month, Nelson tried a new approach, incorporating 'a division of howitzer boats', aimed at capturing French vessels at anchor; but clever defensive devices in Boulogne's harbour, including nets and chains, rendered this a complete fiasco, with 170 British casualties. One bright spot in the summer's operations was British gunboats' capture near Etaples of three French 'flats', each mounting an 8-inch brass howitzer, despite opposition from five field guns on the shore. Three other invasion vessels of identical design were destroyed on the same evening.[79]

In this Gillray engraving, Prime Minister Henry Addington 'evacuates' territories 'eaten' by Britain during the French Revolutionary War. In fact, the British evacuation of Malta promised in the 1802 peace treaty was never carried out, and this was one of the reasons France re-commenced its preparations to invade Britain in 1803.

It is something of an open question whether Bonaparte's 1801 invasion preparations were legitimate, or just 'a form of blackmail to force the British government to come to terms'.[80] Certainly, 'England was ill prepared for a really serious attack'[81] in the summer of 1801, with the fencible cavalry disbanded, volunteer numbers capped, and coastal batteries in their usual state of under-manning and disrepair. Yet, as of the fourth week of July, not only Nelson but the Duke of York and the adjutant-general, Sir Robert Brownrigg, thought on the basis of 'unquestionable intelligence' that the invasion would be 'immediate'.[82] In reality, a 'really serious' attack was hardly possible, given that Bonaparte had placed 'no artillery at Boulogne, and no soldiers at Dunkirk' as recently as June;[83] and that the number of French troops earmarked for this particular invasion was lower, by tens of thousands, than in the parallel efforts of 1779 and 1798. In any case, with France unassailable on the Continent, and Britain looking much the same at sea, peace negotiations commenced in October 1801, and with Prime Minister Addington unsteadily at the helm, the Peace of Amiens was signed six months later. It was generally unfavourable to the British, who handed back Saint-Marcouf, Minorca, and the Cape of Good Hope, among other territories acquired since the start of the war. But vital breathing space had been gained.

FATHERS OF THE MARTELLO

The modern British Army has been described as one of the world's great learning organisations. I would argue that it was also thus in the time of George III, 'a keen apprentice of military science from a young age' whose 'thirst for knowledge led him to collect more than 55,000 maps, charts, prints and manuals'.[1] During my undergraduate study of recruitment policy in various eras and places, I was astonished by his grasp of detail, and care for those serving in his armed forces – especially in comparison to the previous century's King Charles I, a much less intelligent and less curious person, who routinely fobbed such matters off onto Sir Edward Nicholas and other underlings. As so often happens, the attitude of mind at the top filtered down; and the Navy, Army, and Ordnance in the late Georgian period were rich in individuals who concurrently or subsequently excelled in almost every sphere of human endeavour.

Frederick Augustus, Duke of York and non-ordained Lutheran prince-bishop of Osnabrück, the king's second and favourite son, was made commander-in-chief of the British Army in early 1795,[2] despite his mediocre showing in the Flanders campaigns of the preceding two years. He subsequently helped organise a successful opposed landing at Callantsoog in North Holland by some 19,000 troops from '250 craft of all sizes [...] [c]overed by a hot fire' from Royal Navy warships and three highly effective close-support gunboats. After pushing aside a Franco-Dutch field army there, the British seized the Dutch naval facilities of Den Helder and Nieuwe Werk, together with twenty-four ships of war including the seventy-gun *Washington*, plus an armed sloop, three Indiamen, and ninety-seven garrison guns.[3] Unfortunately, as had happened to the French in Ireland the previous summer, the expected mass popular revolt in favour of the invaders never materialised. Attempts over the following three months to push much beyond the bridgehead all failed, with the loss of around 5,000 British killed, wounded and prisoners, the latter category including hundreds of soldiers' wives and children.[4] Though clearly no genius as a field commander, the duke took after his father and proved an unusually talented administrator of the Army at home: he 'supported the commanders' efforts to revive military spirit with some success [...] looked after the soldiers and their comforts, and sternly put down the influence of personal favouritism'.[5] In short, even if the regular army remained 'ill-coordinated' with the Ordnance, volunteers, and militia, the duke's 'years of vigorous reform' that began in 1795 meant that 'Bonaparte would have faced in England a far more dangerous British army than the one he had driven out of Toulon in 1793'.[6]

Though requiring 'but a feeble garrison', the duke noted on 25 August 1803, coastal towers had the advantage of 'keep[ing] possession of the coast defences to the annoyance of an enemy during the whole operation of his landing – and the probable prevention of his disembarking stores until he can bring his artillery against them'.[7] In the same year, he ordered that preparations be made to flood Romney Marsh and Pevensey Level, 'by opening the three sluices in the Dymchurch Wall,

Scene from the landing of the second wave of British troops in Holland in 1799, showing the complex process of re-fitting a field gun's barrel to its carriage after sea transport.

The Dutch might have proved reluctant invaders of England, as suggested in this cartoon by Temple West, but they were formidable foes indeed when defending their own territory.

a fourth at Scots Float on the Rother and a fifth at East Guldeford near Rye', and that the dykes on the River Brede also be breached.[8] However, there was no agreement regarding whether this flooding should be undertaken only during an invasion, or immediately.[9] In the event, the planned construction of defensive towers in some of the areas that would be flooded militated against the opening of the sluices pre-invasion – flooding being, in any case, a 'measure of ruinous consequence', as the duke himself noted on 27 September 1804.[10] Apparently, disagreement about when or if to open the floodgates was one of the issues that prompted the famed Rochester Conference of 21 October 1804, which was attended by the duke; the prime minister – again Pitt, who had returned to power in May; Lord Chatham, master-general of the Ordnance and Pitt's elder brother; Lord Camden, secretary of state for war and colonies; Sir David 'Old Pivot' Dundas, by then commanding general of the Southern Military District (Kent and Sussex); Robert Morse, the nation's first inspector-general of fortifications; Brownrigg, who had succeeded Dundas as quartermaster-general; and John Brown, Brownrigg's deputy and the originator – earlier that year – of the rival, and also as-yet unfunded, Royal Military Canal project.

About the prime minister, little more needs to be said, except that his 'bold approval of costly plans for fortifying the south coast was to transform the whole business of defending England against invasion'.[11] Specifically, it was at Rochester that the Ford-Twiss design of Martello towers for that coast, as endorsed with various further modifications by Dundas, Morse, and D'Aubant, was approved at cabinet level. As Ford had noted back in 1803, '[t]heir main advantage was that they would be so substantially built that they would be long-lasting and their maintenance [...] negligible'; and 'in peacetime, the guns could be dismantled and stored inside'.[12] The conference attendees, though few in number and not now remembered as experts on the subject, in fact represented a vast reservoir of practical knowledge of coastal-attack and coastal-defence matters, gleaned from experience in Canada, America, the West Indies, Gibraltar, Ireland, and the hostile shores of France, Corsica, and the Netherlands.

As the Hon. John Pratt, Lord Camden had been a Cambridge contemporary and friend of Prime Minister Pitt. Elected MP for Bath in 1780, he was outspoken against the American War, but continued to serve as an officer of the West Kent Militia until 1782. He became viceroy of Ireland in 1795, aged just 36, and proved inventive in the sphere of cavalry recruitment. But he 'came across as irresolute' during the Irish Rebellion of 1798, which in fairness he 'probably did little either to provoke or to contain', and was replaced by Gen. Lord Cornwallis on 20 June.[13] It was Camden who gave the Board of Ordnance its specific implementation instructions for the towers (i.e. to commence obtaining sites, contractors, bricks, and all else that was necessary) on 27 December 1804.

Despite being the son and brother of two prime ministers, Lord Chatham had spent his entire career in the armed forces. He resigned his commission on Whig grounds when the American War broke out, but purchased another when the French joined in on the American side. As a captain in the 86th Foot, he served throughout the Great Siege of Gibraltar. From 1788–94 he was first lord of the Admiralty, and in 1799 – by now a major-general – commanded a brigade under the Duke of York in the invasion of Holland. Having been appointed master-general of the Ordnance in 1801, he was one of the recipients of the original Ford-Twiss memo on 'Towers as Sea-Fortresses' in mid-1803. As of the following February, he was decidedly lukewarm on the idea of tower defence, penning a Sir Humphrey-esque memo in which he ignorantly called it 'entirely novel in principle' and bemoaned its 'infinite variety of details'.[14] But by the end of the Rochester Conference, he was won round like the other members of the privy council. Later, Chatham would serve as governor of Plymouth and Jersey, and would command the ill-fated 'conjunct' expedition against Antwerp in 1809 (pp. 179-81).[15] Like the Duke of York, he emerges from the records as a mediocre field commander, but a brilliant administrator, who managed the British artillery arm to an unprecedented level of excellence.

The other key recipient of 'Towers as Sea-Fortresses' was Sir David Dundas, who in August 1796 had led a War Office team that drew up '[t]he first detailed and systematic scheme of defence' since Tudor times, and the most comprehensive up to that point.[16] Now remembered chiefly for his advocacy of 'Prussian' precision infantry manoeuvres over the 'American' light-infantry tactics favoured by Moore, Dirom, Cornwallis, and others, Sir David was, in fact, a Woolwich-trained artillery and latterly, engineer officer who had participated in the Lowland phase of William Roy's mapping of the whole of Scotland at a field-by-field level. He was concurrently an engineer and an infantry officer when he participated in the 'Descents'

Sir David Dundas, right, oversees a 'Prussian' drill practice about to degenerate into comical catastrophe.

of 1758 and the Battle of Saint-Cast. By the time he went to the Siege of Havana, he was a light dragoon; and his subsequent career took him on a whirlwind tour of British infantry and cavalry regiments, with pauses to observe the peacetime camps and manoeuvres of France, Prussia and Austria. After participating in the Torra di Mortella operation in Corsica in 1794 and the Duke of York's campaign in Flanders, Dundas wrote a second drill manual – this time, for the cavalry – and became a staff officer in London in November 1796. From then until 1799, he continued to play 'an instrumental role in the preparations for Britain's home defence', and in 1800–01 was made governor of the Landguard Fort and Fort George, concurrently with his role as quartermaster-general. Though widely made fun of, both for the style of his drill and manuals and his 'austere' appearance and demeanour, Dundas was 'among the most intelligent and knowledgeable of his officer contemporaries', and 'assisted throughout in the Duke of York's reforming efforts, which were of untold value'.[17] In the specific sphere of coastal defence, however, he can be summed up as an alarmist, whose key insight – that when we were at war with any Baltic power plus France or Spain, 'every [...] point of the circuit of the two islands [was] exposed'[18] – could hardly have led to practical remedial action, even if it had been true. His fears that Lincolnshire was 'ill-placed to receive help from outside' conversely meant that its value as a bridgehead was highly questionable.[19] Likewise, the difficulty he highlighted of preserving the city of Exeter was perfectly counterpoised by the difficulty of sending enough attackers out of it to deal a knockout blow to any other part of the country. The best that can be said is that Dundas took a clear-eyed view of just how bad things might get if the Royal Navy were ever comprehensively defeated in home waters;[20] and in such circumstances, for good or ill, Martello towers and other coastal fortifications would certainly have come into their own. He proposed that the coastal areas of his Southern Military District be protected by a hundred new redoubts of 'strong stone', each mounting a complete battery, as early as 1797.[21]

Perhaps at Dundas's behest, the first detailed proposal to the War Office that defensive towers be built on the coast of the British mainland – indeed, 'as close to the beach as possible', in the case of seven towers to be built between Worthing and Littlehampton[22] – was not made by an engineer, but by Thomas Reynolds, an officer of the 30th Foot. If one's aim was to prevent an enemy landing, Reynolds argued in 1798, nothing could be better than 'a Simple Tower of Brickwork defended by a Handful of Resolute Men'.[23] Though he specifically cited the Torra di Mortella as an inspiration for his scheme, the towers he proposed were of a broadly Conway pattern: less massive than the eventual south-coast Martellos (i.e. each containing only 300,000 rather than half a million bricks), and 'a line of twelve loopholes in the wall'.[24] He thought that ninety-eight towers in all should be built between Littlestone in Sussex and Yarmouth, and nominated specific sites for each of them. While no part of Reynolds's plan was adopted at the time, it would have been remembered, albeit perhaps vaguely, in the defence-planning circles of five years later.

Brown was born in Elgin in 1756 and went to work as a surveyor in Tobago, with considerable acclaim, but not much financial success, and in constant fear of disease. Having failed in the first half of his goal – to 'make as much money in this place [...] to go anywhere else like a Gentleman, or perish in the attempt' – he joined the 27th Foot in 1782.[25] After serving around the Caribbean and in England and Ireland as a junior officer for seven years, he transferred to the Royal Irish Engineers as a captain-lieutenant, thereafter specialising in defensive works in southern Ireland. Along the way, he discovered a literal gold mine in County Wicklow in 1795. In response to the French near-invasion of Bantry Bay in the following year, Brown oversaw the construction of five batteries, at Ardnagashel Point, Chapel Island, Eagle Point, Horse Island, and Whiddy Point, and an expensive set of improvements to Fort Camden in Cork Harbour. Roundly praised for his 'ability and topographical science',[26] he became in July 1802 assistant quartermaster-general at Horse Guards, where his responsibilities included London's invasion preparedness. This involved actually implementing many of the recommendations that had been made in the *Times* on 25 April 1798, including the construction of blockhouses in the city's squares, and equipping a responsible person in each street with a box of grenades.[27] In addition to seeing his canal essentially as an alternative coastline that could replace the non-defendable Romney Marsh, Brown originally anticipated that a flotilla 'stationed in the port of Rye for the defence of Pevensey Bay' could move up and down it as a further form of defence against attacks by land.[28] A similar idea was expressed by David Dundas in his endorsement to Brown's canal proposal of 19 September 1804.[29]

Robert Morse was commissioned into the 12th Foot 'while still a cadet' at Woolwich, and served, aged about 16, in Gen. Bligh's raid on Cherbourg during the Seven Years War. The following year, Morse was 'employed on the coast defences of Sussex', and present at the capture of Belle Île off Brittany in 1761. He was in the Caribbean in both that war and the next, latterly as commanding engineer of Dominica, St Vincent, Grenada, and Tobago, before returning to the defence of Sussex, and latterly Plymouth and Falmouth, in the crisis year 1779. He was then sent to look after the defences of Nova Scotia, where he 'warned of the potential for boundary disputes with America on the Sainte Croix River' and the need for improvement to the fortifications at Annapolis Royal and Halifax. By the following year, 1784, Morse had been appointed chief engineer in British North America. After various other appointments, including half a decade as commander, RE at Gibraltar, he became inspector-general of fortifications in April 1802.[30] In that role, he took a great interest in the standardisation of the traversing carriages for garrison guns that had started appearing in British outposts in the early 1790s. In 1804, he asked the Earl of Chatham to convene a combined committee of RA and RE officers to ascertain whether traversing platforms were 'generally or in what particular cases preferable to the common Stone or Wooden Platform', as well as how high and how long they ought to be, and whether the pivot should in general be at the front, centre, or rear, 'and for what reason'.[31] It is quite possible that Chatham never obliged him, but once it had been decided that Martello towers would be round and lack any embrasures, only rear-pivot traversing carriages for their armament made any sense at all.[32]

The remarkable William Twiss, son of a Kentish waterman, joined the Ordnance department at age 15, and at 17 – more than a year before being commissioned into the Engineers – was sent to Gibraltar as overseer of the king's works. A man 'of strongly aviform appearance, with a great beak of a nose and a receding forehead', he worked on the defences of Portsmouth Dockyard in 1771, and in 1776 went to North America, where he 'took part in the operations to clear the insurgent Americans from Quebec province'; oversaw 'the construction of a fleet to wrest possession of Lake Champlain from the Americans, an objective accomplished [...] in October 1776'; and planned the siege-works 'that led the Americans to abandon Fort Ticonderoga'. After a brief spell as a prisoner, he returned to Canada, supervising the construction of field-works at Quebec City, choosing the site of Fort Haldimand, and designing the Côteau-du-Lac 'fortified canal'. Back in England after the war, he wrote reports on the defences of Plymouth and Portsmouth and 'supervised the construction, among other fortifications, of Fort Cumberland at the entrance of Langston harbour' before moving on to serve as commander, RE, for the Southern Military District from 1792. In that role, by now a lieutenant-colonel, Twiss added four new bastions to the eastern side of Dover Castle, served in the Den Helder expedition of 1799, and 'made tours of the Channel Islands (1800) and Ireland (1802) [...] to report upon their defences' before returning to Dover to improve the fortifications on its western side, including the 'grand shaft' leading from the barracks to the town.[33] His Irish report, dated 15 January 1803, led directly to the building of defensive towers on Bere Island and Garinish in Bantry Bay, as well as in the vicinity of Dublin – though he rejected Dundas's opinion that the coastline of the whole island could be fortified, instead favouring strong-points on islands in rivers as combining 'the maximum of advantage with the minimum of cost'.[34] Twiss also performed a coastal survey on the mainland with John Moore in the summer of 1803, which rated the 1790s defensive works around Dungeness as so bad that it was 'hardly possible [...] to make them defensible': a finding that led in short order to the planning of the Royal Military Canal.[35] The following summer, Twiss travelled from Beachy Head to Dover and selected fifty-eight sites for bomb-proof towers, not counting the Tudor Device Fort at Sandgate. This old structure, he said, could be made into a 'secure sea battery' by placing bomb-proof arches over the existing towers[36] – a technique he had previously employed at Dover Castle.[37] All of his findings were communicated to Morse promptly. Of course, it was impossible for fifty-eight towers to be evenly spaced over more than seventy miles of coastline and still be 'within five or six hundred yards of each other' as required for mutual support, so they were to be sited in clusters where the local topography tended most to favour the attackers.[38] This would later lead John Brown to criticise the scheme as 'in some parts of the coast [...] too scanty, in others too profuse';[39] but, in fact, it was in keeping with theoretical writings on how to oppose beach-landings and river-crossings going back to Lloyd, and probably beyond.[40] On 3 October 1804, another report, this time containing a 'lucid' description of the towers' design features, was signed by Twiss, D'Aubant, and Lt-Col Thomas Nepean RE. The trio's eagerness is indicated by the fact that they submitted this document 'without waiting until the drawings [...] are finished'.[41]

D'Aubant, as chief engineer at the British defence of Rhode Island, produced various plans of forts, earthworks, and fortified towns in that colony, eight of which survive in the University of Michigan's William L. Clements Library.[42] At a time when standards of draughtsmanship among British military engineers

Napoleon's medal for veterans of the invasion of England, bearing a false claim that it had been 'Struck in London in 1804'. The theme is the victory of Hercules over Antaeus, whose rather fishy appearance reflects that, thanks to Sir Sidney Smith, Sir Home Popham and others, the true boundaries of Great Britain at this time were not her own coasts, but the enemy's. Another variant of the medal, lacking the reference to London, continued the Hercules theme but with England cast as the Nemean Lion. Image copyright National Maritime Museum, Greenwich, London.

Napoleon inspecting the troops at Boulogne, 15 August 1804.

and artillery officers were quite high, D'Aubant's work was outstanding for its ability to capture the overall topographical setting as well as the details of the focal structures. We last encountered him in 1787, criticising the uselessness of the defensive towers built on Guernsey and relegating them to barrack use; but he had since been present during the British destruction of Corsica's Torra di Mortella, and was now an enthusiast for towers, provided that they were 'everywhere equally strong', i.e. including around the staircases, chimneys, drains, and shot-lockers that would be built into the thickness of the walls.[43]

Not much is known about Thomas Nepean's earlier career, except that he infuriated Gen. Charles Stuart at the siege of Calvi in Corsica in 1794 by being a whole day late in constructing a battery.[44] Importantly, however, he was the son of the keeper of the Green Dragon Inn in Saltash, and therefore the brother of a civil servant who had accrued so much influence as to deform the governance of the country and empire around himself. At the age of 21, Evan Nepean began an eight-year career as a civilian clerk and, latterly, purser on a series of Royal Navy warships stationed in England and America. But at the end of the American War, he was suddenly appointed under-secretary of state at the Home Office. This 'astonishing' promotion has generally been taken to indicate that he was, in fact, a spy of considerable merit. Of course, it could hardly have hurt that he was a man of 'unremitting diligence and integrity', regularly in danger of 'killing himself by his labours'. At the Home Office, as well as overseeing intelligence operations, the younger Nepean

> was involved in the negotiations for the peace of 1783, regulations for the government of Ireland [...] and arrangements for botanical expeditions. These last included [Lt William] Bligh's search for breadfruit in the *Bounty* and Archibald Menzies's voyage with Captain George Vancouver in the *Discovery* to the Pacific coast of America in 1790. He also planned, with Arthur Phillip, the first convict settlement in New South Wales, in 1788.[45]

By 1793, Evan Nepean was considered a personal friend by the prime minister, and giving regular briefings directly to the king, for whom he drafted a top-secret plan for a British invasion of Spanish America in 1797.[46] In 1804, he was busily plotting the overthrow of Napoleon via a coup. Given his immense attention to detail and demonstrated family loyalty, the involvement of his brother in the Martello project implies, at the very least, that the then-equivalent of MI5 and MI6 was not dead-set against the idea.

A similar comment could be made about Brownrigg, newly appointed quartermaster-general at the time of the conference. Quite unlike Nepean, he was something of a nonentity, whose career had prospered simply due to his status as 'the protégé and personal friend of the "grand old duke of York"'.[47] However, the nature of his official role and his close ties to the commander-in-chief meant that he could probably have strangled the Martello programme at birth. Thus, if only in a negative sense, it could not have happened without him.

John Moore finished the American War as a captain, and served as MP for Linlithgow Burghs in his native Scotland from 1784 to 1790 before returning to active service as lieutenant-colonel commanding the 51st Foot. Having played the part in the Torra di Mortella escapade described in Chapter 6, he proceeded to the siege of Calvi, forty-two miles west of San Fiorenzo town on the same side of the island. There, he worked closely with an improvised shore battery of heavy naval guns, slothfully built by then-Capt. Thomas Nepean and commanded by an as-yet obscure Capt. Horatio Nelson RN. It was in this action that Nelson lost

Sir John Moore.

the sight of one eye, while Moore was wounded in the head by a shell fragment. Sacked as adjutant-general of the Anglo-Corsican Kingdom for maintaining too-close ties with the mercurial Pasquale Paoli, Moore led a brigade in the recapture of St Lucia in 1796 and stayed on as its governor during a French-backed slave revolt, during which 'he tirelessly visited outposts, sleeping in the open and sharing the same sparse rations as his men in a determined attempt to regain control of the region'. Unlike many of his brother officers and the local planter fraternity, he was evidently not against the arming of freed slaves to fight in the British cause (which had been normal practice in the American War) and would eventually accept the titular colonelcy of the 9th West India Regiment. But after two bouts of yellow fever, he returned home in mid-1797 and recovered enough to be given command of the forts of Cork and Kinsale in December. During the 1798 Irish rising he re-took the town of Wexford without a fight, after defeating Fr. Philip Roche's insurgents at the Battle of Foulksmills, and was promoted to major-general. He remained in Ireland until the Anglo-Russian invasion of Holland, where as a brigade commander he had 'a finger of his right hand broken by a shot deflected from his spyglass'. Shot through the face at the Battle of Egmont-op-Zee, he nearly died after drinking a lead-based topical solution in his confusion, but recovered from both these mishaps and was in Minorca by the summer of 1800, from where he prepared an amphibious assault on Cadiz. That operation being cancelled at the last second (Moore's men were already in the landing boats), he was sent to join Koehler with the Turkish army at Jaffa, but unlike his friend, did not contract the plague there. He played a leading role in the opposed landing at Aboukir Bay in 1801, where he was wounded in the leg, and was awarded the Turkish Order of the Crescent. It was in July 1803 that Moore 'took command of a brigade centred on Shorncliffe, near Folkestone in Kent, where he established his celebrated training camp for light infantry' in a new fort laid out by Twiss in the 1790s; and took responsibility, under Gen. Dundas, 'for the coast of Kent from Deal to Dungeness [...] primarily concerned with the threat of invasion'.[48]

George Hanger was about as unpromising a piece of human material as has ever been spawned by the Anglo-Irish aristocracy. '[I]rascible, violent, dissipated, extravagant, and individualistic sometimes to eccentricity', he was involved in three duels before his twenty-first birthday and 'claimed to have worn the first satin coat in England'. A committed Whig, he helped Banastre

Tarleton (under whom he had served in America) organise a gang of party-political 'bludgeon men' in an apparently successful attempt to sway a Westminster by-election in favour of the Foxite candidate, Lord John Townshend.[49] Despite his flaws, however, Hanger was an intelligent man who rightly saw the loss of London to the enemy as an irrecoverable blow. He also perceived – presumably due to his personal experiences at the capture of Charleston, South Carolina – that Tilbury Fort could simply be raced past in ships, or circumvented by land on its northern side. To prevent the latter, he proposed that the most vulnerable part of the north bank of the Thames be fortified with four

George Hanger's characteristic haughty sneer.

redoubts, arranged in 'a portion of a circle concave towards the enemy' around the probable landing beach, and armed 'en barbett'[50] (i.e. with their guns able to fire in any direction, like a Swedish *udema*). Though the barbette mounting on land was hardly a new idea – D'Aubant had used it at Fort Brown, Rhode Island in 1779 – the new traversing carriages that greatly facilitated it would be widely introduced in 1800,[51] and installed on the roofs of English Martello towers from the latter's inception. Unlike the later Martello proponents, however, Hanger argued that his beach-defence redoubts 'should not be nearer to the deep water than 1,000 yards', to preserve them from the fire of enemy ships and floating batteries, and leave them free to pursue their main function: slaughtering enemy infantry in the beachhead with 'converging fire'.[52] As such, remarkably, Hanger's widely publicised proposed system of coastal fortification anticipated both Martello towers and the Royal Military Canal: being, in effect, a version of the latter composed of the former.

In the American War, Viscount Keith – then George Elphinstone – had constructed a floating battery ballasted with empty barrels, 'so that if she was shot through and through, it was not possible to sink her', and passed this secret on to Hanger, who was serving alongside him there.[53] Keith authorised the building of early Martello towers at the Cape of Good Hope, and in 1801 commanded the naval element of the signally successful British amphibious landing in Egypt. On the latter occasion, Sir Sidney Smith served under him as the commander of 'a battalion of 1,000 seamen who were put ashore to co-operate with the army',[54] which I take as evidence of Keith's forward-thinking as much as Smith's. In 1803, Keith was appointed commander-in-chief North Sea, a brief that 'stretched from Selsey Bill in Sussex to the Shetland Islands' and 'gave him the heavy responsibility of preparing the defence of the coast against a likely invasion'. Installing himself at East Cliff Lodge by Ramsgate, he set about 'organizing the sea fencibles from Hampshire to the Forth, the signalling and telegraph systems on shore, the extension of the chain of Martello towers, and liaising with the army'. Most importantly,

> French ports had to be blockaded, and all movements of the enemy, real or pretended, had to be watched since a feint might always be converted into an actual attempt at invasion, and this might come from either Boulogne or the Texel.[55]

Lastly, and perhaps most unexpectedly, our ancient enemy Charles Dumouriez, monarchist to the bone, had 'become the advisory expert of the British War Office',[56] a confidant of Pitt, Camden, and the Duke of York, offering them copious and detailed advice on how to defeat the sorts of invasion schemes he had devised from 1777 to 1793. Such was Napoleon's fear of Dumouriez that, when he heard a rumour that the Duke d'Enghien, an exiled French prince, had become friendly with 'his neighbour [...] Dumouriez' in the German state of Baden, the dictator sent a party of dragoons across the border to kidnap d'Enghien, who was executed in March 1804. In fact, the neighbour in question was 'a harmless old man, Thumery'.[57] In the country where he actually lived, too,

> Dumouriez [...] never seems to have been quite fully trusted, which in the context of a prolonged war with France is hardly surprising, and he had to base his defence suggestions and recommendations on his own ideas rather than with the aid of British military facts and figures which were purposely withheld from him as a foreign citizen.[58]

Nevertheless, 'many of the places he highlighted were subsequently defended with batteries and Martello towers'.[59] In the autumn of 1803, Dumouriez began writing a thorough report on invasion weak points. On its completion in May 1804, it echoed Dirom's arguments[60] that coastal fortresses should not be so strong on the landward side that they can, if taken, be held indefinitely by the enemy. Indeed, Dumouriez said, they 'must be fortified only on the front parallel to the sea'.[61] In place of rear fortifications of the standard type, there should be 'redoubts [...] within reach of seaports or of beaches [...] constructed on a height or at the confluence of streams [...] with room for four or five hundred men'.[62] In terms of siting, this echoed Twiss's views on the siting of smaller forts in Ireland; and in terms of scale and purpose, it anticipated the largest size of redoubts that the Rochester Conference would approve later in the year. Dumouriez's report went on to recommend isolated, enclosed batteries, each 'surrounded with a moat full of water [... and] placed as near the beach as possible inside bays and coves'.[63] While he did not propose that these should take the form of towers, the import of the general idea is clearly parallel to that of previous and subsequent coastal-tower schemes:

> They prevent the descent of the enemy and his deployment should he manage to land. They form an obstacle which he is bound to overcome before he can advance; and since they can be supported from behind and act as *têtes de colonne* to the defender's troops dispatched from the [... redoubts,

they] might entirely stop the enemy's movements and expose him, ere he could deploy completely on the strand, to an attack by land or sea. It is chiefly on the east and south-east coasts where the water is less deep and the beaches spacious and cut up by marshes and canals that these isolated batteries would be most useful.[64]

Dumouriez did not specify these batteries' sizes in terms of either guns or gunners. However, all else being held equal, he noted that it was less effective to build one large battery than several small ones that supported each other within a limited area. 'Six batteries of four pieces each, spaced on the two flanks of an anchorage, would be of more avail than a single battery of twenty-four', which 'might be easily silenced by the vessels and gunboats moored below', whereas small batteries in a carefully dispersed group 'could not all be silenced at once'.[65] Lastly, in focusing on the relative ease with which the Dungeness Peninsula could be landed upon,[66] Dumouriez's work provided an important intellectual spur to the Royal Military Canal, which would surround that peninsula and, it was hoped, effectively transform it into an island. The canal's position, in turn, helps explain the non-construction of any Martello towers on the nearly twenty-mile stretch of coast between no. 27 in St Mary's Bay and no. 28 on the west bank of East Sussex's River Rother.

Above left: Gen. Charles Dumouriez, *c*.1792.

Above right: Mezzotint of the Duke of York, by William Dickinson after John Hoppner.

Adm. George Elphinstone, Lord Keith.

11

'AN ALL-ENCOMPASSING ATTACK'[1]

Conveying the unprecedented scale and geographic scope of Bonaparte's post-Amiens plans to invade 'at one and the same time [...] the east and south of England and the south-west and west of Ireland' stretched Dumouriez's powers of description to the limit. After spending an entire paragraph struggling to explain which of the Dutch, Flemish, French, Spanish, and Portuguese invasion ports' thrusts would be real attacks as opposed to feints, he threw up his hands: 'In this project of invasion there is, properly speaking, no sham attack.'[2] For the French had finally adopted, albeit on an unimaginably grander scale, Dumouriez's own 1777 plan for a ship-less invasion using small, specialist boats only. As well as being harder to detect, both out at sea and on approach, they would be much faster to unload – for no man, gun, or horse could be buried deep in the hold, as in a conventional transport ship. Moreover,

> Every expedition is to be pushed forward [...] with equal vigour; in every case they will attempt to strengthen the *tête de pont* and settle in force; for even if the first point they succeed in occupying is not the one best adapted to the furtherance of their ulterior aims, it will serve at least to divide the English forces, to perturb the nation and the capitalists, and to confuse the general plan of defence.[3]

Navigationally, this lack of a definitive target also obviated 'the difficulty of making the coast exactly at the predetermined spot'.[4] That is, if you are an inexperienced sailor heading in darkness or fog toward Gosport or Sandgate, you might on a good day miss it by half a dozen miles; but missing England is altogether harder. In short,

> the thing is bold but not absurd. An army of 40,000 men will not require 1,000 [fast fishing-luggers, and once in England...] they will find everything to hand. In 1779 we only numbered 17,000 men for embarkation at St. Malo and we had nearly 400 vessels to take us over. At Havre 12,000 men had 270 at their disposal. William III's fleet was of 400 sail to carry 14,000 men. An army taking much baggage with it tries to preserve it, but one with little or none at all tries to acquire it. This is a great motive power for all nations, but especially for the French, who for the past fifteen years have been used to living by rapine.[5]

The resumption of the war in 1803 coincided neatly with Bonaparte's receipt from America of 60 million francs (£2.4 million then or up to £16 billion now), in exchange for a vast territory known as 'Louisiana'. It included not only much of that future US state, but all or part of fourteen others, plus bits of the future Canadian provinces of Saskatchewan and Alberta. '[M]uch of the money received

The 'old' volunteers, as those formed in the 1790s became known after the Peace of Amiens, often wore fanciful uniforms of their own invention, and elected their officers. The 'new' volunteers who came forward later were expected to wear standard-issue red coats, and found the experience much more regimented as well as less well paid, breeding resentment between 'old' and 'new' units.

was spent on preparing for the execution of his third and greatest project for the long-talked-of invasion of England',[6] though 35 million more was donated by individuals, firms and towns in France and French-occupied Italy, and a further 20 million borrowed from the banks.[7] Improvements to the roads leading from Paris to Brest, Cherbourg and Boulogne absorbed 20 million by themselves.[8]

> He made the most gigantic and determined efforts to collect a formidable flotilla, revised the plans for its organization a dozen times, built new docks and enlarged existing ports, and when it was proved to him beyond the shadow of a doubt that a temporary command of the sea was indispensable, he worked towards that end with almost superhuman energy.[9]

Dumouriez agreed with Cornwallis's and Twiss's view that Ireland was 'easy to invade' and thus recommended that its defenders be concentrated mainly in 'entrenched camps and depots' near four towns – Cork, Limerick, Athlone, and Enniskillen – each occupied by a complete field army of more than 10,000 men.[10] But for Britain, the renegade Frenchman's answer to Napoleon's almost atomistic strategy of attack was its exact counterpart: 'a very complicated and murderous guerrilla war'.[11] Clearly, the British government agreed with this approach and was prepared to underwrite it with enormous sums, not least those associated with keeping 81,000 regulars in the home islands through the Peace of Amiens.[12] After that peace was broken in May 1803, George Cruikshank described every town in England as 'a sort of garrison' filled with the sounds of fifes, drums, bugles, and musketry from five in the morning onwards.[13] In Aberdeenshire, three times more men volunteered than were wanted, while on the beach at Musselburgh, the young Walter Scott fashioned Frenchmen with turnips for heads, which he practised lopping off with his yeomanry sabre.[14] At that time, the 'old' militia and the supplementary militia who had been actually called up in England and Wales numbered 75,000, and the volunteers and yeomanry, more than 300,000. However, personal firearms could at first only be found for half the volunteers.[15]

As soon as the war resumed, both 'the sea fencibles and the navy's armada of small craft for shallow water defence [were] revived and expanded',[16] to include 127 gun-vessels based between Dungeness and Beachy Head alone.[17] It was also in or around 1803 that the River Fencibles were formed, 'to deal with the transport of troops and military stores to any threatened point' along the Thames.[18] They frequently trained in embarkation and debarkation alongside the Honourable Artillery Company, a military 'fraternity or guild' dating back to at least the reign of Henry VIII and renowned for their marksmanship. The latter were, by 1803, more than 600 strong: an increase of 50 per cent since 1799, due to the greater intensity of the post-Amiens invasion threat.

Unknown artist's impression of London light-infantry volunteers at target practice. As of 1798, red coats were the norm and 'helmet hats' were popular. Only in 1801 would the mid-1790s estimates of the minimum number of troops necessary to the defence of the home islands at last be exceeded: with 158,000 regulars, embodied militia, and volunteers serving there, in addition to 90,000 regulars abroad.[19]

The previous decade's proposal by George Hanger to create corps of riflemen on the Hessian model of the 1770s and 1780s had also borne spectacular fruit. The entire 5th Bn, 60th Royal Americans were issued with rifles imported from Prussia in 1797, and further issues of these weapons were made to other battalions in 1799. A separate Experimental Corps of Riflemen was formed by Gen. Moore in January 1800. Designed by Ezekiel Baker of Whitechapel, the new British issue rifle of that year was of a smaller calibre than the venerable 'Brown Bess' smoothbore infantry musket – .62 vs .75 – as well as shorter-barrelled and slower to load; but it was accurate to three times the range.[20] Such was the success of this experimental corps that it entered the line as the 95th Regiment of Foot (Rifles) in 1803. These rifle units, and the Honourable Artillery Company's rifle company formed in 1803, were clad in green: both as a reference to the Hessian Jägers' original gamekeeper-inspired uniforms, and as an early form of camouflage, thoroughly in keeping with the Duke of York's full-throated endorsements of guerrilla warfare.[21] Moore also encouraged the Rifles and other light infantry under his command to ignore 'Old Pivot' Dundas's Prussian-style formations, think for themselves, and fight individually from behind cover or prone. This, no doubt, would have made them

Above left: The Inverness-shire Militia in 1804. Under the Militia (Scotland) Act 1802, childless men under 30 were balloted first; then childless men who were older; then fathers whose children had all reached age 14; then those with one child 13 or younger; and only then the fathers of two or more children 13 or younger.

Above right: A member of the Experimental Corps of Riflemen prepares to fire his Baker rifle.

The British volunteers as a swarm of bees, with French corpses littering the beach beyond.

even more dangerous to the enemy in the country just beyond Romney Marsh, 'wooded and intricate and except in fine weather difficult of passage for a large corps'.[22] Dumouriez, too, called for the volunteers to work hand in hand with a new 12,000-strong British regular army division of 'chasseurs', incorporating light artillery (possibly horse artillery) and light cavalry as well as riflemen.[23] Though the eventual Light Division would not reach such a size even on paper, the fact that it was formed at all was an extraordinary departure from pre-American War norms. For Britain, at least, we are witnessing the birth of a philosophy that would later be termed 'manoeuvrism': defined as 'an attitude of mind in which doing the unexpected and using initiative [...] is combined with a ruthless determination to succeed'.[24]

It was a further indicator of the British government's faith in the British people's military skill and sheer stubbornness in defence that the policy of 'driving the country' slowly died. In 1801 some argued that it be downgraded to 'the burning of all mills and the removal of all vehicles'; by 1804, it was generally agreed that only draught animals and horses, and not sheep, pigs, fowl, or human beings, would be sent inland.[25] The impulse to remove the whole human population could have been tied to the prevailing legal notion that the residents of an invaded territory should give their full obedience to the occupying enemy, a concept also echoed in religious texts such as the *Thirty-Nine Articles of the Church of England* and the *Confession of Augsburg*, which taught Protestants to obey whomever was placed in authority over them irrespective of their characteristics. Among the many other things destroyed by the wars covered by this book was that idea. Many would be stunned by the King of Prussia's 1813 order to his subjects to resist the French occupation not only with any weapons available, but in the spirit of the Spanish partisans, who were renowned for their cruelty.[26] In Britain, too, repeated, credible invasion threats from 1779 onward helped to forge a sense of loyalty to the nation that transcended both religion and international law.[27] This, in turn, helps to explain both Nelson's attitude toward Copenhagen, and Dumouriez's exhortation to the British people to 'map out a great inland war' and 'dispute the ground foot by foot'.[28] Such things would have been unthinkable in the 1750s heyday of Henry Lloyd, when war was still a vast game played by rulers against other rulers, and in which the civilians whose cities, towns, and villages changed hands were expected always to acquiesce. The clearer this transformation became to those in authority, the less inclined they were to denude the coasts of their people. It was also reflected in arrangements for the defence of the capital. Amid 'the decline of democratic sentiment and the corresponding rise of patriotism which resulted from the aggrandisement of Napoleon', measures for the security of London that in the 1790s had been 'directed mainly to the repression of malcontents within [...] now turned to the warding off of an attack from without'.[29] On the northern side of the Thames, in the event of an invasion, the Hackney Marshes were to be flooded and twenty-six earthwork redoubts thrown up by 5,000 civilians and 800 horses in four days – assuming, of course, that the enemy took longer than that to arrive. (Dumouriez expected that '[e]ight days will decide the fate of the war' and Napoleon planned to reach London in five.) To the southeast of the city, the main defences would be centred on Shooter's Hill, athwart the London-Dartford road in the Borough of Greenwich.[30] This prominent feature had 'the merit of giving some protection to Deptford and Woolwich' as well as to the capital itself; but Britain's chronic shortage of trained artillerymen made it unclear whether full advantage could be taken of it.[31]

Dumouriez felt that the British blockade of the enemy's Channel ports, while good for building and maintaining Royal Navy sailors' skills and morale, was 'not so beneficial as was fancied at the outset', since an enormous increase in the numbers and firepower of French shore batteries now effectively protected the invasion vessels 'that singly or in small divisions proceed from Flanders and Normandy to swell the great gathering at Boulogne'.[32] He also criticised the British Sea Fencibles' lack of fire-ships, and argued that '[h]ad Lord Nelson been provided with fire-boats in his attack on the Roadstead of Boulogne [in 1801] he would not have failed'.[33]

Boulogne naturally remained one of Britain's prime targets. The Royal Navy, having 'turned' Robert Fulton of *Nautilus* fame with the tidy sum of £800 (about £918,000 today), had him develop a waterproof clockwork ship-killing bomb, known alternately as a 'torpedo' and a 'catamaran'. More than a yard in diameter and 21 feet long, each was filled with 4,000 pounds of gunpowder. By the night of 2 October 1804, Lord Keith had provided himself with enough of these to launch them in a 'stream' for seven hours against 150 French invasion vessels that were moored outside Boulogne's main harbour. But they 'achieved nothing', even on a return visit in December, when on the bright side, they at least achieved detonation.[34]

English news picture of a French
bateau cannonière, 1803. Image
copyright National Maritime
Museum, Greenwich, London.

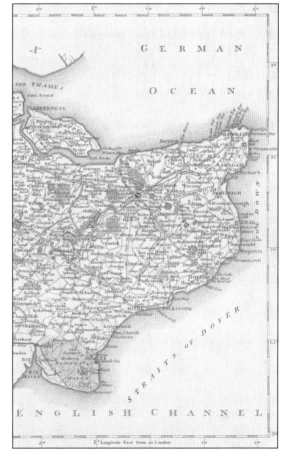

The road system, woodlands and
settlements of East Kent in 1793.

Napoleon's invasion craft of 1803–05 can be divided into four main types. The most numerous and cheapest to build were known as *péniches* or pinnaces. These single-masted, un-decked howitzer boats with thirteen pairs of oars could each hold fifty-five to sixty soldiers in addition to the crew of five or six, and were about 60 feet in length. As of August 1805, they numbered at least 349 but not more than 542, and thus could have carried between 20,000 and 32,000 troops.[35] Their main disadvantage was that they 'could not survive a strong squall', let alone a direct hit from a roundshot.[36] The fact that they needed no wind to reach the correct landing places on time was positive on the face of it, but negative in that any military unit embarked in a mixture of pinnaces and non-oared vessels might be split up over a wide area. At worst, that could mean that the whole first wave to land 'would find itself no more than a jumbled medley of petty detachments'.[37]

The next smallest invasion vessels, up to 70 feet long, were the *bateaux cannonières*. These were essentially similar to the fore-and-aft armed English gun-brigs, in that each had a 24-pounder in the bow 'and a howitzer or field gun in the stern'.[38] However, having three masts rather than two, they were not brigs in English parlance, and neither of their guns was aimable other than 'by pointing the boat itself'.[39] One *bateau cannonière* crewed by six men could carry a complete hundred-man company of field artillery, plus at least some of its horses. Presumably, such a company's ordnance – i.e. either six 8-pounder guns and two howitzers, or eight 8-pounders – would have been disassembled before embarkation and reassembled on arrival, or else carried assembled on a separate vessel. However, there were enough *bateaux cannonières* to carry 57,200 men, nearly triple the number of artillerymen in the whole French army, so other purposes were inevitable. Moreover, the flotilla's auxiliary vessels included 405 specialist horse transports, and in Calais, '81 fishing boats adapted to carrying men and horses'.[40] However, 24-pounders – at a minimum – would have been needed to reduce the Lines of Chatham: a rare-for-Britain *trace italienne* begun around Fort Amherst in 1755 to protect Chatham naval dockyard and, in extremis, to prevent an approach to the capital by land from eastern parts of Kent. Such weapons would have been sent in conventional transport vessels once one or more of the small ports near Pegwell Bay had been secured.[41]

Next in size, at up to 80 feet in length, were the *chaloupes cannonières*: brig-rigged and armed with three 24-pounders and a howitzer. Numbering 320 in August 1805, these carried crews of twenty-two and 130 soldiers, for a total carrying capacity of 41,600 of the latter. Last and biggest were the eighteen three-masted *prames*, 100 to 110 feet long, each mounting twelve 14-pounders. These only held 120 soldiers, presumably due to their much larger crew requirements (for thirty-eight men). This, in turn, probably related to their armament, which alone among the four types was comparable to that of a British ship-sloop.[42] Be that as it may, the presence of the *prames* would push the grand total of troop-carrying capacity for the four main classes of vessel to 133,480, of which 46 per cent was in the vastly improved anchorages of Boulogne itself.[43] As the total carrying capacity of all types of French invasion vessels was claimed to be 167,000 in the same month and year as the per-class totals given above, it must be assumed either that the auxiliary vessels such as converted fishing boats had sufficient capacity for at least 33,000 men more, or that the headline figure is incorrect.

Boulogne also seemed curiously under-supplied with horse transports, having only forty-four, or less than 11 per cent of the total that had been built.

The invasion craft have been widely critiqued for their presumably poor sailing qualities. However,

> [t]hey were still navigable, or those built in Holland, Le Havre, Brittany and the Bay of Biscay ports would never have reached Boulogne. In reasonable summer weather, and with the French fleet in command of the sea, they should have made the crossing somehow.[44]

Following 'his own maxim "Disperse to feed, concentrate to fight"', Napoleon kept 93,000 troops in the Channel ports and the others at various points around the hinterland.[45] Dumouriez thought that the total number of men who could be brought across in a single lift by the flotilla was just 60,000, due to it being 'encumbered with artillery, munitions, supplies, horses, camp and hospital effects, etc',[46] but with the benefit of hindsight this seems a gross underestimation. Certainly, though it would take at least two and up to six tides to launch them all, Napoleon meant as of July 1804 to strike with 'an immensely strong first wave' of between 120,000 and 150,000 men, 'landing simultaneously'.[47] The targeted area of northeastern Kent would be replete with food and fodder at harvest time, and the three harbours of Margate, Broadstairs, and Ramsgate were 'very readily assaulted from the sea' but just as easy to take by land; thus, for the enemy to secure them as links in his supply chain was 'little more than a matter of marching'.[48] Moreover, given that Britain's volunteers had no field artillery, and her militia, neither field artillery nor cavalry, the numerical advantage in both of these arms that would normally accrue to a field army defending its own territory against an amphibious assault was absent in the British case. And '[i]t would be childish to suppose that these weaknesses were not perfectly well known to the great artillery officer who commanded the legions of the enemy across the Channel'.[49]

Nor should the mere fact of the vast Boulogne flotilla's existence be taken as proof that a smaller enemy army in conventional troopships would *not* land somewhere in the British Isles. Specifically, it was still possible that 30,000 or 40,000 soldiers 'from the Maas and Scheldt ports' would attack in the vicinity of Tilbury, as George Hanger had warned they might back in 1795.[50] Dumouriez seemed more worried about this possibility than about the Boulogne flotilla itself: 'In no case must the foe be allowed to penetrate higher than Tilbury, which covers the shipyards, the powder-stores, the arsenals and the Metropolis itself – it must be defended to the last extremity.'[51] He also recommended that the Isle of Sheppey be reinforced, as 'the predetermined pivot of […] the safeguarding of the river',[52] no doubt because in 1667 the Dutch had captured it, along with its then-new naval dockyard of Sheerness, and used it as a base for their further up-river depredations.

The possibility of London being captured quickly was entertained very seriously by the British side as of November 1803, albeit clearly from the point of view that the war would go on regardless. The contents of Woolwich Arsenal, including a thousand tons of gunpowder as well as weapons of every description, were to be shipped via the Grand Union Canal to Weedon Bec in Northamptonshire, roughly as far from the sea as it's possible to get, where an '[a]dmirably laid out, architecturally attractive, and soundly built' Royal Military Depot, including a large house for the king himself, had been built.[53] The gold from the Bank of England, whose employees had formed themselves into a volunteer infantry battalion complete with grenadiers, would be moved to the cathedral city of Worcester, fifty-five miles west of Weedon Bec, along with those members of the royal family who were not serving in the armed forces. The choice of Worcester was probably symbolic as much as practical, for it was there that King Charles II had made his final, doomed stand against Oliver Cromwell in 1651 – and yet, escaped to fight another day. Such preparations, coupled with the enthusiasm of the volunteers, suggest that even the fall of London would have been 'only the beginning' of any French attempt to subdue the nation.[54] Perhaps the strongest evidence for this is the battle plan drawn up by the Duke of York and David Dundas. If Britain's main field army were mauled and pushed inland by invaders in any part of Kent, it would withdraw not northward or westward toward Chatham and Shooter's Hill, but into the fortress of Dover, where it could be reinforced and, if necessary, re-equipped before menacing the French from the flank and rear (if they continued to advance), or fight them again head-on (if they gave chase).[55] As it happens, bureaucratic bungling meant that the vital western heights of Dover would not be rendered 'unassailable' by the British engineers until 1805.[56] Seen in a positive light, however, the steady improvement to the western heights was another factor, alongside the rising quality and quantity of England's volunteers, that made Napoleon's third invasion project a race against time, had he but known it.

A total of ten French squadrons were able to run the British blockades of Brest and Rochefort between 1796 and 1806.[57] This was easy enough to foresee. As Hanger had noted in 1795:

[W]hen I say, they *may land any where, in spite of our grand fleet*, (except in the deeper waters of the western shores) it is with this intent, to destroy that vulgar opinion, founded in ignorance and supported by national insolence, presuming too much on our powers at sea, that the French can never invade us as long as our grand Channel fleet has the superiority[.][58]

Signed, sealed and delivered
The south coast towers

Eventually, the prehistory of a technology must end, and the thing itself be designed, approved, and built. The actual proposal on which mass-production Martellos were based was written by Capt. William Henry Ford RE. About him very little is known, apart from the fact that he went on to command 3rd (Dover) Company, Royal Military Artificers, for fourteen years beginning in 1806, and later served on the board of governors at the Royal Military Academy, Woolwich, which had opened near the Warren in 1741. Like other officers of the artillery and engineers of this period, he would almost certainly have been trained there himself – probably in his early teens, but possibly from as young as 10 – in history, geography, geology, mathematics, engineering, drawing, surveying and mapping, principles of fortification, French, and German, in addition to the practical use of a broad range of personal and heavy weapons.

Ford's towers were to have been square, but were modified in various ways by Twiss, now a brigadier-general, before the latter got them approved at Cabinet level – albeit with more-or-less round plan, which was preferred due to its lower projected cost.[1] To have gained approval for any particular design was a fairly remarkable achievement, given that '[n]ot only was the whole country divided on the subject of towers, but so was the army'.[2] Twiss's proposal of 3 September 1804 suggested that the new English towers be 29 feet in diameter and mounted with 'one heavy Gun' and two carronades, all on the roof.[3] Having no guns on the lower floors would seem at first sight to place both guns and gunners, and thus the tower itself, at unnecessary risk. However, it addressed Dirom's much-publicised criticism of traditional batteries with embrasures: that, 'as the guns are to be pointed against a moving object', it was absurd that they not be capable of pointing 'in any direction'.[4] The compromise solution – an aperture in a defensive tower wide enough to allow its main armament to 'track' a passing ship, as at Simonstown – was probably a hazard in itself, both tactically and structurally.

The memorandum on 'Bomb Proof Towers' signed in early October 1804 by Twiss, D'Aubant, and Thomas Nepean proposed a height of 33 feet to the top of the parapet, an interior diameter of 26 feet, and that the gun and two carronades on the roof all be 24-pounders. Soon after this, at the Rochester Conference of 21 October, all were downgraded to 18-pounders. Nevertheless, the difference in length between a long 24-pounder and long 18-pounder being only 6 inches, it would have been tricky even to fit all three of these weapons onto the roof of a tower of the size chosen – and almost unimaginable that all three could then be brought to bear on the same target. Lt-Col Nepean promised that he would make it work via an 'ingenious contrivance'. However, his contrivance having either not been so ingenious, or having failed altogether to materialise, the scheme for mounting two carronades on each south-coast tower was quietly abandoned;

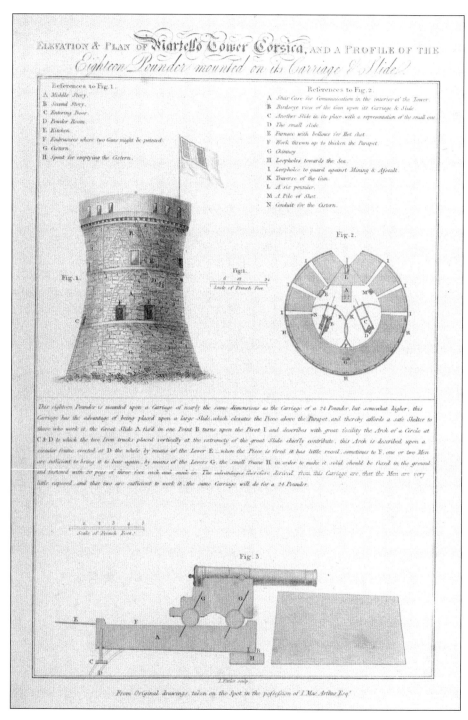

Plan and view of the Torra di Mortella after a drawing by I. MacArthur, including a detail of the main gun's traversing carriage with front pivot. Image copyright the National Maritime Museum, Greenwich, London.

and for the one remaining weapon, the long-barrelled 24 was chosen over the 18-pounder.[5] (By April 1810, one-third of the south coast towers would also mount, or at least possess, a 5½-inch iron howitzer, though when they were given such weapons is unclear.[6]) Two higher classes of bomb-proof towers were also proposed and approved, to be armed with four and eleven pieces of ordnance, respectively. But only one of the former and three of the latter were actually built.[7]

In 1803, the projected price of one Martello tower, as reported to the Defence Committee by Twiss, had been £2,000. In the event, however, only £1,456. 6s. 2½d per tower was actually budgeted. This meant that the entire programme was expected to cost less than the £200,000 allocated to the Royal Military Canal.[8] Nevertheless, due to strikes, spiralling transport costs, and profiteering, the final figure 'must have been much larger' even than the £3,000 per tower originally projected by Ford,[9] and one historian has suggested that it was actually £7,000 per tower.[10] In any case, except among some radicals who opposed war in general or favoured the French cause, Martellos were highly popular, and construction was spurred on in part by 'an outcry by local people for protection by towers' almost as soon as they were heard of.[11]

Each south-coast Martello contained half a million bricks, sufficient to build 'thirty four-bedroomed houses'. Canals, rivers, coastal vessels and road vehicles were all used to transport the necessary building materials at various times and to various places.[12] The official complement per tower was twenty-four privates, usually from the militia, and one non-commissioned officer. The lone door always

Eastbourne Redoubt, begun in 1805, mounted ten of the planned eleven heavy guns, and had accommodation for more than 300 troops. Like its siblings at Dymchurch and Harwich, it is around 225 feet in diameter and 40 feet high.

Eastbourne Redoubt's 'drop bridge' was designed to be removed in great haste in an emergency; this replica was created with the help of the Royal Engineers in 2003. Drastically different from Martello towers as the three redoubts were, they were devised simultaneously as a part of a complete menu of off-the-peg coastal fortifications, which also included structures of an intermediate size that were never built, apart from a lone example at Aldeburgh, Suffolk, northernmost tower in the east-coast chain.

Constructed of five million bricks, each redoubt's ground floor was divided into twenty-four 'casemates', in that word's early sense of self-contained artillery-proof chambers, with or without embrasures. They were used for a variety of purposes including soldiers' accommodation. At Eastbourne, Casemate no. 11 housed the main magazine.

faced the landward side, and was either 20 feet above ground level, or 20 feet above the bottom of the moat, in cases where moats were provided. At least twelve south-coast Martellos (and nine east-coast ones) had moats, but these additional defences were not part of the original plans, and the reasons for them being added in some places and not others has never been definitely ascertained. I suspect it may relate to Dumouriez's above-mentioned proposal for 'isolated batteries'.

Two embrasures were provided in south-coast Martello towers, both at right angles to the door. They were 6 feet deep and lined with stone. On the side of the tower from which an enemy attack was deemed most likely to come, the walls were 13 feet thick at the bottom and 9 at the top; elsewhere, they were 7 feet thick at the bottom, tapering to 5. A central brick column ran the whole height of the structure, and was 5 feet in diameter. Its chief function was to support the 2½-ton weight of the building's main armament on the roof. The basement was divided in half: with a water cistern or well and fireplace-fuel supply on one side, accessed from above by a ladder; and the main magazine on the other side, accessed laterally from the water-and-fuel room via a door. Internal divisions were of oak, and copper was used extensively in place of iron for hinges, locks, keys and so forth as it was less likely to spark if struck.

The troops' quarters, musket armoury, and stores were, like the door to the outside world, located on the middle level, which had one window and one fireplace for the commander, and one other window and fireplace for everyone else. The quarters for the commander and his family, and the armoury/store, each took up roughly one-sixth of the available space on that level, and the main sleeping quarters, the remaining two-thirds.

The two fireplaces' chimneys protruded through the gun-platform's parapet, and Glendinning has suggested that they served 'as a visual stop to prevent overshooting of the adjacent fort'.[13] However, it is hard to disagree with Sutcliffe's argument that the traversing 24-pounder main armament would simply knock the chimneys off if it needed to – an idea supported by the fact that the whole circle of the parapet was marked with degrees.[14]

William Twiss's siting plan of mid-1804 called for dense concentrations of Martellos in certain places, notably Pevensey Bay, where up to fifteen towers could have fired simultaneously at the same ship. The eight-mile stretch of Kent coast from Dymchurch to Sandgate would also be well-covered, by no fewer than twenty Martellos – including the best-preserved, no. 24, seen here – plus a 'Martello-ised' Sandgate Castle. From Cliff End to the far side of Hastings, on the other hand, Twiss regarded the shore as 'so high that Towers do not seem applicable to its Defence', which would be better conducted 'by a movable force'.[15]

Here, roughly in the middle of the Dymchurch-Sandgate stretch, we see Martellos nos 14 and 15 from the Army rifle ranges at Hythe. No. 14, which 'survives well, and retains many of its original components',[16] is on the left because the south-coast towers were numbered in ascending order westward from East Wear Bay. No. 19, at the far western end of the range, is in a picturesque state of collapse due to coastal erosion, and nos 16–18 have disappeared altogether, for the same reason.

At the Rochester Conference, the lone dissenter to the basic design of Martello described above was Lt-Col John Brown, 'perpetrator' of the Royal Military Canal, to which the tower programme always seemed opposed rather than complementary at the time.[17] Indeed, Brown vehemently opposed what he called, in his diary entry from that day, 'the expensive and diabolical system of Tower Defence'.[18] However, if his loathing for Martellos was partly prompted by a fear that they would supplant his own scheme, he need not have worried, for in the end, the government adopted both. Some Martello towers 'were placed in pairs to defend the sluice gates' that would be opened as the 'ultimate deterrent' – though plans to rush troops *to* the coast and farm animals *from* it along the same roads, which were also to be destroyed to prevent the enemy travelling along them, were inherently implausible.[19] In Norfolk, where there were no Martellos, some roads leading inland from the coast actually were destroyed simply as a precaution.[20]

In October 1804, the Royal Military Canal was hailed in the press not merely as 'one of the greatest military works in this or any other kingdom!' but for its future commercial potential, as a relatively inexpensive means of sending bulk goods from the interior of Kent to the coasts.[21] Using relays of horses to tow boats,

The Royal Staff Corps barracks, Hythe, and Royal Military Canal as they appeared from the Ashford Road about 1816.

The eastern extremity of the Royal Military Canal today. Brown's plan called for it to be 60 feet wide at the surface, 9 feet deep, and 40 feet wide at the bottom. It was also to mount 180 12- and 18-pounder cannon at intervals of around 500 yards, and thus presumably in pairs, given its overall length of twenty-eight miles. Its route contains periodic 'staggers' to allow artillery to be fired straight along it, taking enemy boats or pontoons in flank, without hitting the next British post.

an average speed of 7mph on it was attained in August 1806; it had taken just twenty-two months 'from the cutting of the first sod' to the creation of 'a tolerable work of defence'.[22] As the quartermaster-general explained, 'the sea now acting from both ends, there is no doubt [...] that the effect of one spring tide, would make an island of Romney Marsh': the 'advantage' that Pitt had originally foreseen.[23] However, the military road remained to be completed, and would consume a quarter-million tons of shingle at a cost of about £18,000; barracks and stables at Hythe would cost another £8,000; and maintenance was estimated at £6,000 per year. 'Such is the laborious, unwholesome and dirty nature of the work that it is not desirable to employ soldiers upon it,' Brown wrote.[24] Nonetheless, in sharp contrast to the Martellos, it ran only 17 per cent over budget. Whether it was money well spent, however, continued to be questioned by many. William Cobbett, sergeant-major of the 54th Foot turned famous radical journalist, mocked the canal as a risible obstacle to French armies 'that had so often crossed the Rhine and the Danube'.[25] Pontoon bridges, whether purpose-built or improvised, were far from being a novelty in this period, having occasionally appeared in wartime since the days of King Darius of Persia. As of the 1770s, they seem to have been carried to war chiefly by the French artillery, who had by then improved them to the point that they could support river crossings by 24-pounder siege guns.[26] As such, if attackers reached the canal at all, its status as an obstacle would have been chiefly a function of how ferociously defended it was. But it was first mounted with artillery, captured from the Danish navy, only at some point after 1807.[27]

An unexpected benefit of the canal emerged somewhat later. In April 1809, Brownrigg noted that troops returning from Spain were travelling by canal-boat to Hythe from the lock on the Rother in just four hours, 'thus performing the march from Rye to Hythe in one day which before always occupied two'; and he estimated that the 40-mile journey from Dover to Hastings or Dover to Battle could now also be completed in a day, given that half the distance would be by canal. In practice, the formerly three-day journey from Dover to Rye was cut to just one.[28] The canal historian P. A. L. Vine lamented

> that no detailed account exists of these troop barges. The sight of 500 troops in their red coats being speedily carried in five barges each drawn by a pair of horses from the Royal Waggon Train across Romney Marsh at 5 miles an hour, must have aroused as great an interest as did the passing of the first steam trains.[29]

Dover Castle, as improved continuously since the end of the American War, 'had been chosen as the last stronghold of the British Army where the final stand against the enemy would be made', and housed a mobile force of 5,000–6,000 troops in addition to its garrison *per se*.[30] There were already six batteries on the most vulnerable stretch of the coast, between Beachy Head and Dover, on the eve of the English Martello-building programme; of these six, two were in Eastbourne, three at Hythe (part of 'an epidemic of military building' there[31]), and one at Folkestone. The south coast from the Solent westward was usually deemed safe because any wind favourable to a French landing in that quarter would have tended to raise such surf as to make getting ashore impossible, much as had happened to the French troop transports that reached Bantry Bay in 1796.[32] The king himself fretted that an enemy who gained a lodgement in Dorset could simultaneously threaten both of his great naval bases, and he was actually in Weymouth in May 1804 when, in heavy fog, a French landing at Portland was falsely reported.[33] But, by and large, the 'invasion coast' as understood by both sides in the war extended no farther west than the boundary between Hampshire and Dorset. And Hampshire itself was deemed sufficiently well defended without any Martellos, as it contained a heavy concentration of older coastal-defence facilities that were still viable.

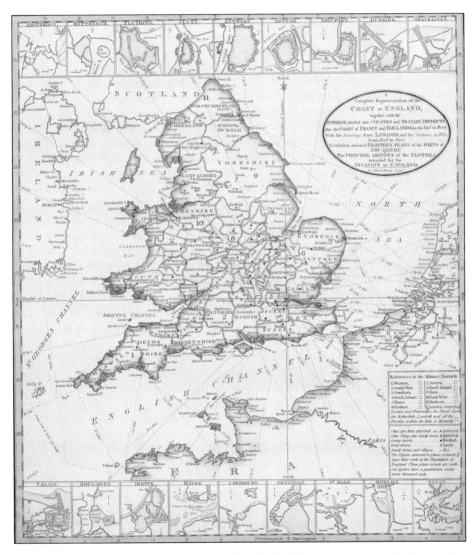

A Complete Representation of the Coast of England (1804) showed all probable invasion routes and the boundaries of England's military districts, and included inset plans of eighteen enemy invasion ports. The French were just as systematic, dividing their invasion coast into six *Arrondisements maritimes*.

Due to a range of problems with land-leasing, contractors, building materials and weather that anyone who has ever tried to build something in England will be familiar with, only six true Martellos had been completed by the late summer of 1806. In fairness, however, it should be noted that seventy-three of the original eighty-one south coast towers that had been proposed in October 1804 had been finished before the end of 1808, and the other eight deemed surplus to requirements. None of the east-coast Martellos were built prior to the completion of the main south-coast chain in 1808, but one on the south coast – at Seaford, Sussex (1810) – was added after the east-coast works were underway, making for a south coast total of seventy-four, and a grand total of 103.

In a neat inversion of Col John Campbell's 1790s plan to arm existing signal towers with cannon,[34] some of the 'Towers as Sea-Fortresses' were used as signal stations beginning in January 1812, using 'a union jack and three black canvas balls hoisted on a flagstaff mounted on the roof above the door'.[35]

Of course, none of this should be taken to suggest that fortification-building other than of Martello towers and Brown's canal totally ceased after 1804. The already elaborate Lines of Chatham, for instance, had their brick-faced Lower Lines added by the early summer of 1804, and remained integral to defence planning. This was just as well, since it was at London from somewhere between Margate and Deal, via the Lines, that the French actually planned to strike in 1803–05.[36]

PEAK DANGER

There is a widespread if illogical belief that the real danger to Britain during the Revolutionary and Napoleonic Wars rapidly ebbed away due to her victory at Trafalgar in October 1805.[1] To the extent that one holds such a view, the intensity of Martello-building and other coastal-defence measures after that date becomes a mystery to be solved. The real mystery, however, is the view itself: for a rather more compelling case can be made that the two to four years immediately *after* Trafalgar were the period of acutest danger to Britain during the whole of the eighteenth and nineteenth centuries, notwithstanding the departure of the 'Army of England' from the invasion ports. For one thing, Nelson himself had been removed from the board, mortally wounded by a French sniper. Just six weeks later, Napoleon defeated more than 70,000 Austrians and Russians at Austerlitz, his crowning achievement as a tactician and effectively the end of Austria as a world power. Arthur Wellesley, the future duke of Wellington, was a thirty-something obscurity, most of whose military exploits had been in India and, while impressive, still paled in comparison to the achievements of Robert Clive in that theatre in the 1750s. William Pitt the Younger, in hindsight his country's only really effective civilian war leader until Winston Churchill, and likewise a hopeless alcoholic, died of a perforated ulcer of the stomach or duodenum in January 1806. Though only 46, he was said by his physician to have died 'of old age'.[2] The next month saw the rise to power of a mostly Whig government that included the execrable William Windham, destroyer of the volunteer movement.

Later that year, Pitt's great political opponent Fox died, and 'with him any further prospect of peace', even on grovelling terms.[3] Between August and October, Napoleon defeated and dismembered Prussia, hitherto an important British trading partner. Shortly afterwards, from the 'Imperial Camp' outside his new city of Berlin, he decreed that the whole continent of Europe was closed not only to British ships, but to all forms of British trade and communication whatsoever. '[L]etters or packets, addressed either to England, to an Englishman, or in the English language, shall not pass through the post-office and shall be seized'; and any of King George's subjects found on the Continent would henceforth be treated as prisoners of war, whether they were combatants or not.[4] From this point on, in other words, Britain would have to crush France, or be crushed, in what was looking perilously like a total war of a more modern sort.[5] With some justification, Dumouriez warned that the Berlin Decree could merely be the prelude to 'a great attack on England in 1808 by all the naval forces of the Continent', followed up by a 'direct invasion' that would have a reasonable prospect of success.[6]

In January 1807, news reached London that the British forces who had re-captured the Cape of Good Hope the previous year had sailed west – without the prior knowledge or approval of the government – to take, and in short order humiliatingly lose, the Spanish colony of Argentina.[7] Throwing good money after bad, the British administration followed this up with a much larger 'conjunct' that lost 2,200 men killed, wounded, and prisoners in a single horrendous day of street-to-street fighting in Buenos Aires. This deeply embarrassing South American misadventure also temporarily removed the ingenious Sea Fencibles impresario Sir Home Popham from the playing field, as the unauthorised first expedition had been his idea.[8] In July 1807, Napoleon would make a separate peace with the Russians, who agreed to join him in closing the whole of Europe to British goods; and as night follows day, the British bombarded Copenhagen, capital of Russia's leading client state, this time leaving many of its neighbourhoods as mere piles of rubble, reminiscent of twentieth-century cities that had been bombed from the air.

This time, however, Russia and Denmark–Norway both responded by declaring states of war, which would last for nearly five years in the Russian case and six and a half in the Danish. The Danes emerged as particularly wily and dangerous opponents in this *Kanonbådskrigen* (Gunboat War), so called due to their extensive and effective use of tiny, fast, cheap, heavily armed craft – again designed or inspired by Fredrik af Chapman – against larger Royal Navy vessels. On numerous occasions, swarms of Danish gunboats surrounded and overpowered conventional British sloops of war, including HMS *Allart* (18) and HMS *Turbulent* (12); and on 15 October 1808, thirty-two of them mounting a total of seventy pieces of heavy ordnance caused sixty casualties and massive damage aboard HMS *Africa*, a 64-gun ship of the line on convoy-escort duty. Britain's perennial problem of defence against privateers was also a problem 'multiplied […] by the hostility of the Danes',[9] who remained a 'formidable enemy' of the British merchant marine: with five Danish brigs capturing forty-seven British merchantmen off the Skaw in July 1810 alone.[10]

A print of the Second Battle of Copenhagen, 1807. Produced in the Kingdom of Bavaria, then a Napoleonic client state, it was apparently aimed at the French market.

Post-war artist's impression of Danish gunboats closing in on the stern of a British sloop of war.

Most importantly, however, the eleven ships and 8,000 sailors the French had lost at Trafalgar were as nothing, when weighed against their Continental empire's ever-growing stock of existing warships, shipyards, shipyard workers, experienced seafarers, forests, ironworks, and specie. And, though the French capture of Spain and Portugal would soon be challenged by the British Army and by those countries' own inhabitants, it was seen in the moment as dramatically increasing the danger to Ireland, to the point that Dumouriez had to draw up a complete new defence plan.[11] For those keen to draw parallels between the Napoleonic War and Second World War, Trafalgar was – at best – Britain's 'Dunkirk moment': a terrible, seemingly inevitable fate, briefly postponed. As Vine put it, Trafalgar

> did but reaffirm the strength of British naval power which was clear before; it did not materially increase that supremacy. [...] Had the battle not been fought at all the issue of the struggle would probably not have been seriously altered.[12]

In this context, post-1805 Martello-building was not a Quixotic or panicky response to a threat that had already passed, but reasoned and reasonable. Even the shift in counter-invasion planners' attention from the south coast to the east coast reflected a shift in Napoleon's invasion plans from Boulogne, opposite Dover and Folkestone, to his puppet regime in present-day Holland and Belgium, ruled by his brother Louis. Britain may only have escaped invasion in 1807 or 1808 because – led in this respect by future prime minister George Canning, then the foreign secretary – it had narrowly prevented Napoleon from capturing the Danish and Portuguese fleets, and thus 'spoilt the emperor's master plan of wresting the maritime initiative from Britain', at least until his new ships being built for a descent on England's east coast could be completed.[13] But it is equally possible that the completed Martello towers and Royal Military Canal 'had transformed the nature of the war' by making it 'pointless to attempt an invasion across any beach within the range of the Boulogne flotilla'.[14]

Beginning in 1799, fear of an invasion of southern England 'would not abate for […] ten years',[15] so there is no mystery in why the British government embarked on the building of the east-coast chain of Martello towers only in 1808 – or, for that matter, sent thousands of men to their deaths on Walcheren Island in 1809. That expedition's objective was to wreck the port of Antwerp, which was known to be engaged in the creation of yet another 'great French fleet that might finally breach England's invasion defences'.[16] And the ongoing danger from fleets built and manned throughout coastal areas of France's ever-expanding empire was only compounded by the fact that Britain's economy and political system both 'almost buckled under the strain' of waging a land war in Spain and Portugal from 1808 to 1814.[17] Such was the horror of the British government at French control of the Antwerp shipyards that, as late as 1813, they made it known they would not sign any peace treaty in which such control – or even merely 'the influence of France' over Antwerp – was maintained.[18]

On the east coast, Martello towers mounted three artillery pieces 'according to their position and needs', with the subsidiary weapons usually consisting of two carronades or one carronade and one 5½-inch iron howitzer.[19] This, in turn,

Rear-Adm. Sir Sidney Smith taunts Napoleon and the French foreign minister through a megaphone as the Portuguese royal court, treasury, and more than a dozen ships of war escape to Brazil, 29 November 1807. It was immaterial to Britain whether these ships fled or were destroyed, provided only that they never fell into French hands; and when the Portuguese prince regent vacillated about leaving, Smith threatened to flatten his capital in the same manner as Copenhagen.

These small circular redoubts formed part of the Lines of Torres Vedras. Laid out by British, German, and Portuguese engineers in October 1809 and built by Portuguese civilians, they stretched from the broad estuary of the River Tagus to the Atlantic Ocean, making Lisbon impregnable. The outermost line, which was never breached, contained around eighty forts, batteries and redoubts, but was ready for occupation after just one year. The country to the north of it was also 'driven', and this led to starvation in an attacking French army in 1811.

As well as all being of slightly later vintage than their south-coast counterparts, the twenty-nine east-coast Martellos were larger and of a slightly different, oblong shape, clearly shown in this photo of Tower 'D' at Jaywick, Essex before its restoration. Also, their traversing carriages pivoted at the front rather than the rear, implying a maximum arc of fire of something less than 180 degrees for each of their three artillery pieces. The east-coast towers were assigned letters A-Z northward from St Osyth's Point, Essex, with the final three being AA, BB, and CC.

mandated that they have more spacious roofs than their south-coast counterparts, and thus that they be bigger altogether, each comprising 700,000 as against 500,000 bricks. The Grays Brickyard in Essex employed 500 men in 1808, this being the main reason; and a Board of Ordnance cement works was established at Harwich in 1811, almost certainly 'to produce the requisite amount of stucco to render the towers' on that side of the country.[20] The construction work itself was

> undertaken by local subcontractors of varying abilities under the supervision of the Royal Engineers. [...] [T]he towers on the east coast are, in general, better constructed than those on the south coast. This seems likely considering that the south coast towers were built first and it was therefore in these that the lessons were learnt with regard to how the towers needed to be built, [and] this process led to the alterations to the design that can be seen in the east coast examples as well as the more careful selection of the building contractors employed.[21]

Fear of endemic contagious disease on the Essex Coast, however, led to a decision to leave all eleven Martello towers in that county standing empty, and to man them with troops from the new barracks at Weeley only if word arrived of an invasion in progress.[22]

A howitzer-armed east-coast Martello tower's ammunition supply included half a ton of powder; 100 24-pounder roundshot; ten to twenty rounds each of 24-pounder case and grape; forty rounds of 5½-inch howitzer case; forty howitzer carcases; '280 various types of shell'; and eighty hand grenades.[23] As well as for use against assault parties that got ashore, the grenades could have been used for creating ballons: anti-personnel rounds consisting of a mixture of live grenades and loose gunpowder (at the ratio of 2lb of powder per grenade), stuffed into a sturdy canvas sack sealed with pitch.[24] This would presumably have been protected from premature detonation by a plug known as a sabot, made of elm or alder wood.

Dumouriez, for all his good points, was no economist, and he seems to have shared the fantasies expressed by his countrymen Hoche and Bonaparte regarding the endless wellspring of England's treasure. So, having done as much as anyone to sell the idea of vast numbers of small coastal forts and a hugely augmented force of light troops and volunteers for home defence, he decried Britain's 'perpetual defensive' posture, and argued that unless the war was carried to the enemy on land, Napoleon was likely to win in the end.[25] In particular, he noted in 1803 that Portugal – which 'must be looked upon as the outwork covering Ireland' – had '40,000 troops of the line and as many militia, all good of their kind' and would be 'suitable for a protracted and stubborn defence' if sent money and 'a [British] commander of ability and repute'.[26] In the event, of course, it was not ignoring Dumouriez's advice but attempting to put it into practice that nearly broke the British state, not only in the Iberian Peninsula but on the invasion coast of the Continent.

The year of 'the largest British expeditionary force ever assembled', 1809, had not begun particularly well.[27] The previous year's campaign – to aid the Spanish monarchist revolt against a new puppet regime headed by one of Napoleon's brothers – had been conducted with 'almost reckless aggression', capped by a fierce winter battle against an army of French pursuers within sight of the

Anticipating Dumouriez's firm critique of Britain's 'perpetual' preparations to be invaded and the resulting 'protracted disquietude', John Bull takes the fight to the enemy in this August 1803 print by Roberts after Woodward.

Britannia bestowing King Ferdinand VII of Spain's 1808 revolt against 'King' Joseph Bonaparte with a literal cornucopia of guns, powder, edged weapons and at least three different types of cannon ammunition. The small round objects could equally be musket-balls or gold coins: an acknowledgement that Britain's deepening engagement in Iberia would come at a heavy price.

evacuation beaches.[28] It left behind thousands of dead including its commander, Sir John Moore, struck in the torso by a roundshot, and thousands of prisoners, including a large number of soldiers' wives. Though now remembered as an eerie precursor to the Miracle of Dunkirk,[29] the disembarkation of the remaining 'filthy, exhausted soldiers on the south coast of England caused consternation and appeared more like an unprecedented disaster'.[30] A replacement force was found by re-purposing Arthur Wellesley's troops, who were in County Cork training for a long-planned descent on Venezuela that was now quietly shelved. But Spain and Portugal were, as of this stage of the war, mere targets of opportunity. The potentially mortal threat to the British Empire was still the port of Antwerp.

In March, Sir David Dundas, who had replaced the Duke of York as commander-in-chief of the Army, was asked by the cabinet to provide men for a 'conjunct' against Vlissingen, where there was a strong French naval squadron that 'could only emerge one by one after removing all their guns', due to the shallowness of the water.[31] Elsewhere in the Scheldt Estuary, moreover, there were a further twenty ships of the line destined for French use under construction, and the cabinet naturally wished to destroy them. Unfortunately, all the British soldiers who might otherwise have been available to do this were either still recovering from Moore's campaign in Iberia or returning there with Wellesley. Even if enough troops could be assembled later in the year, the ever-cautious Dundas was sceptical of their chances of success, as was the king. However, Brownrigg and Dumouriez both supported the effort, the latter enthusiastically,[32] while the newly rehabilitated Popham did not actually object; and the cabinet heard what it wanted to hear, as cabinets usually do. Thus, it was decided on 21 June 1809 'to throw the main strength of England' against Vlissingen and Antwerp, despite the country's 'general exhaustion of [...] military and pecuniary resources', chiefly through support for the continued independence from France of Portugal, Spain, and Sicily.[33] As the plan gathered pace, it also gained in grandiosity, and Vlissingen came to be seen as a springboard for a British thrust into the heart of Europe in support of anti-French rebels in Hesse, Hanover and Prussia, among other places; or even the permanent restoration of Hanover to the King of England's dominions. Lord Chatham, for whom 'the troops were ready to make unusual exertions [...] for his great brother's sake', was placed in command. By late July, assisted by Brownrigg, Chatham had embarked 33,000 infantry, 3,000 field artillery, and 2,000 cavalry on 'incomparably the greatest armament that had ever left the shores of England': fifty-eight ships of the line and frigates, nearly 200 sloops and smaller vessels of war, and more than 300 transports.[34]

Chatham's instructions were to destroy the enemy ships in Vlissingen and Antwerp, along with those towns' arsenals, and a third arsenal at Terneuse. And, in a strange echo of Hoche's orders to Tate regarding the harbours of Chester and Liverpool in 1797, Chatham was – 'if possible' – to render the River Scheldt itself 'no longer navigable by ships of war'.[35] Unsurprisingly, given its importance to Napoleon, the estuary was by this time a hornet's nest of redoubts, batteries, and well-armed fortresses, Antwerp foremost among them. Worse, all had recently been repaired, due to a blatant profusion of Royal Navy scouting expeditions through the spring and early summer. Though undermanned in comparison to the previous decade, due to the constant drain of the emperor's vast wars in the

Near-contemporary aquatint of the British bombarding Vlissingen in 1809.

Continent's interior, they were hardly empty: Vlissingen alone having a garrison of between 4,000 and 5,000 men.

In the event, the British landing on the northern side of Walcheren Island was more troubled by darkness, unfavourable tides, and heavy surf than by the seven heavy guns of the fort of Den Haak. Middelburg, in the centre of the island, surrendered without a fight on 31 July. By this time, the town of Veere on the east side of Walcheren had been substantially destroyed by Popham's gunboats, though two of them had been sunk by its fort. Veere surrendered to advancing British land forces the next day, but only after 200 of its garrison had escaped to Vlissingen. On the southwest side of the island, at least four batteries were either found deserted 'or evacuated after a trifling resistance'.[36] On the neighbouring island of Zuid-Beveland, immediately to the east,[37] a different British division discovered 'a battery which commanded the usual anchorage of the French fleet' abandoned and spiked, and found no enemy troops in the formidable redoubt at Batz, on the eastern tip of Zuid-Beveland nearest to Antwerp. However, a planned British assault on a third island, Cadzand[38] – located to the south of Walcheren and on the opposite side of the main channel of the river – had to be abandoned when it was discovered that the defenders numbered 6,000, whereas the 2,000 British attackers only had enough boats to land 700 men at a time. This arguably meant 'the failure of the whole enterprise', since the British fleet would not be able to sail safely up the river between the guns of Breskens on Cadzand and those of Vlissingen on Walcheren, unless and until the British land forces' siege of the latter town reached a favourable conclusion.[39] And even if that only took a few days, the chance to strike Antwerp in a state of semi-readiness – let alone take it completely by surprise, as originally intended by the British government – would be hopelessly lost. Worse, rowboats full of enemy troops could pass freely between Cadzand and Vlissingen in 15 to 20 minutes, and by this method the garrison of the latter was increased by some 2,000 men over the course of three days.

Vlissingen was bombarded with carcase rounds and roundshot from fifty-one heavy siege guns, as well as with rockets and by gunboats and other vessels, and fell on 16 August. By that point, the British had taken 7,600 prisoners for the loss of 738 killed, wounded, and missing. However, the defenders of Walcheren had cut its sea-dykes, so that the whole place started filling up with water. The physical damage was reparable, but by the 20th, 1,600 British had fallen ill with fever, which 'was increasing among the troops every hour'.[40] One medical officer blamed the local topography:

> The bottom of every canal that has direct communication with the sea is thickly covered with an ooze which, when the tide is out, emits a most offensive effluvia. Each ditch is filled with water which is loaded with animal and vegetable substances in a state of putrefaction, and the whole island is so flat and near the sea that a large proportion of it is little better than a swamp, and there is scarcely a place where water of tolerably good quality can be procured.[41]

Mosquitoes were also common, and while the exact nature of the fever in medical parlance remains 'open to speculation', one learned modern observer has suggested it was

> a lethal combination of [...] malaria, typhus, typhoid, and dysentery – acting together in a group of men already debilitated by previous campaigning and a life of poverty and drunkenness in the lower reaches of society. The reduced mortality in officers compared with the troops (only 3% compared with over 10%) was probably as much due to their better general health as to the more attentive care they undoubtedly received.[42]

Including those who had been or would be sent home to England, the sick numbered 4,000 on 1 September, 8,000 on the 3rd, and 11,000 on the 7th. Among the 18,000 British soldiers who remained to garrison Walcheren, despite the expedition's main objective of Antwerp now being hopelessly out of reach, the proportion with fever rose from 39 per cent on 10 September to half on 1 October.[43] If the whole force had been evacuated there and then, the episode would have rated as a disaster; but unaccountably, they were left in place for nearly five more months, rendering it an unparalleled catastrophe. As of 12 November, death and the departure of the worst cases for England had reduced the garrison to below 10,000 – 52 per cent ill – and by the time of the final abandonment of the area in February 1810, some 4,000 sufferers had died, either there, at home, or aboard ship. The survivors of the disease, moreover, were never completely well again, and in subsequent phases of the war in Spain, it was said that 'the Walcheren regiments were always the first to fall ill'.[44]

For our purposes, however, the important thing about the expedition was neither the virulence of the disease nor the inadequacy of the response, but rather the fact that it failed on its own terms before the fever struck. Dumouriez, who had advocated the capture of Walcheren in the strongest terms as far back as 1803 as 'one of the branches of the defence of England',[45] undoubtedly saw it not only as an extension and vindication of his ancient Wight-to-Portsmouth strategy,[46] but also as an inverse version of the attack on London via Tilbury that he had so feared since settling in England. Yet the French, without the benefit of his advice, were able to utilise some of the same countermeasures he had proposed. In particular, the reinforcement of Vlissingen from Cadzand in oared vessels, at times when winds and tides prevented the British sail of the line from doing anything to stop them, was in line with what Dumouriez had recommended for mutual reinforcement by the defenders of Kent and Essex – especially if one sees in Cadzand a cognate of Dumouriez's heavily reinforced Isle of Sheppey. Likewise, the resistance of Vlissingen, though not especially protracted by the standards of Napoleonic siege warfare, bought Antwerp and the French fleet there just enough time to put themselves in perfect readiness for an attack: indeed, even an attack by Britain's largest invasion force in history down to that date. The excellent showing of the British gunboats against the town and fort of Veere was, from the point of view of the defence of the Kent coast against their French counterparts, fairly worrying. However, if one can accept Tilbury Fort as comparable to the fortifications of Vlissingen, at least in the context of up-river *coup de main* attacks on London and Antwerp, then the wisdom of Dumouriez's exhortation that Tilbury 'be defended to the last extremity' is self-obvious.[47]

Another parallel worth considering is that of the Lines of Chatham – which Napoleon in 1804 intended to take and hold as a forward base – to the whole scheme of fortifications on the islands of Walcheren and Zuid-Beveland. Only vast luck on the landing beaches and an astonishing rate of march would have allowed him to take this subsidiary target quickly enough that he could move on into London before British forces outnumbering his own concentrated there. Politically, likewise, the Napoleonic regime shuddered to its core at the approach of Britain's own Great Armada to Antwerp – by then, a more significant naval base even than Brest; but the regime did not actually collapse. On that basis, it can be argued that a French landing in Kent, even by 95,998 fighting men,[48] would not *of itself* have caused the disintegration of a British state that had three times that many troops at its immediate disposal, a considerable proportion of them directly across the invaders' path.[49]

14

Endgame

For a 'fleeting moment' in 1811, Napoleon

> did revive the idea of invasion by planning to spend two millions [*sic*] francs on repairing the flotilla; but nothing was done and after his return from Moscow little more than the ruined frames of prams and pinnaces, half-buried in mud along the river banks of Northern France, remained as evidence of the emperor's wishful plans.[1]

At least one French officer aboard the Great Armada of 1779 had been of the opinion that the English, including the Cornish, were so deeply law-abiding that they would obey any order of the French and Spanish invaders, provided it was conveyed to them through their own minor public officials.[2] Those who know the English a bit better have drawn starkly different conclusions. Vine, for instance, believed that if Napoleon had effected a landing in England, and beaten the regular army in the field, 'there can be no doubt that a fierce national resistance would have followed under conditions favourable to the defence', leading to a long war of

attrition 'that would have anticipated the exhausting war in Spain, and might have proved as fatal as his march on Moscow'.[3] Nor should one discount the effect of simple fear among

Napoleon's armies included thousands of enthusiastic rapists, and this detail from a print by Williams was meant to suggest that their officers – emblematised by the male figure's sash and gorget – were more than merely complicit. Those who condemn the brutal physical violence of British military discipline in this period would do well to consider the alternative.

the French soldiery, who would be fighting with their backs to a 'river' more than twenty miles wide, and whose comrades were routinely castrated, raped, boiled alive, buried alive, sawn apart, and even crucified by the civilian populations of the other countries they 'liberated'.[4]

Historian Richard Glover believed that the volunteers would be pivotal to England's defence. However, because their state of training and equipment was continuously improving, the invasion's precise timing was just as key to the outcome:

> In 1803 they might have released some regular troops from the police duties required of the Army. By 1804 a considerable number of them were ready for active service; and if Bonaparte had landed in 1805 he would have found in the Volunteers about as formidable a citizen army [...] as any nation has ever raised.[5]

It is this factor of steady change over time in the quality of the defences and defenders that makes 'what-if' scenarios so difficult and unprofitable in this case. That is, even if opposition by the British fleet were to be ruled out in all scenarios, the expected outcomes of French invasions would differ wildly month by month, not only within 1803–05 but across the entire forty-year period covered by the present book.

The Grande Armée's first step on the road to Moscow did, in the event, mark the final end-point to Napoleon's dreams of knocking Britain out of the war via direct

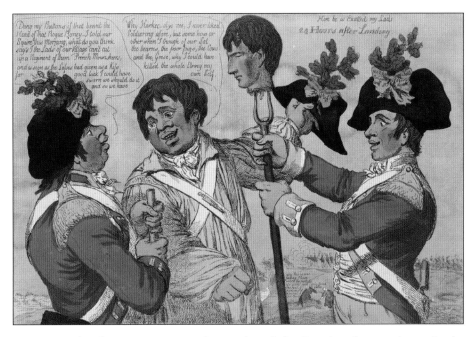

Inexperienced volunteers rejoice at the repulse of the French, who are shown in the background leaping from a cliff to escape the deadly impact of an English volley. The latter image evokes the deathly bugle-call of the contemporary *Rifle-Corps Song*: 'To the echoing woods,/ To the mountainous floods/ Around let it go, and around:/ Down the terrible Steep/ To the bellowing Deep,/ When the host of Invaders are drown'd'.

assault. However, it was not the end of her need to defend her coasts, as well as the coasts of new outposts, notably Heligoland. This pair of islands in the North Sea, some forty miles from the mouth of the River Elbe, was seized from Denmark at the start of the Gunboat War in September 1807. Much larger than Saint-Marcouf, Heligoland was subsequently used as a centre for espionage; a transit point out of Europe for thousands of recruits to the King's German Legion;[6] and a depot for the shipment of arms, ammunition, and uniforms to more or less anyone in the German-speaking lands who expressed a credible plan of rebellion against the French.[7] Most importantly, Heligoland was the main base for government-condoned smuggling of 'a vast amount of British manufactured goods and sugar, coffee and tea' into German ports.[8] The island of Anholt, occupied by Royal Marines in May 1809, also served such useful purposes that it was subjected to 'a most determined attempt by the Danes to recapture the place' in May 1811, which the defenders barely withstood.[9] Since '[m]ore than anything, the conflict at sea [...] was marked by aggressive commercial blockades by both Britain and France', smuggling on an industrial scale saved Britain's financial and credit structures from buckling, and was thus absolutely vital to the war effort.[10]

Moreover, '[a]s each side raised the stakes, the operation of neutral shipping in European waters, particularly American shipping, became impossible'.[11] It was therefore no great surprise when, in June 1812, France's hitherto neutral friend the United States declared war on the British Empire. In part, this was done in the hope of cleansing the North American continent of Britons and pro-British Indians; but the official justification involved the Royal Navy's 'restraints on maritime trade and the impressment of seafarers', both of which were 'essential to the success of economic war against France'.[12] This strategic background meant that both

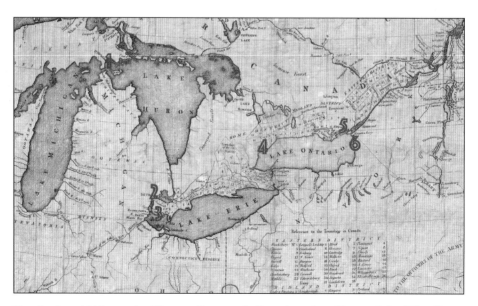

Detail of an 1812 map by Thomas Kensett, dedicated to the officers of the US military, annotated to show the relative positions of Mackinac Island (1), Detroit (2), Amherstburg (3), York (4), Kingston (5), and Sackett's Harbour (6).

Canadian lake warfare and the Atlantic privateer war, dormant since the 1780s, would resume. However, 'the lessons of the American Revolutionary War had been clear enough: Britain could not defeat America while [...] engaged in an existential war with other major powers', so whatever strategy she adopted would need to be 'cheap'.[13] Extension of the Martello programme to lakeside and riverine areas ticked that box. So did the re-purposing of the local shallow-draught boats, known as batteaux, used by fur trappers.

   In the opening days of the war, acting on his own initiative, the sickly Capt. Charles Roberts of the 10th Royal Veteran Battalion – an 1804 rebranding of the Invalids, known for its 'unconquerable drunkenness' – scratched together a force of some 600 British, Canadians, and Indians, a 6-pounder gun, and some batteaux and war canoes and made for the American fort on Mackinac Island, which dominated the narrow passage from Lake Huron into Lake Michigan. The sixty-one defenders, having heard nothing about war being declared, surrendered without a fight. The verve with which the island was captured, 'a decisive stroke in the successful defence of Upper Canada', inspired many hitherto neutral Michigan Indians to join the British cause.[14] This, in turn, made the Americans feel that their position at Detroit was untenable, and in August 1812 they surrendered that town and fort to the Shawnee leader Tecumseh (nicknamed 'the Wellington of the Indians') and Guernsey-born Maj.-Gen. Isaac Brock, who had served in both the Anglo-Russian invasion of Holland and the First Battle of Copenhagen.[15] The new owners of Mackinac Island, assisted by the Royal Newfoundland Fencibles and a company of Michigan Fencibles newly raised by Roberts, rebuilt the fort on a higher point of the island, tantalisingly just above the reach of naval broadsides, as the Americans would discover to their consternation when they tried to retake the place later in the war.

Quebec City Martello no. 1, one of four 'interdependent' towers on the Plains of Abraham planned by Quebec-born Lt-Col R. H. Bruyeres RE, was begun in 1808 due to 'the deterioration in Anglo-American relations' of the previous year.[16]

Surrender of the Canadian-built and partly Canadian-crewed thirty-gun frigate HMS *Confiance* at the Battle of Lake Champlain, 11 September 1814. She had been hit more than a hundred times and sustained 53 per cent casualties. Engraving by Benjamin Tanner after a painting by Hugh Reinagle.

British naval losses on the Great Lakes and Lake Champlain are mocked in this cartoon by William Charles, published in Philadelphia in 1814.

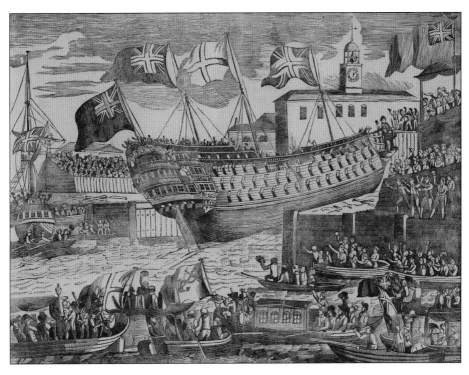

Woodcut commemorating the launch of the 120-gun first-rate HMS *Howe* at Chatham, 1815.

From a Canadian perspective, the defining moment of the conflict came on 27 April 1813, when 2,700 American troops based in the lakeside town of Sackett's Harbour, New York, landed from schooners just to the west of York (now Toronto), capital of Upper Canada (Ontario). Attacking the low-lying town's western defensive battery and fort from both land and water, the invaders overwhelmed the 750 British and Ojibwa defenders led by Massachusetts-born loyalist Gen. Roger Sheaffe. As the British forces withdrew towards their much stronger base at Kingston, they set their fort's powder magazine on fire. The resulting explosion killed more than 200 Americans, including their leader, Gen. Zebulon Pike, squashed by a huge falling stone. In revenge, the remaining Americans looted and burned the undefended town: an act 'of little strategic benefit', and one that demanded revenge.[17] Probably without knowing it had occurred, 150 Royal Marines led by Nova Scotia-born Hanoverian Lt George Westphal RN appeared to deliver it six days later. Firing as they approached from fifteen or twenty carronade-armed launches and a 'rocket boat', they stormed a six-gun coastal battery by Havre de Grace, Maryland, taking it and its guns without loss as the Americans fled – possibly because one of them had been spectacularly killed by a Congreve rocket. Westphal's force swiftly went on to destroy the 'complicated heavy machinery [...] of the Cecil or Principio Foundery', one of America's leading gunmaking concerns. There, as well as the equipment, they disabled forty-one guns, mostly of large calibres.[18]

On 24 June, a much larger force of Americans with a seven-gun coastal battery at Hampton, Virginia, were routed by a landing party of 2,400 British from the fleet

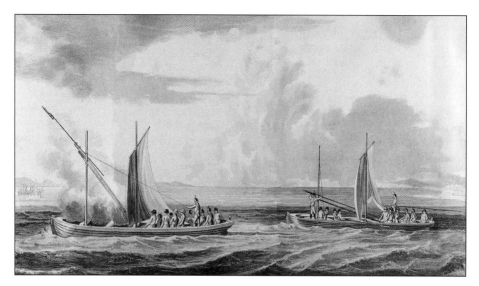

British rocket boats in action.

blockading Chesapeake Bay, who committed 'every horror [...] with impunity', or
so the Americans claimed at the time.[19] But Havre de Grace and Hampton were
just two incidents in a larger pattern of aggressive blockade-related activity on the
Chesapeake.[20] Indeed, it would seem that the British forces had learned little from
the overly vindictive amphibious raids on the Connecticut shore in the previous
war, each of which was of more value to the losers – in the form of propaganda –
than it was to the winners.

Nonetheless, Britain's grand strategy during the first two years of the War of
1812 was thoroughly defensive, as the government were

> more concerned with defeating Napoleon in Europe than fighting a minor
> war with the United States. Because of this, they had been content to defend
> their territory from American invasions without launching any of their own.[21]

This defensive outlook was reinforced with the May 1813 arrival of Cdre Sir James
Yeo as 'commander-in-chief of the warships on the North American lakes'. As
the burning of York had occurred less than three weeks earlier, Yeo concentrated
his attention on Lake Ontario, 'on whose control the entire British position in
Upper Canada depended'. Within less than a month, he had gathered

> an efficient squadron of two ships of 24 and 20 guns, with a 14-gun brig
> and some smaller vessels, and [... planned] an attack on Sackett's Harbour,
> where the enemy had a couple of large vessels on the stocks. [...] Yeo took his
> squadron up the lake in June, capturing or destroying enemy storeships and
> depots and reversing the American army's invasion.[22]

Unfortunately, Yeo's focus on Lake Ontario implied the neglect of the British
squadron on Lake Erie, which was resoundingly defeated on 10 September 1813,

leading to the American capture of the gunboat and all five sloops of war that were engaged. Less than three weeks later, the British forts at Detroit and Amherstburg also fell. As with Mackinaw Island the year before, a sudden reversal of fortune on the water had made multiple lakeside garrisons suddenly untenable: in this case, chiefly due to the local scarcity of food. So short were supplies of all kinds at Amherstburg, in fact, that the largest British vessel in the Erie squadron, HMS *Detroit*, had been armed with a hotchpotch of old garrison guns as well as naval ordnance, amounting to seventeen pieces of no fewer than four different calibres, as well as two sizes of carronade.

Point Frederick, Ontario, headquarters of Canada's Provincial Marine since 1789, would be transformed over the course of the war into a locally important naval dockyard. However, Yeo's carronade-armed vessels had simply to run away from newly built American lake-ships with 'heavier and more efficient armament':[23] notably, the same general type of gun – the long 24-pounder – that was mounted on Martello towers at home. After the various disasters of September 1813, however,

> Yeo built two large ships at Kingston, and with these added to his squadron embarked a large body of troops and attacked Oswego on 6 May 1814. After a sharp contest the place was carried, and a large quantity of ordnance stores and provisions was captured or destroyed.[24]

This miniature naval arms race see-sawed across the lake through the summer, but in September 1814, it was decisively won by the British and Canadians, who somewhat astonishingly had managed, over just ten months, to complete and launch that awesome engine of war, HMS *St Lawrence*: the Royal Navy's first and only fresh-water ship of the line. A first-rate, no less, it mounted 108 guns, six more than HMS *Victory* had carried at Trafalgar.[25] An American attempt to destroy *St Lawrence* using a so-called torpedo failed, and the war would come to an end before any further escalation on the inland seas could occur.[26]

The late summer of 1814 also saw the event remembered in Canada as the definitive act of revenge for the burning of York, almost exactly one year earlier. This was the destruction of the not-yet-white Presidential Mansion, the US Capitol Building, the Supreme Court, the Washington Navy Yard and a bridge over the Potomac River, by 3,400 British Peninsular War veterans and 1,100 Royal Marines under Irish Maj.-Gen. Robert Ross. Unlike in Upper Canada, however, 'most private property was left untouched'.[27]

The War of 1812 ground on obliviously after the peace treaty had been signed, with a gigantic, failed 'conjunct' against Louisiana in December 1814. The land forces in that campaign were led by Wellington's brother-in-law, Maj.-Gen. Sir Ned Pakenham, a last-minute replacement for Robert Ross, who – leading from the front – had been mortally wounded by small-arms fire in a failed 4,000-man attack on Baltimore in September. Pakenham was killed too, and some 3,000 other British soldiers, sailors and marines killed or wounded.[28]

Over the course of the War of 1812, the enemy had clearly been impressed by the Martello-tower idea, especially as a potential means of defending their southern states. They accordingly assigned the name 'Martello' to defensive structures

British mortar-boats of Danish inspiration at the destruction of the Navy Yard in Anacostia, during Maj.-Gen. Robert Ross's dramatic 1814 assault on Washington DC.

It tends to be conveniently forgotten in Canada that Ross's equally large amphibious attack on the militarily far more important city of Baltimore, Maryland, was repulsed by the Americans three weeks later, despite the firing of up to 1,800 rounds into Fort McHenry by the Royal Navy over a period of twenty-four hours. The lit fuses of the mortar bombs are clearly visible here. The US national anthem commemorates this action, which by its lack of success was Britain's main spur to peace negotiations.

Pf. 7, 15-17.   Der Februar 1814.   Jef. 14, 15-20.

The repressed return to slay the beast. The motley Prussian army was receiving some of its uniforms from Britain by this point in the war, which could explain why the coat of the jäger at right so closely resembles those of the 60th Foot.

The campaigns that culminated in the fall of Paris also included up to 112,000 plainly clad members of the Prussian Landwehr. The cheap iron cross on the shako (in fact, probably brass) would have borne a German motto meaning 'With God for King and Country 1813'. In theory consisting of all adult males under age 46, the Landwehr's solid performance can be taken as collateral evidence that the British volunteers of 1794–1807 would not simply have been brushed aside.

Remains of the Wallbach Tower, a so-called Martello built in Portsmouth, New Hampshire in 1814.

of various plans, including at least one square and one hexagon, and another made partially of timber at Tybee Island, Georgia. This brought the development process full circle, for nearby St Augustine, Florida – oldest European settlement in what is now the United States – had a system of wooden defensive/signal towers, presumably modelled on the corsair towers of the Mediterranean.[29] New York City and Portsmouth, New Hampshire, would each receive a Martello, and the present coat of arms the US 41st Infantry Regiment features a purported Martello tower as part of its crest.

As well as the places already mentioned above, Martellos or Martello-like structures were built during or slightly prior to the Napoleonic War in British-held Sicily, Trinidad, Sierra Leone, and Ceylon, as well as an island off the coast of Croatia. Including other parts of the British Isles, the non-English total appears to have been ninety-one.[30] After the conflict ended, one was constructed in Bermuda in the 1820s; five in Jersey, five in Mauritius and one in Cape Colony in the 1830s; and four in Upper Canada in the 1840s. The last Martello to be built in the British Empire was an addition to the defences of Sydney Harbour in Australia. On Pinchgut Island, it was authorised in response to a menacing visit by American warships in 1839, but the tower was not actually completed until eighteen years later, due to a new threat from the Russians. The British volunteer movement was suddenly and spectacularly revived in 1859 due to

A post-Napoleonic War Martello tower in the South Indian Ocean nation of Mauritius, a British colony from 1810 until 1968.

an invasion threat made by France's Emperor Napoleon III, though by that time, enormous, rifled naval artillery had outpaced any conceivable defensive construction techniques on land; and this innate superiority of attack over defence would remain the case until the perfection of steel-reinforced concrete in the 1870s. America, too, desisted from building so-called Martello towers after 1873.[31]

Most of England's surviving Napoleonic and pre-Napoleonic coastal batteries are located in Devon and Cornwall. However, Harwich's Bath Side battery of three 24-pounders, approved in 1809 and built in 1810, outlived its siblings at Angelgate and Beacon Hill, and was the subject of archaeological investigations in the 1990s. Martellos on the east coast also tended to be constructed in the immediate vicinity of three- to seven-gun shore batteries of 1790s vintage, and those at towers A, B, K, L, and AA survived into the present century in some identifiable form. Martellos were first considered to be of archaeological as opposed to current military interest only in 1937, when J. P. Bushe-Fox surveyed most of them for the Ministry of Works.[32] Of the seventy-four built in Kent and Sussex between 1805 and 1810, twenty-six survive, whether as visible ruins, private residences, visitor attractions, or simply intact but empty. A real treasure is Martello no. 24, run since 1969 as a museum, which boasts a Blomefield 24-pounder authentically mounted on a traversing carriage on the roof. The survival rate of the heftier Martellos built in northern Essex and southern Suffolk was higher, despite some having been sold off as building materials as early as 1819.

> Of the original 29 towers built [on the east coast …] 18 survive, if Tower R is included despite its having been partially demolished and incorporated into the Bartlet Hospital, Felixstowe, in the 1920s. Of those which survive three are on the Buildings at Risk Register because they are perceived to be steadily decaying, one as a result of coastal erosion and two [...] of prolonged neglect.[33]

This is not to suggest, however, that the south coast towers were weak. It took no fewer than 150 rounds fired at 1,000 yards from new Armstrong rifled muzzle loaders, some of calibres larger than anything that had existed in Napoleonic times, to demolish Tower no. 68 near Eastbourne during a Royal Artillery field day in 1860.[34]

The ebb and flow of offensive and defensive military technologies, with one and then the other gaining the upper hand, will probably continue as long as

Located on a high bluff above the town of Sandgate and below Shorncliffe Camp, Martello no. 8 is a fairly typical modern house conversion.

The 1820s Martello tower at Ferry Reach, Bermuda.

Kingston, Ontario's Shoal Tower was built in the 1840s, and is unusual in being surrounded by water. However, the now-landlocked 'Tally Too'er' in Leith, Scotland, planned in 1807–10 but not completed until the mid-century, was originally in a similar position on the Mussel Cape Rocks.

This British-made Armstrong rifled muzzle loader, seen here in a rebel fortress in North Carolina known as the 'Southern Gibraltar', would have been a match for any masonry then in existence. It was a necessary but not sufficient condition for the US Civil War that paramilitary rifle clubs, modelled loosely on the British volunteers of 1794–1807, spread like wildfire through the Anglosphere at the end of the 1850s.

Adm. Adam Duncan.

there are human beings. But one critically important aspect of war springs eternal. It can be assisted or thwarted by technology but is not itself technological. It is deception. Time and again, we were saved by our ability to fool the enemy: that Lord Cawdor's eager misfits with pitchforks were backed up by thousands of disciplined regular troops; that Adm. Duncan's fleet in the run-up to Camperdown had not mutinied over pay and conditions, and were still taking his orders; that Adm. Villeneuve's fleet covering the invasion of 1805 was about to be attacked by three dozen non-existent British sail of the line.

Likewise, we were saved time and again by the enemy's inability to deceive us about invasion plans that were too big to conceal, and thus, in a sense, too big to succeed. Had Napoleon got across, moreover, our planned fighting withdrawal to Dover rather than to Chatham would probably have given him the surprise of his life, by implying that what was, in fact, our main field army was just the advance guard of some much larger army already gathered between Chatham and London. And every day he delayed his advance in fear of that other army would add to its reality, as volunteers poured into the capital from inland districts (exactly as happened at Antwerp the moment we moved against it). Where we failed most dismally, as at Boulogne in 1801 and Walcheren in 1809, we had been telegraphing the punch – in the latter case, for years on end. Thus, if the saga of British coastal defence in the reign of King George III holds one crucial lesson for the young person of today, it is this. Whatever game you are playing, you cannot think too early or too often about deceiving your opponents, or about how they may be deceiving you.

Though it depicts a rousing victory for the Royal Artillery, James Gillray's 1803 image of an opposed landing in England also highlights the grave exposure of the defenders, who have nothing between them and the enemy's fire but a quarter-inch of 'starvation cheap' wool. As well as protecting its crew from death, capture, and wounds, the advent of the single-gun 'Bomb Proof Tower' would make the gun itself considerably harder for the enemy to steal.

NOTES

Foreword

1. 'Introduction to the modern edition', in H. F. B. Wheeler and A. M. Broadley, *Napoleon and the invasion of England: The story of the great terror* (Stroud: Nonsuch, 2007 {1908}), pp. 7–10, p. 8.
2. A concise explanation of the naval-funding controversy is provided in Norman Longmate, *Island fortress: The defence of Great Britain 1603–1945* (London: Pimlico, 2001 {1991}), p. 17.
3. Longmate, *Island fortress*, p. 174. Even the Grand Old Duke of York's disastrous Flanders campaign, which will barely be touched on in these pages, can be been seen to have 'served as a subsidiary defence of the British Isles': Wheeler and Broadley, *Napoleon and the invasion*, p. 41.
4. Jeremy Black, *War in the eighteenth-century world* (Basingstoke: Palgrave Macmillan, 2013), p. 128. As the leading military theorist of the century, Henry Lloyd, remarked, 'the Russian infantry is by far superior to any in Europe; insomuch that I question whether it can be defeated by any other infantry whatever': *The history of the late war in Germany, between the King of Prussia, and the Empress of Germany and her allies*, Vol. 1 (London: S. Hooper, 1781), p. 145.
5. Roger Knight, *Britain against Napoleon: The organization of victory 1793–1815* (London: Penguin, 2014), p. xxii, who stresses not merely the scale or geographic scope of the war, but also the sufferings of the civilian population and Britain's vulnerability, both aspects that are normally ignored.
6. I remain grateful to my undergraduate tutor P. J. Cain for alerting me to the long-running debate over the accidental aspects of imperial expansion, launched by John Gallagher and Ronald Robinson's 'The imperialism of free trade' in *The Economic History Review* Vol. 6, No. 1 (1953), pp. 1–15.

Chapter 1: Defence against what?

1. G. M. Anderson and A. Gifford Jr., 'Privateering and the private production of naval power', *Cato Journal* Vol. 11, No. 1 (1991), pp. 99–122, p. 102, n. 4. All calculations of the present-day buying power of Georgian-era currency in this book have been made using https://www.measuringworth.com/calculators/ppoweruk/.
2. History.com editors, 'Congress authorizes privateers to attack British vessels', 13 November 2009, https://www.history.com/this-day-in-history/congress-authorizes-privateers-to-attack-british-vessels.
3. Bryan Mabee, 'Pirates, privateers and the political economy of private violence', *Global Change, Peace and Security*, Vol. 21, No. 2 (2009), pp. 139–152, p. 139. See also I. A. A. Thompson, '"Money, money, and yet more money!" Finance, the fiscal-state, and the military revolution: Spain 1500–1650', in C. J. Rogers, ed., *The military revolution debate: Readings on the*

military transformation of early modern Europe (Boulder, CO: Westview, 1995), pp. 273–298, p. 290.

4. Such an argument was advanced in D. A. Baugh's *British naval administration in the age of Walpole* (Princeton: Princeton University Press, 1965), p. 22, but subsequently criticised by the economists Anderson and Gifford, who note that privateering could just as easily have lessened both the duration and destructiveness of eighteenth-century wars: 'Privateering', p. 113, p. 113n.

5. The low end of this range was levied by Britain and Spain, and the high end by the American revolutionaries. See Anderson and Gifford, 'Privateering', p. 102, n. 6.

6. Anderson and Gifford, 'Privateering', p. 105, n. 9.

7. Anderson and Gifford, 'Privateering', p. 101. The *Encyclopaedia Britannica* entry 'American Revolution' claims there were 70,000 US privateer crewmen spread across 2,000 ships, but this appears to be an error arising from the fact that new letters of marque were issued for each cruise, i.e. multiple times to any privateering vessel that set forth from America more than once. I have found no other source suggesting that there were more than 800 American privateers in total, including the tiniest, non-ocean-going vessels. In any case, American privateers 'constituted the only sustained offensive pressure brought to bear by the Americans' and were a major factor in the British civilian population's eventual desire for peace: https://www.britannica.com/event/American-Revolution/The-war-at-sea.

8. Anderson and Gifford, 'Privateering', pp. 100, 104.

9. https://allthingsliberty.com/2014/11/the-bermuda-powder-raids-of-1775/.

10. J. W. Fortescue, *A history of the British Army*, Vol. 3 (London: Macmillan, 1911), p. 184.

11. Beamish Murdoch, *A history of Nova Scotia, or Acadie* (Halifax, NS: James Barnes, 1866), Vol. 2, p. 619.

12. https://www.massar.org/2011/06/23/privateers-of-the-revolution/. The Continental Congress's total was 1,697, but the total issued by individual states is not definitively known; therefore the grand total might be as low as 2,639 or as high as 2,848.

13. https://www.massar.org/2011/06/23/privateers-of-the-revolution/.

14. Compensation for the livestock was promised but apparently never received by the islanders: E. Ames et al., *The acts and resolves, public and private, of the Province of the Massachusetts Bay* (Boston, MA: Wright and Potter, 1922), p. 245.

15. 'Pounder' designations referred to the weight of a single cannonball, though, in extreme situations, two or even three projectiles might be loaded into the same gun simultaneously. This, as well as the relation of 'pounder' ratings to calibres and ranges, will be discussed in detail in a later chapter.

16. http://www.whitehavenandwesternlakeland.co.uk/johnpauljones/raid.htm.

17. When a nail for literally 'spiking' its touch-hole was unavailable, a gun could be 'spiked' by the expedient of wrapping one of its own roundshot in 'a man's hat' and ramming it 'as close in the chamber as possible': John Ardesoif, *An introduction to marine fortification and gunnery [...]* (Gosport: W. Dawkins, 1772), p. 152.

18. http://www.whitehavenandwesternlakeland.co.uk/johnpauljones/raid.htm.
19. The US sailors and marines who raided Whitehaven and other places in 1778 were mis-identified as privateers in both a local newspaper and the *Morning Chronicle and London Advertiser*: Longmate, *Island fortress*, pp. 191–192.
20. Longmate, *Island fortress*, p. 204.
21. Daniel MacCannell, *Lost Banff and Buchan* (Edinburgh: Birlinn, 2012), p. 28.
22. Royal Commission on the Ancient and Historical Monuments of Scotland, Canmore Database, item 21190.
23. MacCannell, *Lost Banff and Buchan*, p. 154.
24. K. W. Maurice-Jones, *The history of coast artillery in the British Army* (Uckfield: Naval and Military, 2005 {1957}), p. 51.
25. Frontispiece.
26. *The London Gazette*, 4–8 May 1779, p. [2]. After *c*.1770, all Royal Navy vessels mounting fewer than twenty guns were termed 'sloops of war', but subdivided into 'ship-sloops' with three masts (including the fourteen-gun HMS *Swan*, in which my ancestor Thomas Thomas served); 'brig-sloops', usually with two masts; and 'cutters', normally with one. Presumably, British officials and newspaper reports applied such terminology to French craft based on their number of masts. The contentious planning phase of this expedition is detailed in J. Holland Rose and A. M. Broadley, *Dumouriez and the defence of England against Napoleon* (London and New York: John Lane, 1909), pp. 321–324.
27. https://morethannelson.com/battle-cancale-bay-13-may-1779/.
28. Visually similar to cannon, these weapons generally used less propellant and fired in much higher trajectories – but not as high as those of mortars, which were fixed to their bases at an angle of 45 degrees.
29. https://morethannelson.com/battle-cancale-bay-13-may-1779/.
30. It should be noted here that both small-calibre, anti-personnel swivel guns, and carronades, the high-calibre but short-barrelled, short-range, low-velocity artillery pieces first deployed in the 1770s, were often carried on warships during the period covered by this book, but they were not included in formal counts of guns aboard until 1817.
31. https://morethannelson.com/battle-cancale-bay-13-may-1779/.
32. Maurice-Jones, *Coast artillery*, p. 49.
33. Ordnance order, *c*.1756, quoted in Maurice-Jones, *Coast artillery*, p. 52.
34. Maurice-Jones, *Coast artillery*, p. 52.
35. Though it should be borne in mind that they were organised into 150 companies, and not grouped as battalions in practice at this date. Longmate, *Island fortress*, p. 201.
36. Fortescue, *British Army*, Vol. 3, p. 294.
37. Abercromby Gordon, 'Parish of Banff', in *The Statistical Account of Scotland* (Edinburgh: William Creech, 1791–1799), ed. by John Sinclair, Vol. 20, pp. 319–382, quotations at p. 359.
38. Horace Walpole, *Memoirs of the Reign of King George III*, Vol. 3 (London: Richard Bentley, 1845), p. 107.

39. Fortescue, *British Army*, Vol. 3, p. 41.
40. Walpole, *Memoirs*, Vol. 3, p. 107.
41. Longmate, *Island fortress*, p. 199.
42. Maurice-Jones, *Coast artillery*, p. 49. Fortescue concurs that the number of regulars assigned to the defence of the British Isles as of 1777 was 'very insufficient': *British Army*, Vol. 3, p. 198.
43. This was recommended not only by Dumouriez, but by a renegade former Royal Navy lieutenant, Robert Hamilton, who – working independently – had considered and rejected 'Plymouth, Dartmouth, Torbay and Harwich': Longmate, *Island fortress*, p. 197.
44. Quoted or perhaps paraphrased in Maurice-Jones, *Coast artillery*, p. 50.
45. For the sake of narrative flow, I have deemed 18-pounders and above to be 'heavy' and 12-pounders and below to be 'light', on two grounds: first, that by 1793, no European army used guns larger than 12-pounders as field artillery, and relegated all larger calibres to coastal-defence, garrison, and siege use: see Terence Wise, *Artillery equipments of the Napoleonic Wars* (London: Osprey, 1979); and second, that 18, 24 and 32-pounders all had a similar extreme range of around 1.3 nautical miles, as compared to substantially less than 1 nautical mile for all smaller calibres. In Georgian parlance, however, the term 'light guns' probably meant 9-pounders or smaller.
46. Maurice-Jones, *Coast artillery*, p. 50.
47. Elizabeth Montagu, quoted in Longmate, *Island fortress*, p. 196.
48. The two fleets had linked up on 22 July, substantially later than planned.
49. Maurice-Jones, *Coast artillery*, pp. 52–53 seems to accept the contemporary official view that Plymouth would be the real target of the attack, while rejecting its then-governor's opinion that 'if attacked [it] must unavoidably fall'. Fortescue, on the other hand, took it as read that the dockyard could have been taken 'in six hours' and that 'strong censure of the neglect that had left Plymouth defenceless was perfectly justified': *British Army*, Vol. 3, pp. 295, 299. And Longmate (*Island fortress*, p. 210) calls the governor a 'useful scapegoat' for wider failings by the Army. In any case, the survival of a contemporary plan for taking Plymouth via Cawsand Bay and then establishing 'bomb-batteries or guns firing red-hot shot' on the Maker Heights or Mount Edgcumbe (Longmate, *Island fortress*, pp. 202–203) does not by itself prove that the Great Armada was going to implement it. Less than a month after its sickness-stricken ships began limping into Brest, the French army – all dressed up, but with nowhere to go – were planning amphibious attacks on 'Weymouth, Portland, Torbay, Dartmouth, Start Point, Fowey [...] the Lizard [...] Plymouth, Falmouth and Helford River', none of which ever came to anything: Longmate, *Island fortress*, p. 209.
50. Warley Barracks would not be built until 1804.
51. Longmate, *Island fortress*, p. 202.
52. Longmate, *Island fortress*, pp. 204, 207.
53. Longmate, *Island fortress*, p. 209.
54. Maurice-Jones, *Coast artillery*, p. 53.

55. Maurice-Jones, *Coast artillery*, p. 55.

56. On the guns themselves, Phil Carradice, *Britain's last invasion: The Battle of Fishguard 1797* (Barnsley: Pen and Sword, 2019), pp. 64-65, quotation at p. 65. These guns' small calibre meant that Goodwick Sands, a 'perfect landing site for any army', was out of range: *ibid.*, p. 65. On ammunition quantities, Maurice-Jones, *Coast artillery*, pp. 88–89; and on the response by the local smuggler, Longmate, *Island fortress*, p. 194.

57. His Majesty's Engineers were given their Royal title in 1787.

58. Carradice, *Britain's last invasion*, pp. 165–166.

59. Longmate, *Island fortress*, p. 204.

60. Likewise, the extant Martello tower by the Channel Islands Military Museum would not be constructed until nineteen years after Napoleon's final defeat and exile.

61. Fortescue, *British Army*, Vol. 3, p. 416.

62. Fortescue, *British Army*, Vol. 3, p. 308.

63. Maurice-Jones, *Coast artillery*, p. 81.

64. Fortescue, *British Army*, Vol. 3, p. 356.

65. Fortescue, *British Army*, Vol. 3, p. 306.

66. As of 1790, garrison guns were routinely operated by as few as three men, who 'doubled up on the jobs that had to be done', with the maximum crew being eight: Robert Wilkinson-Latham, *British artillery on land and sea 1790–1820* (Newton Abbot: David and Charles, 1973), p. 67. Still, I see no merit in Longmate's suggestion (*Island fortress*, p. 277) that south-coast Martello towers' guns would have been worked by just two men as a matter of routine, while the other twenty-two just waited inside. British shipboard gun crews tended to be larger, i.e. ten men and boys for 12- and 18-pounders, twelve for 24-pounders, and fourteen for 36-pounders, in part because of the need to raise and lower the gun ports, and in part because of the potential need to tell off half the members of each gun crew to man the guns on the other side of the ship (sea-fights involving simultaneous action by both sides of the same ship being rare, but not unknown): Wilkinson-Latham, *British artillery*, p. 74. Members of naval gun crews were also frequently called away to fight fires, repel boarders, board enemy ships, fire at the enemy with muskets, or work aloft.

67. Maurice-Jones, *Coast artillery*, p. 63.

68. Knight, *Britain against Napoleon*, pp. 42–43. In 1778, Richmond in the Lords and Charles James Fox in the Commons had 'moved simultaneously that no more of the old regiments should be sent out of the kingdom, which, as they had already condemned the raising of new regiments, amounted practically to a motion for the sacrifice of all external British possessions whatever': Fortescue, *British Army*, Vol. 3, p. 248.

69. Wise, *Artillery equipments*, p. 26.

70. Fortescue, *British Army*, Vol. 3, p. 344.

71. *British Army*, Vol. 3, p. 149.

72. Robert Beatson, *Naval and military memoirs of Great Britain, from 1727 to 1783* (London: Longman, Hurst, Rees, and Orme, 1804), Vol. 5, p. 368.

73. Beatson, *Naval and military memoirs*, Vol. 5, p. 369.

74. *The new annual register [...] for the year 1781* (London: G. Robinson, 1782), p. 35.
75. *The London Gazette*, 13–16 January 1781, p. [1].
76. Because Corbet was court-martialled and forced into retirement after this episode, accounts of his role in it vary considerably: from being surprised asleep in bed by the French, to having been warned of their arrival by Capt. Clement Hemery of the militia artillery, whom he sent on to warn the Royal Glasgow Volunteers at Grouville: https://www.theislandwiki.org/index.php/The_Battle_at_Platte_Rocque.
77. Beatson, *Naval and military memoirs*, Vol. 5, p. 378.
78. *The London Gazette*, 13–16 January 1781, p. [1].
79. Maurice-Jones, *Coast artillery*, p. 68.
80. Maurice-Jones, *Coast artillery*, p. 68.
81. Fortescue, *British Army*, p. 419.
82. James Falkner, 'Eliott, George Augustus, first Baron Heathfield of Gibraltar (1717–1790)', *Oxford Dictionary of National Biography online [ODNB]*.
83. Maurice-Jones, *Coast artillery*, p. 65. Fortescue, *British Army*, Vol. 3, p. 417, notes that half of the defenders had lived on salted provisions for three years, and the other half for six years, making virulent scurvy inevitable.
84. Maurice-Jones, *Coast artillery*, p. 70; the number of ships is from Frederick Sayer, *The history of Gibraltar and of its political relation to events in Europe [...]* (London: Saunders, Otley and Co., 1863), p. 373.
85. Sayer, *History of Gibraltar*, p. 372.
86. Sayer, *History of Gibraltar*, p. 372, who gives the minimum number as eight and the maximum as twenty; the numbers I have given are from Maurice-Jones, *Coast artillery*, p. 72.
87. Spanish orders, quoted in Sayer, *History of Gibraltar*, p. 374.
88. Sayer, *History of Gibraltar*, p. 379.
89. Maurice-Jones, *Coast artillery*, p. 71.
90. Maurice-Jones, *Coast artillery*, p. 71.
91. Sayer, *History of Gibraltar*, p. 387.
92. Quoted in Sayer, *History of Gibraltar*, p. 392.
93. Sayer, *History of Gibraltar*, p. 387.
94. Falkner, 'Eliott', *ODNB*.
95. I.e. 19.9 vs 13.6 rounds per gun per hour, the per-gun average at Waterloo having been 129 rounds fired during the entire battle.
96. Fortescue, *British Army*, Vol. 3, pp. 424–425.
97. I am self-consciously adapting the nickname 'University of War', ascribed to the similarly lengthy Siege of Ostend of 1601–04: see https://www.gla.ac.uk/myglasgow/library/files/special/exhibns/month/mar2004.html, which includes superb contemporary bird's-eye views of *trace italienne* fortifications in action.
98. Alastair W. Massie, 'Koehler, George (1758–1800)', *ODNB*.
99. According to Fortescue, *British Army*, Vol. 3, p. 266, less than one hour elapsed between the last French ground forces surrendering and the sails of the French relief fleet being sighted.
100. Fortescue, *British Army*, Vol. 3, p. 268.

101. Fortescue, *British Army*, Vol. 3, p. 269.
102. Maurice-Jones, *Coast artillery*, p. 58.
103. Maurice-Jones, *Coast artillery*, p. 62. Likewise, per Fortescue, 'whatever the power of the British Navy for protection, a fleet requires naval bases, and naval bases require garrisons': *British Army*, Vol. 3, p. 25.
104. Maurice-Jones, *Coast artillery*, p. 60.
105. Maurice-Jones, *Coast artillery*, p. 32. Another such proclamation, which Richard Glover thought might be the first of its kind, was issued on 9 July 1779: *Britain at bay: Defence against Bonaparte, 1803–14* (London: Allen and Unwin, 1973), p. 54.
106. Wheeler and Broadley, *Napoleon and the invasion*, p. 9.

Chapter 2: The role of forts in coastal defence to 1783

1. Though it was originally a description of a shift in infantry tactics, the 'revolution' as re-theorised around defensive architecture remains a dominant theoretical armature in the field of military history today. An excellent overview is provided by Rogers, ed., *Military revolution debate*.
2. Lynn, 'The *trace italienne* and the growth of armies: the French case', 169–199 in Rogers, ed., *Military revolution debate*, pp. 171–172.
3. Black, *War*, pp. 48–49 quotation at p. 49.
4. Though now inextricably linked with America, thanks to Francis Scott Key, the phrase was used without irony to describe George III's England in Wheeler and Broadley, *Napoleon and the invasion*, p. 79.
5. This date is per https://historicengland.org.uk/listing/the-list/list-entry/1290222; other sources place the commencement as early as 1550, or as late as the 1560s.
6. Tellingly, the first *trace italienne* fort in Britain was built by English troops holding Eyemouth, Berwickshire in 1547; after it was dismantled pursuant to treaty terms in 1550, it was rebuilt by French troops in 1556 and demolished, again by agreement, in 1559. On the roles of Pelham and Lee in an unsuccessful assault on the Italian-designed fortifications of the port of Leith in 1560, see Christopher Fleet and Daniel MacCannell, *Edinburgh: Mapping the city* (Edinburgh: Birlinn, 2014), pp. 8–10.
7. Brian Lavery, 'Dockyards and industry', in in Quintin Colville and James Davey, eds., *Nelson navy and nation: The Royal Navy and the British people, 1688–1815* (London: Conway, 2013), pp. 58–75, p. 62.
8. Black, *War*, p. 176.
9. Ardesoif, *Marine fortification*, p. 30.
10. *War*, p. 216.
11. Ardesoif, *Marine fortification*, pp. 2–3, 22, 29. One additional seldom-considered advantage of shore batteries over warships was that enemy round shot falling on land could be picked up and fired back, paralleling the defensive advantage in the Battle of Britain regarding where shot-down pilots fell, i.e. in enemy vs home territory.
12. Ardesoif, *Marine fortification*, pp. 4, 6, 70.
13. Ardesoif, *Marine fortification*, p. 134.

14. The term actually used by Ardesoif was 'half a cable's length', a cable for this purpose being 101 fathoms, i.e. either 606 or 608 feet, depending on whether one meant the 'warship fathom' of exactly 6 feet, or exactly 1/1,000 of the Admiralty mile of 6,080 feet.
15. Ardesoif, *Marine fortification*, pp. 2–4, 6, 22, 29, 30.
16. Ardesoif, *Marine fortification*, p. 33. It was presumably on this basis that HMS *Swan* served as a fireship from 1779 to 1783, but survived, and returned to 'normal' service for a further eighteen years.
17. Ardesoif, *Marine fortification*, pp. 36–37.
18. Ardesoif, *Marine fortification*, pp. 29–30.
19. Now Maine. The other side of the border, now New Brunswick, was then still part of Nova Scotia.
20. *Pace* Bernard Cornwell's otherwise excellent *The fort* (London: Harper, 2011), p. 166, His Majesty's Marines would not become known as Royal Marines until 1802.
21. https://npgallery.nps.gov/NRHP/GetAsset/NRHP/69000007_text.
22. Knight, *Britain against Napoleon*, p. 17.
23. J. K. Laughton, rev. by Nicholas Tracy, 'Collier, Sir George (1738–1795)', *ODNB*.
24. For a rare defence of the Connecticut raid's aims and outcomes, see Fortescue, *British Army*, Vol. 3, pp. 287–288.
25. The tale that the American defenders of Fort Griswold were tortured and murdered by the British appears to have been invented by one Sgt Stephen Hempstead: https://www.mountvernon.org/library/digitalhistory/digital-encyclopedia/article/connecticut-raids/.
26. Fortescue, *British Army*, Vol. 3, p. 399.
27. I am thinking especially of the attacks on Sag Harbor (24 May 1777) and Manor St George (23 November 1780), though other examples from my ancestors' 'whaleboat war' in the Sound could no doubt be multiplied.
28. Fortescue, *British Army*, Vol. 3, pp. 414, 417, 474–475, quotation at p. 417.
29. http://www.english-heritage.org.uk/visit/places/forts/.
30. Interesting details of pre-Dartmouth 'artillery towers' in England, and the Mediterranean gun towers of the fifteenth century onward, are provided by Bill Clements in his excellent *Martello towers worldwide* (Barnsley: Pen and Sword Military, 2011), pp. 9–15.
31. Sidney Toy, *A history of fortification from 3,000 BC to AD 1,700* (Melbourne, London and Toronto: Heinemann, 1955), p. 236.
32. Toy, *History of fortification*, p. 237.
33. http://www.english-heritage.org.uk/visit/places/forts/.
34. Each of the three Harwich blockhouses has been counted separately here. Though sometimes counted as a Device Fort, the Devil's Point Artillery Tower by Plymouth was privately funded and pre-dated the programme by two years. Today, the five best-preserved examples of Henry VIII's coastal-defence forts of *c.*1540 can be found at Walmer (Kent), Deal (Kent), Camber (Sussex), Pendennis (Cornwall), and St Mawes (Cornwall).
35. However, it is possible that St Helen's Bulwark on the Isle of Wight, and Camber Castle by Rye, were both brought into action during this invasion attempt or large raid, which lasted six days in the summer of 1545.

36. Lord Grey or Sir Thomas Palmer, quoted in Norman Longmate, *Defending the island from Caesar to the Armada* (London: Pimlico, 2001 {1989}), unpaginated e-book.
37. Longmate, *Island fortress*, pp. 10, 16, quotation at p. 16, though he does not mention Harwich, near which the Device Fort site now known as the Landguard Fort was comprehensively rebuilt in James I's time: https://historicengland.org.uk/listing/the-list/list-entry/1030415.
38. Longmate, *Island fortress*, pp. 13, 17.
39. Daniel MacCannell, *Cultures of proclamation: The decline and fall of the Anglophone news process, 1460–1642* (unpublished PhD dissertation, University of Aberdeen, 2009), p. 40.
40. Clements, *Martello towers worldwide*, p. 14.
41. Rose and Broadley, *Dumouriez*, p. 238.
42. J. J. Crooks, ed., *Records relating to the Gold Coast settlements from 1750 to 1874* (London: Taylor and Francis, 1973), esp. p. 55.
43. Though the Black Pioneers were an unarmed labour unit, they were working near Bull's Ferry at the time, and one of the dead was described as 'a Negro' in the number of *The New York Gazette and the Weekly Mercury* that appeared three days after the fight, which can be seen in transcript form at http://www.royalprovincial.com/military/rhist/lrv/lrvdead.htm.
44. *Royal Gazette* (New York), 22 July 1780 and 9 December 1780. Full transcripts of these items can be seen at http://www.royalprovincial.com/history/battles/lrvrep1.shtml and http://www.royalprovincial.com/military/rhist/lrv/lrvlet3.htm respectively.
45. Fortescue, *British Army*, Vol. 3, p. 406.

Chapter 3: 'Making provision [...] against a future war', 1784–93

1. Adm. Sir Charles Middleton to Prime Minister William Pitt, 12 December 1785, who called the progress of such preparations 'very great'; quoted in Knight, *Britain against Napoleon*, pp. 38–39, but I have changed the initial 'M' to uppercase.
2. Knight, *Britain against Napoleon*, p. xxxii. The firm of Templar and Parlby was responsible for 'the major civil engineering works at Portsmouth and Plymouth' over a nearly forty-year period ending in 1787, and had its own 'quarries, lime kilns, regional depots and transport system': *ibid.*, p. 34.
3. Knight, *Britain against Napoleon*, p. 27.
4. Paul L. C. Webb, 'Sea power in the Ochakov Affair of 1791', *The International History Review*, Vol. 2, No. 1 (1980), pp. 13–33, p. 13.
5. Knight, *Britain against Napoleon*, p. 27n. Cumulative inflation for the relevant twenty-year period was 15.8 per cent, i.e. a commodity that would have cost £1 in 1764 was worth £1 3s 2d in 1784, an annual rate of just 0.74 per cent: https://www.measuringworth.com/calculators/ppoweruk/.
6. Knight, *Britain against Napoleon*, pp. 7–8.
7. As of early 1804, Pitt – then a member of the loyal opposition – remained in favour of building yet more gunboats, partially due to the advice of Capt. Sir Home Popham RN, who had successfully blown up the lock gates at Ostend

in May 1798, specifically as a pre-emptive invasion countermeasure (Knight, *Britain against Napoleon*, p. 88); but the concept was roundly dismissed as 'contemptible' in a fiery speech in Parliament by Adm. Sir Edward Pellew MP (*ibid.*, p. 223), nowadays famed chiefly for his fictionalised role in the *Horatio Hornblower* novels and television series.

8. Initially, this was on Carleton Island in Lake Ontario, nominally a part of the State of New York but home to a prosperous community of loyalists. In 1789, it moved to Point Frederick, Ontario.

9. Knight, *Britain against Napoleon*, p. 94n.

10. Knight, *Britain against Napoleon*, p. 56.

11. Ardesoif, for one, expressed indignation at the prevailing system whereby 'an officer should be sent by another corps, to command and direct [Royal Navy officers] even in the simple operation of firing a bomb': *Marine fortification*, p. xi. The practice of deploying hundreds of Royal Artillerymen and some infantrymen with the fleet to serve the guns 'was discontinued in 1804 with the formation of the Royal Marine Artillery', in the wake of widespread refusals by RA personnel of all ranks to perform any non-artillery-related shipboard duties whatsoever: Wilkinson-Latham, *British Artillery*, p. 76.

12. Jonathan Spain, 'Blomefield, Sir Thomas, first baronet (1744–1822)', *ODNB*.

13. Spain, 'Blomefield', *ODNB*.

14. Spain, 'Blomefield', *ODNB*.

15. Spain, 'Blomefield', *ODNB*.

16. Landmann's appointment as Professor of Fortifications and Artillery at the Royal Military Academy, Woolwich, occurred on 25 November 1777, and his initial salary was £100 per annum plus a house in 'the Warren', as the Royal Arsenal was known prior to 1805. 'He was highly thought of and [... a] great influence over the many young men he taught for a period of nearly thirty-eight years': R. H. Vetch, rev. by P. G. W. Annis, 'Landmann, Isaac (1741–1826), military educationist', *ODNB*.

17. David McConnell, *British smooth-bore artillery: A technological study to support identification, acquisition, restoration, reproduction, and interpretation of artillery at national historic parks in Canada* (Ottawa: Environment Canada, 1988) pp. 18–19.

18. McConnell, *British smooth-bore artillery*, p. 19.

19. McConnell, *British smooth-bore artillery*, pp. 17–18. On Schalch's many failings and run-ins with the military authorities, see also Ruth Rhynas Brown, 'Schalch, Andrew (1692–1776)', *ODNB*.

20. According to McConnell, *British smooth-bore artillery*, p. 21, the assay process was as often 'by eye' as by immersion in nitric acid. The proportion of copper in this copper-tin alloy tended to fall between 86 per cent and 91 per cent: https://www.arc.id.au/Cannon.html.

21. McConnell, *British smooth-bore artillery*, p. 27. By 1801, an even more stringent test would again be applied to suspect guns: thirty consecutive discharges, executed as quickly as possible, each with two roundshot rather than the usual one: *ibid*.

22. Longmate, *Island fortress*, p. 45.

23. https://www.arc.id.au/Cannon.html.
24. Meaning that the men had their own mounts, rather than riding on the gun-limbers or other vehicles, or marching beside them. In the British case, horse artillery drivers were, from the outset, soldiers rather than hired civilians: another important step towards greater efficiency.
25. Battalion guns' demise could have been influenced by the writings of the Chevalier Jean du Teil in the 1770s. Nevertheless, by mid-1809 Napoleon had captured so many Austrian and Prussian 3- and 4-pounders that he reinstated battalion guns in his field army, essentially to 'mop up' this sudden increase in supply, and to chase his dream of having a ratio of five guns to every thousand soldiers. This dream was never achieved, though his Russian enemies would deploy six guns per thousand men at the Battle of Eylau in February 1807.
26. Black, *War*, p. 152 for the quote; on Austria's leadership in artillery in the 1750s and 1760s, Wise, *Artillery equipments*, p. 4.
27. It would not be replaced by a steam-powered version until 1842, and remained incredibly labour-intensive, not least because each gun was modelled individually, and the model destroyed in the mould-making process.
28. Pursuant to an Ordnance instruction of 9 August 1775.
29. Brett D. Steele, 'Robins, Benjamin (1707–1751), *ODNB*.
30. The question of whether Lt Shrapnel was aware of Samuel Zimmerman's work on this type of ammunition in the 1570s remains an open one, but on balance, given the obscurity of the earlier inventor, reinvention seems more likely than copying.
31. Maurice-Jones, *Coast artillery*, pp. 75–76. Black, *War*, p. 186, points out that the total tonnage of Western navies rose by a third over the course of the 1780s.
32. Black, *War*, pp. 5–6. Moreover, those who argue that one or many *technological* military revolutions occurred in or around that same period have often bound up such ideas with the *political* revolutions that occurred in America and France in the last quarter of the eighteenth century: a questionable approach that 'downplays the vitality as military systems of the leading Western powers, Britain and Russia', while also ignoring non-Western developments, including the military success of China: Black, *War*, pp. 128, 216, quotation at p. 128.
33. Spain, 'Blomefield', *ODNB*.
34. Wilkinson-Latham, *British artillery*, p. 54.
35. Maurice-Jones, *Coast artillery*, pp. 77–78.
36. That is, only eleven of these thirty companies were posted to all other parts of Britain: Maurice-Jones, *Coast artillery*, pp. 80–81.
37. Maurice-Jones, *Coast artillery*, p. 81.
38. Maurice-Jones, *Coast artillery*, p. 81.
39. Fortescue, *British Army*, Vol. 3, p. 265.
40. Robin May and G. A. Embleton, *The British Army in North America 1775–1783* (London: Osprey, 1994 {1974}), p. 6.
41. Fortescue, *British Army*, Vol. 3, pp. 172–173, quotation at p. 173.

42. Fortescue, *British Army*, Vol. 3, p. 350.

43. Wheeler and Broadley, *Napoleon and the invasion*, pp. 20, 23.

44. Fortescue, *British Army*, Vol. 3, pp. 520–521.

45. 'Report of the proceedings of a committee of general officers regarding the equipment of soldiers', 15 June 1784, quoted in May and Embleton, *British Army in North America*, p. 8.

46. Fortescue, *British Army*, Vol. 3, p. 542.

47. See MacCannell, *Lost Banff and Buchan*, pp. 155–158.

48. Vol. 4 of Fortescue's *British Army*, covering the years 1789 to 1801, several times describes British operational groups of twenty-four infantry companies as constituting a body of 1,100 men.

49. Fortescue, *British Army*, Vol. 3, p. 525. In practice, however, most deserters who were caught were sent as replacements to the 60th (Royal American) Regiment of Foot in the West Indies, sometimes in batches of more than a hundred: 'Nothing is more remarkable than the splendid record of this regiment in the field, at a period when few soldiers entered it untainted by crime': *ibid*.

50. Lt-Gen. Edward Harvey, 13 February 1772, quoted in Fortescue, *British Army*, Vol. 3, p. 538.

51. May and Embleton, *British Army in North America*, p. 6.

52. Fortescue, *British Army*, Vol. 3, p. 41.

53. Quoted in Glover, *Britain at bay*, pp. 129–130.

54. Knight, *Britain against Napoleon*, p. 51.

55. Fortescue, *British Army*, Vol. 3, p. 528.

56. Fortescue, *British Army*, Vol. 3, pp. 515–516. Windham changed his tune completely by 9 December 1803, when he argued strongly in the House for a system of tower defence for East Anglia, not unlike the Martello programme that later emerged. However, I have not included him in my 'Fathers of the Martello' chapter, first because his proposal, lacking in detail, was not actually adopted, and second, because I doubt the fundamental sincerity of his desire to defend this country by towers or indeed any means whatsoever.

57. Knight, *Britain against Napoleon*, pp. 9–10.

58. Nick Lipscombe, 'Napoleon's obsession – The invasion of England', *British Journal of Military History*, Vol. 1, No. 3 (2015), pp. 115–133, p. 118.

59. Wheeler and Broadley, *Napoleon and the invasion*, p. 19.

60. Though not in Scotland, where James Tytler had already ascended on 27 August: Elizabeth Baigent, 'Lunardi, Vicenzo (1759–1806)', *ODNB*.

61. G. Goold Walker, *The Honourable Artillery Company 1537–1947* (Aldershot: Gale and Polden, 1954), p. 179.

62. Walker, *Honourable Artillery Company*, p. 179.

63. H. S. Torrens, 'Sadler, James (*bap.* 1753, *d.* 1828)', *ODNB*.

64. Wheeler and Broadley, *Napoleon and the invasion*, p. 109.

65. Quoted in Caren Kaplan, *Aerial aftermaths: Wartime from above* (Durham, NC: Duke University Press, 2018), p. 6.

66. https://www.gutenberg.org/files/874/874-h/874-h.htm.

67. Sven Widmalm, 'Accuracy, rhetoric, and technology: The Paris-Greenwich triangulation, 1784–88', in T. Fraengsmyr et al., eds., *The quantifying spirit in the 18th century* (Berkeley, Los Angeles and Oxford: University of California Press, 1990), pp. 179–206, p. 202.

68. *An authentic account of the debates in the House of Commons, on Monday, February 27, and Tuesday, February 28, 1786, on the proposed plan for fortifications, by his grace the duke of Richmond [...]* (London: James Ridgway, 1786), p. 48.

69. Charles Wolfran Cornwall, a former Whig who had turned his coat in 1774 and firmly supported the war in America. The convention that, in the case of deadlock, the speaker should always vote for the status-quo option was not firmly established until Victorian times.

70. Knight, *Britain against Napoleon*, p. 88.

71. Widmalm, 'Accuracy, rhetoric, and technology', p. 203.

Chapter 4: Theory and practice of amphibious operations in the eighteenth century

1. Black, *War*, p. 171.

2. He seems to be assigned credit for the term by Alexander Dirom, in *Plans for the defence of Great Britain and Ireland* (London and Edinburgh: Cadell and Davies/Creech, 1797), p. 137.

3. James Jay Carafano, 'Lloyd, Henry Humphrey Evans (*c*.1718–1783)', *ODNB*.

4. In Lloyd's words, '[t]rees cut down, and placed so as to form a parapet; behind which the troops, particularly infantry, are placed': *History*, Vol. 1, p. 100.

5. Lloyd, *History*, Vol. 1, pp. 14–15. See also *ibid.*, p. 103.

6. Black, *War*, p. 171.

7. Fortescue, *British Army*, Vol. 3, p. 158.

8. Fortescue, *British Army*, Vol. 3, p. 183.

9. Fortescue, *British Army*, Vol. 3, pp. 345–346. At the pyrrhic victory of Bunker Hill, bloodiest for Britain within the Thirteen Colonies, there were 236 killed, a death rate of roughly 9 per cent: *ibid.*, p. 161. See also Todd Andrlik, 'The 25 deadliest battles of the Revolutionary War', *Journal of the American Revolution* online (13 May 2014), unpaginated.

10. Robert Harvey, *The war of wars: The epic struggle between Britain and France, 1789–1815* (London: Constable, 2007), p. 277. At the second British capture of the Cape of Good Hope, in 1806, the surf was so bad that 41 highlanders were drowned (Knight, *Britain against Napoleon*, p. 231): a number equal to one-fifth of all the British casualties sustained at the ensuing Battle of Blaauwberg.

11. The Rifles Museum's Facebook page published an informative article about this action on 20 February 2020.

12. Fortescue, *British Army*, Vol. 3, p. 189. On the East River, the area today is bounded by East 34th Street in the north, East 27th Street in the south, and Third Avenue in the west.

13. Fortescue, *British Army*, Vol. 3, pp. 308–309.

14. George Hanger, *Military reflections on the attack and defence of the city of London [...] in the year 1794* (London: J. Debrett, 1795), pp. 105–106. Hanger took this American episode to be clear evidence of the uselessness of Tilbury Fort to the defence of London against a swift and determined fleet.

15. Fortescue, *British Army*, Vol. 3, pp. 312–313.

16. Black, *War*, p. 169; J. W. Hall, ed., *The Cambridge history of Japan*, Vol. 4 (Cambridge: Cambridge University Press, 1991), p. 475.

17. Knight, *Britain against Napoleon*, p. 65.

18. Knight, *Britain against Napoleon*, pp. 193–194.

19. Knight, *Britain against Napoleon*, pp. 180, 189, quotation at p. 189.

20. J. W. Fortescue, *A history of the British Army*, Vol. 4 (London and New York: Macmillan, 1906), p. 136.

21. I take Sir Walter Scott's comments that Britain's effort was not 'worthy' during the Toulon operation to have meant chiefly that the number of troops sent was too small. See his *Life of Napoleon Buonaparte: With a preliminary view of the French Revolution* (Edinburgh: Robert Cadell, 1842), esp. p. 179. The numbers of attackers and defenders are from William Laird Clowes, *The Royal Navy: A history from the earliest times to the present*, Vol. 4 (London: Samson Lowe, 1899), p. 208.

22. Fortescue, *British Army*, Vol. 4, p. 138.

23. Clowes, *Royal Navy*, Vol. 4, pp. 210–211, notes that '[t]he French Government [...] deliberately decreed the death of all the inhabitants, and the demolition of the town', and while this was not carried through, some 6,000 civilians were deliberately killed after the allies and refugees had left.

24. Scott, *Life of Napoleon*, p. 179. Please note that I take Sir Walter's 'night' in this passage to be a metaphorical backdrop for his metaphorical rising star, and not as literally meaning that the fire and the executions occurred on the same evening.

25. Scott, *Life of Napoleon*, p. 180.

26. Knight, *Britain against Napoleon*, p. 159.

27. Knight, *Britain against Napoleon*, pp. 161, 172. On the troop numbers proposed vs actually embarked, see Clowes, *Royal Navy*, Vol. 4, p. 408.

28. Knight, *Britain against Napoleon*, pp. 176–177, 210.

29. I realise that this claim is not normally made, but given that Portugal's royal family lived on the other side of the Atlantic, and that its army was superseded in 1809 by a British-equipped 'Anglo-Portuguese Army' headed by a British general, William Carr Beresford, I will stand by it for the time being.

30. This topic has been dealt with so well by David Gates in *The Spanish ulcer: A history of the Peninsular War* (Cambridge, MA: Da Capo, 2001 {1986}) that I will simply refer the reader to him.

31. Knight, *Britain against Napoleon*, p. 188.

32. Knight, *Britain against Napoleon*, p. 201.

33. Clowes, *Royal Navy*, Vol. 4, p. 455.

34. Knight, *Britain against Napoleon*, p. 201.

35. A league being three nautical miles.

Chapter 5: Powder and shot

1. Quoted in Wheeler and Broadley, *Napoleon and the invasion*, p. 80.
2. The fact that Russia, which was considered one of the most advanced powers of the time, used as few as four horses per gun seems to have had more to do with the hardiness of the horses in question than any other factor.
3. I am not certain of whether Longmate did suggest this in *Island fortress*, p. 261, where he said that this class of vessel was 'primarily for horse and artillery transport and the men attending them', with the men numbering 100 and the horses 'hoisted in or out through a movable roof'.
4. Glover, *Britain at bay*, pp. 93–94.
5. Equating to £53,110 and £59,850 in today's money, based on inflation since 1792 and 1793, respectively.
6. Wilkinson-Latham, *British artillery*, Ch. 3.
7. Wilkinson-Latham, *British artillery*, pp. 21–22, 50, quotation at p. 22.
8. Knight, *Britain against Napoleon*, pp. 42, 45.
9. Ardesoif, *Marine fortification*, p. 92.
10. Wise, *Artillery equipments*, p. 15.
11. Knight, *Britain against Napoleon*, p. 45.
12. https://www.royalgunpowdermills.com/.
13. Wise, *Artillery equipments*, p. 10.
14. He would go on to propose a steam-powered ironclad in 1828: Roger T. Stearn, 'Congreve, Sir William, second baronet (1772–1828)', *ODNB*.
15. Wilkinson-Latham, *British artillery*, p. 18.
16. Wise, *Artillery equipments*, p. 27.
17. Wise, *Artillery equipments*, p. 29.
18. Wise, *Artillery equipments*, p. 29.
19. Wise, *Artillery equipments*, p. 29.
20. Ardesoif, *Marine fortification*, pp. 114, 117.
21. Ardesoif, *Marine fortification*, pp. 106, 108.
22. Ardesoif, *Marine fortification*, p. 105.
23. However, double-shotting of carronades was unknown. Importantly, the roundshot element was always loaded last 'because it had greater velocity than either bar or grape': Wilkinson-Latham, *British artillery*, p. 74.
24. Wise, *Artillery equipments*, p. 18.
25. Wise, *Artillery equipments*, p. 29. Nevertheless, due to the relatively small sizes of its targets, counter-battery fire was widely regarded as too wasteful of ammunition, and sometimes actively prohibited, including by Wellington at Waterloo: *ibid.*, p. 20.
26. Shrapnel was awarded a life pension of £1,200 per annum in 1814, and – unlike so many serviceman-inventors of the period – lived to enjoy it for more than a quarter century.
27. Ranging from 0.2 to 1.33 inches, depending on the calibre of the weapon and its degree of elevation.
28. Wise, *Artillery equipments*, p. 19.
29. Wilkinson-Latham, *British artillery*, p. 37.
30. In the 1770s, French carcases were referred to by English officers as 'fire-balls', presumably because they were actually round, rather than rugby-ball-shaped like the British ones. Ardesoif, *Marine fortification*, p. 147.

31. Wise, *Artillery equipments*, p. 18.
32. Ardesoif, *Marine fortification*, p. 131.
33. Rocket sticks were never less than 8 feet or more than 24 feet in length, with the 42-pounders' being 17 feet. Sheet iron replaced the rockets' original paper cases in 1806: Wilkinson-Latham, *British artillery*, pp. 25–37.
34. Ardesoif, *Marine fortification*, p. 71.
35. Wise, *Artillery equipments*, pp. 28–29, quotation at p. 29.
36. As of August 1805, not including carronades, British coast defences boasted more than 850 24-pounders and more than 750 18-pounders, but 32-pounders and 12-pounders numbered just 226 and 213, respectively. Calculated based on Maurice-Jones, *Coast artillery*, pp. 94-99.
37. The date at which some of them also received howitzers is unclear.
38. Brass barrels' two main disadvantages were their cost, and that they softened too much under sustained rapid firing, resulting in bore damage. Their main advantage over cheaper cast-iron guns was lightness, resulting from their greater ability to withstand the explosive pressures generated by firing. Hence, brass continued to be used for field guns 'where lightness was of paramount importance' long after its abandonment in static fortifications: McConnell, *British smooth-bore artillery*, pp. 15–16, quotation at p. 16.
39. This length of iron howitzer was 'originally intended for Martello towers', but a longer-barrelled version of the 5½-inch iron howitzer, probably measuring 3 feet 5 inches in length, also existed British service in the first decade of the nineteenth century: McConnell, *British smooth-bore artillery*, p. 158.

Chapter 6: From Mortella to Minorca, 1794–98

1. Fortescue, *British Army*, Vol. 4, p. 179, who incorrectly describes all five vessels as sloops; in fact, they consisted of two 74s, a 64, and two frigates.
2. Fortescue, *British Army*, Vol. 4, p. 181.
3. Not to be confused with Farinole, which boasts an intact Genoese tower, some three miles east of Mortella on the opposite side of the bay.
4. Fortescue, *British Army*, Vol. 4, p. 182.
5. Fortescue, *British Army*, Vol. 4, pp. 182–183, quotation at p. 183.
6. Fortescue, *British Army*, Vol. 4, p. 157.
7. Vice-Adm. Sir William Cornwallis, brother of the much better known Charles, Lord Cornwallis.
8. Quoted in Wheeler and Broadley, *Napoleon and the invasion*, p. 30.
9. Longmate, *Island fortress*, p. 188.
10. Harvey, *War of wars*, pp. 54–55.
11. It helped the French case that, since 1788, Holland had been a *de facto* joint protectorate of Britain and Prussia.
12. Wheeler and Broadley, *Napoleon and the invasion*, p. 30.
13. Hanger, *Military reflections*, p. 3.
14. Knight, *Britain against Napoleon*, p. 67.
15. Knight, *Britain against Napoleon*, p. 51.
16. Fortescue, *British Army*, Vol. 4, p. 144.
17. Hanger, *Military reflections*, p. 116.
18. Maurice-Jones, *Coast artillery*, p. 85.

19. Hanger, *Military reflections*, p. 12.
20. In part, this was because seafaring wisdom held that the North Sea's dangerous sandbanks quite far out from shore, frequent fogs, and relative scarcity of prominent landmarks for navigation (on either side) meant that much – but not all – of the east coast was virtually un-invadable.
21. Specifically, in '[c]amps [that] had been constructed on the hills around Brighton in 1793 and 1794 [...] and in barracks in the town': Rose and Broadley, *Dumouriez*, p. 239.
22. Hanger, *Military reflections*, pp. 24, 75, quotation at p. 75.
23. This seventeenth-century form was shortened to brigadier in the British Army in the 1920s, but is still in use in the United States, and was reinstated in Canada in 1968.
24. Sheila Sutcliffe, *Martello Towers* (Newton Abbot: David and Charles, 1972), p. 102. He was in England from early July to late November or early December that year.
25. Carradice, *Britain's last invasion*, p. 166.
26. J. E. Cookson, *The British armed nation, 1793–1815* (Oxford: Clarendon, 1997), p. 32.
27. P. K. Crimmin, 'Duncan, Adam, Viscount Duncan (1731–1804)', *ODNB*.
28. Knight, *Britain against Napoleon*, p. 77.
29. Knight, *Britain against Napoleon*, p. 75–76.
30. Known as the Directory from autumn 1795.
31. Fortescue, *British Army*, Vol. 4, p. 416.
32. Fortescue, *British Army*, Vol. 4, p. 420.
33. Wheeler and Broadley, *Napoleon and the invasion*, pp. 44–45.
34. Fortescue, *British Army*, Vol. 4, p. 408.
35. Roger Morriss, 'Smith, Sir (William) Sidney (1764–1840)', *ODNB*.
36. Maurice-Jones, *Coast artillery*, pp. 120–121, quotation at p. 121.
37. Maurice-Jones, *Coast artillery*, p. 121. The Saint-Marcouf enterprise strikes me as a close prefiguration of Wellington's signature tactic of 'squatting' on some strong natural feature until the enemy came to feel it was essential to take it away from him. The defence of Hill 937 in South Vietnam in 1969 represents another classic example.
38. James Burnley, rev. by R. C. Cox, 'Gamble, John (1761/2–1811), *ODNB*.
39. J. D. Davies, 'Murray, Lord George (1761–1803), *ODNB*.
40. Dirom, *Plans*, p. 42. Dirom had served as a captain in the 60th (Royal American) Regiment in 1781: Gordon Goodwin, revised by Alex May, 'Dirom, Alexander (1757–1830)', *ODNB*.
41. Knight, *Britain against Napoleon*, p. 137.
42. It fairness, however, it should be mentioned that the vital Isle of Wight signal station in Elizabethan times was already capable of sending 'three different messages': C. G. Cruickshank, *Elizabeth's army*, 2nd edn. (Oxford: Clarendon, 1966), p. 70.
43. A version for ship-to-ship communication was invented by Sir Home Popham in 1800 and entered use immediately. It was retrospectively approved by the Admiralty in 1812: Hugh Popham, 'Popham, Sir Home Riggs (1762–1820)', *ODNB*.

44. The sections omitted as of the latter date were Great Yarmouth to Skegness; Flamborough Head to Hartlepool; and Scotland northward of Edinburgh. Only the Great Yarmouth-to-Skegness gap was ever closed, and not until 1803. Flag towers of this type were also built in the Channel Islands, North Wales, Ireland and Heligoland at one time or another during the wars.
45. Longmate, *Island fortress*, p. 267.
46. Maurice-Jones, *Coast artillery*, p. 94; Longmate, Island fortress, p. 268.
47. Sutcliffe, *Martello towers*, pp. 15, 16, 23, 40, quotations at pp. 15 and 40.
48. Sutcliffe, *Martello towers*, pp. 23, 28, quotation at p. 23.
49. 'Unlike their Canadian counterparts the English towers were not intended to be armed on their barrack floors. This is perhaps indicative of the concept of the home government that they were almost exclusively elevated sea batteries, difficult to escalade but little able to resist a land assault assisted by artillery, and so not requiring an extended flank defence': http://parkscanadahistory.com/series/chs/15/chs15-1e.htm.
50. Sutcliffe, *Martello towers*, pp. 38–39, first quotation at p. 38; second quotation in S. G. P. Ward, 'Defence works in Britain, 1803–1805', *Journal of the Society for Army Historical Research*, Vol. 27, No. 109 (1947), pp. 18–37, pp. 27–28.
51. However, it should be mentioned that the three 'small forts' constructed at L'Eree, Rocquaine and Hommet on Guernsey in 1804 did not share these problems, each being essentially an undersized 'modern' Martello – 26 feet high and 37 feet in base, with walls 5½ feet thick – immediately surrounded by an artillery battery.
52. Wheeler and Broadley, *Napoleon and the invasion*, p. 31, says there were twenty-two, and Longmate, *Island fortress*, p. 217, that there were '12 [...] at Dunkirk, another 12 at Boulogne'. Muskein's orders are also quoted verbatim in Longmate, *ibid*., p. 216.
53. Wheeler and Broadley, *Napoleon and the invasion*, p. 32. This mirrored the carrying of 'uniforms, muskets, and ammunition for twenty or thirty thousand more' men than the 3,500 it actually contained by the British-backed French royalist expedition to Brittany in June 1795: Fortescue, *British Army*, Vol. 4, p. 413.
54. Carradice, *Britain's last invasion*, pp. 27–28.
55. Knight, *Britain against Napoleon*, p. 85. The mutinous mood would continue after the failure at Bantry Bay: 'the rumour that another landing in Ireland was being planned' prompted the desertion of some 8,000 sailors at Brest in 1797: Longmate, *Island fortress*, p. 223.
56. Wheeler and Broadley, *Napoleon and the invasion*, p. 36.
57. Knight, *Britain against Napoleon*, p. 85, from whom the quotation; and on the speed of transmission, Longmate, *Island fortress*, p. 222.
58. MacCannell, *Cultures of proclamation*, pp. 40–42.
59. Hoche, who had no particular reason to inflate his own numbers, enumerated the total force embarked as 14,750, fairly close to Tone's estimate of 15,100 (Longmate, *Island fortress*, p. 219) and the Whig politician Lord Pelham of Stanmer's 16,000 (Cookson, *Armed nation*, p. 52).
60. Marianne Elliot, 'Tone, (Theobald) Wolfe (1763–1798)', *ODNB*.

61. This remarkable document, addressed simply to 'Republicans', is translated in full in Wheeler and Broadley's *Napoleon and the invasion*, pp. 33–34.
62. Longmate, *Island fortress*, pp. 221–222; quotation (from Tone) at p. 222.
63. Wheeler and Broadley, *Napoleon and the invasion*, p. 41.
64. Wheeler and Broadley, *Napoleon and the invasion*, pp. 36–37.
65. Knight, *Britain against Napoleon*, p. 86.
66. The others at this date were Carrickfergus, Kinsale, Drogheda, Dublin Harbour, Dundalk, Waterford, Galway Bay, and Tarbert Island. At that moment, Cork also boasted a sixty-four-gun ship of the line and six frigates: Longmate, *Island fortress*, p. 218.
67. Maurice-Jones, *Coast artillery*, pp. 104–105.
68. Wheeler and Broadley, *Napoleon and the invasion*, p. 40.
69. Longmate, *Island fortress*, p. 227.
70. Wheeler and Broadley, *Napoleon and the invasion*, p. 53.
71. Wheeler and Broadley, *Napoleon and the invasion*, p. 53.
72. Quoted in Wheeler and Broadley, *Napoleon and the invasion*, pp. 54–55.
73. Quoted in Wheeler and Broadley, *Napoleon and the invasion*, pp. 55, 57.
74. Quoted in Wheeler and Broadley, *Napoleon and the invasion*, pp. 58–59.
75. Quoted in Longmate, *Island fortress*, p. 212. As early as 1772, the French military intellectual Hippolyte de Guibert 'criticised reliance on fortifications', instead stressing 'movement and enveloping manoeuvres [...and] living off the land in order to increase the speed of operations': Black, *War*, p. 151. But it is, of course, possible to take anything too far.
76. Longmate, *Island fortress*, p. 229.
77. Quoted in Wheeler and Broadley, *Napoleon and the invasion*, p. 60.
78. Quoted in Wheeler and Broadley, *Napoleon and the invasion*, p. 68.
79. Longmate, *Island fortress*, pp. 175, 181.
80. And prior to that (i.e. in June 1796), the Black Legion or something like it was to have been used as a diversion from a plan to seize Cornwall by landing 1,600 French regulars and fomenting revolt amongst the tin miners. But when Ireland became the target, thanks to 'lobbying' by 'Tone and other Irishmen', the Cornish expedition was itself reduced to the status of a diversion: Longmate, *Island fortress*, pp. 214–215, quotations at p. 214. The Great Armada plan of 1779, whose only actual invasion targets were Wight, Gosport and Portsmouth, included a subsidiary attack on Bristol, another on Liverpool, the destruction at Cork of 'supplies collected there for transport to America', and a purely diversionary concentration of 12,000 troops around Calais: *ibid.*, p. 199.
81. Longmate, *Island fortress*, p. 230.
82. Frank McLynn, *Invasion: From the Armada to Hitler* (London: Crux/ Routledge and Kegan Paul, 2015 {1987}), unpaginated e-book.
83. It has often been said that the Black Legion's field artillery was lost in a small-boat accident during the disembarkation (even by Longmate, *Island fortress*, p. 230). However, in light of their lack of artillery personnel, and their orders to live off the land and to bring with them only 100 musket cartridges apiece, the idea that they were assigned any field guns seems farfetched. Moreover, if they were really felt to need or deserve cannon,

the ships that landed them could easily have spared some of their pieces for shore use, as happened over and over again during the British capture of Corsica. The two forty-gun French frigates alone were carrying two dozen 8-pounders between them.

84. Knight, *Britain against Napoleon*, p. 87.
85. Carradice, *Britain's last invasion*, pp. 114, 157, quotation at p. 157.
86. Longmate, *Island fortress*, p. 235.
87. Longmate, *Island fortress*, pp. 235, 238, quotation at p. 238.
88. Carradice, *Britain's last invasion*, pp. 17–18.
89. Of 17,000 total Irish auxiliary troops in December 1796, a minimum of 10,000 had been deemed necessary simply to keep Ulster under control: Knight, *Britain against Napoleon*, p. 86.
90. Enemy troop numbers, nationalities and destinations in this paragraph are from Wheeler and Broadley, *Napoleon and the invasion*, p. 40.
91. Longmate, *Island fortress*, p. 241. 'It is something of a mystery why the Dutch fleet finally left the Texel on 6 October 1797, too late in the year for an invasion attempt. It has generally been attributed to a display of national prestige by the Dutch government': Crimmin, 'Duncan, Adam', *ODNB*.
92. Longmate, *Island fortress*, pp. 241–242, quotation at p. 241.
93. Maurice-Jones, *Coast artillery*, p. 91.
94. Wheeler and Broadley, *Napoleon and the invasion*, p. 85.
95. Wheeler and Broadley, *Napoleon and the invasion*, p. 87.
96. Quoted in Wheeler and Broadley, *Napoleon and the invasion*, pp. 87–88. That the plans for these specialist craft were actually 'brought from Sweden' has been suggested by Longmate, *Island fortress*, p. 216.
97. As of 9 May 1798: Wheeler and Broadley, *Napoleon and the invasion*, p. 92.
98. '[I]t may be the policy of the French to endeavour, by empty threats of invasion [...] to shake our public credit; to oblige us to exhaust our resources in preparations for defence; and to bring upon us the miseries of famine, by withdrawing too large a portion of our inhabitants from agriculture': Dirom, *Plans*, p. vi.
99. I find it hard to read this document without being put in mind the Reagan cabinet's strategy for spending the Soviet Union into the ground. The defensive equivalent of the same view was put by Glendinning, *The hammers of Invicta: Being a history of the Martello towers round Romney Marsh* (Hythe: Glendinning, 1981), p. 6: the Martello 'was an excellent psychological weapon' *and* one that would 'without doubt' have given a good account of itself if put to the test in combat.
100. Quoted in Clowes, *Royal Navy*, Vol. 4, p. 338.
101. Clowes, *Royal Navy*, Vol. 4, p. 339.
102. Fortescue, *British Army*, Vol. 4, p. 598.
103. Longmate, *Island fortress*, p. 213.
104. And/or Capt. W. H. Ford RE's proposal for square towers in England, which with slight modifications became the basis for mass-production Martellos.
105. This is the number cited by Ward, 'Defence works in Britain', p. 27.
106. *The Hammers of Invicta*, p. 9.

107. Sutcliffe, *Martello towers*, pp. 44–45.
108. Thomas Walsh, *Journal of the late campaign in Egypt* (London: T. Cadell Jr and W. Davies, 1803), p. 15.
109. David Whamond Donaldson, *Britain and Menorca in the eighteenth century* (unpublished PhD dissertation, The Open University, 1994), pp. 491, 493.
110. Donaldson, *Britain and Menorca*, p. 494. The majority of the 'Spanish' infantry were, in fact, poorly disciplined and untried Swiss mercenaries, scores of whom 'deserted to the British immediately': *ibid.*, p. 496.
111. The more commonly cited figure of fifteen towers (e.g. http://parkscanadahistory.com/series/chs/15/chs15-1e.htm) appears to include some 'corsair' towers that were already there, and integrated into D'Arcy's scheme of defence. See Mark Grundy, 'The Martello towers of Minorca', *Fort*, Vol. 19 (1991), pp. 23–58.
112. Donaldson, *Britain and Menorca*, p. 501.
113. Dimensions from http://parkscanadahistory.com/series/chs/15/chs15-1e.htm; all other details from Donaldson, *Britain and Menorca*, p. 504.
114. Walsh, *Campaign in Egypt*, pl. 7 (between pp. 16 and 17). This included a general view, a plan view, two cutaway views from the side, and a cutaway view from above, all on the same sheet.
115. Sutcliffe, *Martello towers*, p. 39.
116. http://parkscanadahistory.com/series/chs/15/chs15-1e.htm.
117. Sutcliffe, *Martello towers*, p. 65.

Chapter 7: Low treason

1. Carradice, *Britain's last invasion*, p. 97. 'If the invasion achieved anything it had to be in the destruction of whatever remnants of radicalism were stored in the hearts and minds of the British': *ibid.*, p. 167.
2. As explained by Leslie Mitchell ('Fox, Charles James [1749–1806]', *ODNB*), leader of the opposition Fox, a descendant of King Charles II through his mother, was 'particular friends [with] Lafayette, Noailles, Talleyrand, Orléans, and Lauzun', who

> were all to be found in that section of the French aristocracy which welcomed the events of 1789. [...] Some had also fought for Washington, thereby linking in their own careers events in England, France, and America. Whenever Foxites visited Paris these men arranged their programmes. [...] Educated in the same classical culture, polished in the same salon society, and travellers with common friends, these men came to call themselves citizens of the world [... and to disavow] substantial national loyalties. Fox called his Parisian friends 'French Whigs', while Talleyrand referred to the Foxites as 'our masters'[.]

3. N. A. M. Rodger, 'Introduction', in Colville and Davey, eds., *Nelson navy and nation*, pp. 8–21, p. 20.
4. Rodger, 'Introduction', in Colville and Davey, eds., *Nelson navy and nation*, p. 16.

5. Rodger, 'Introduction', in Colville and Davey, eds., *Nelson navy and nation*, p. 16. Contrary to well-honed tales regarding the press gang, many of them American propaganda of a slightly later period, 84 per cent of the sailors on British warships during the French Revolutionary Wars were volunteers: *ibid.*, p. 20.

6. Rodger, 'Introduction', in Colville and Davey, eds., *Nelson navy and nation*, p. 11.

7. Charles James Fox, quoted in reference to Gen. Sir William Howe's success at Brooklyn in Fortescue, *British Army*, Vol. 3, p. 198. For more examples regarding the land forces, see pp. 174–175 *ibid.*

8. Daniel MacCannell, 'King Henry IX, or cardinal called York? Henry Benedict Stuart and the reality of kingship', *The Innes Review*, Vol. 58, No. 2 (2007), pp. 196–209.

9. James C. Spalding, 'Loyalist as royalist, patriot as puritan: The American Revolution as a repetition of the English Civil Wars', *Church History*, Vol. 45, No. 3 (1976), pp. 329–340.

10. Fortescue, *British Army*, Vol. 3, p. 245.

11. A 1776 letter from Craister Greathead, Governor of St Kitts, to Johannes de Graaff, Governor of Sint Eustatius, quoted in Louis Arthur Norton, 'Admiral Rodney ousts the Jews from St Eustatius', *Journal of the American Revolution* online (6 March 2017), unpaginated. Norton notes that Greathead's opinion is amply borne out by documentary evidence, and that de Graaff himself was 'was personally sympathetic to the American rebel cause'.

12. Norton, 'Admiral Rodney ousts the Jews'.

13. Fortescue, *British Army*, Vol. 3, p. 298.

14. Elliot, 'Tone, (Theobald) Wolfe', *ODNB*.

15. Clowes, for instance, used such metaphors freely in describing 'mutinous outbreaks such as hardly ever before had disgraced the service [...] more than once accompanied by murder and by treason': *Royal Navy*, Vol. 4, p. 167.

16. Fox allegedly described Bonaparte, five days *after* Britain's declaration of war in 1803, as 'the most stupendous monument of human wisdom'; however, as the only source for this quotation is the stupendous Tory Gen. John Graves Simcoe, founding father of the Province of Ontario, it should be taken with a pinch of salt. Simcoe Papers, quoted in Knight, *Britain against Napoleon*, p. 220. Lloyd George's remarks appeared under his own by-line and the title 'I talked to Hitler' in the *Daily Express* on 17 September 1936.

17. Brian Lavery, 'Dockyards and industry', in Colville and Davey, eds., *Nelson navy and nation*, pp. 58–75, quotation at p. 62; on Aitken's prior criminal career, see his *Life of James Aitken, commonly called John the Painter, an incendiary [...]*, 2nd edn. (Winton: J. Wilkes, 1777). Fortescue, *British Army*, Vol. 3, p. 198, suggests that Aitken's mission was instigated by Silas Deane, secret emissary of the Continental Congress to Paris.

18. Aitken, *Life of James Aitken*, pp. 53–55.

19. Knight, *Britain against Napoleon*, p. 37; dates from J. R. Harris, 'Wilkinson, William (1744–1808)', *ODNB*.

20. Knight, *Britain against Napoleon*, pp. 63, 79.

21. Longmate, *Island fortress*, p. 219.
22. S. M. Farrell, 'Pratt, John Jeffreys, first Marquess Camden (1759–1840)', *ODNB*.
23. Longmate, *Island fortress*, p. 251, from whom the quotation; Wheeler and Broadley, *Napoleon and the invasion*, p. 124.
24. Clowes, *Royal Navy*, Vol. 4, p. 344. Fortescue, *British Army*, Vol. 4, p. 591, specifies that they were met by 'about fifty Yeomen and Fencibles'.
25. Fortescue, *British Army*, Vol. 4, p. 594, who called this 'not mere vainglory'.
26. Fortescue, *British Army*, Vol. 4, p. 593; volunteer numbers from Longmate, *Island fortress*, p. 255.
27. Clowes, *Royal Navy*, Vol. 4, p. 344.
28. Marianne Elliott, 'Emmet, Robert (1778–1803)', *ODNB*.
29. Knight, *Britain against Napoleon*, pp. 63, 79. A US naval landing party in Scotland in 1778, who were hoping to kidnap the Earl of Selkirk, cleared his estate of all the young men who might have been able to defend it simply by claiming to be a Royal Navy press gang: Longmate, *Island fortress*, p. 191.
30. Quoted in Knight, *Britain against Napoleon*, p. 159.
31. Austin Gee, *The British volunteer movement, 1793–1807* (unpublished PhD dissertation, Oxford University, 1989), p. iv.
32. Knight, *Britain against Napoleon*, p. 233.

Chapter 8: Invasion and counter-invasion craft of the 1790s

1. Clowes, *Royal Navy*, Vol. 4, p. 339.
2. Knight, *Britain against Napoleon*, pp. 109–110.
3. Dirom, *Plans*, pp. 38–39.
4. Roger Knight, 'Beyond Trafalgar', in Colville and Davey, eds., *Nelson navy and nation*, pp. 208–227, pp. 208–209.
5. Knight, 'Beyond Trafalgar', p. 209.
6. Longmate, *Defending the island*, unpaginated e-book.
7. These and other details of this extraordinary plan can be found in Longmate, *Island fortress*, pp. 186–188, and Rose and Broadley, *Dumouriez*, esp. pp. 51–54.
8. Knight, 'Beyond Trafalgar', pp. 208–209.
9. Clowes, *Royal Navy*, Vol. 4, p. 340.
10. Price's statement that fifty-*two* boats had attacked him, repeated by Clowes, does not tally mathematically with the former's repeated statements that he captured only one and sank no more than seven, and that forty-three retreated.
11. *The London Gazette*, 8–12 May 1798, p. 390.
12. Clowes, *Royal Navy*, Vol. 4, pp. 340–341.
13. Quoted in Wheeler and Broadley, *Napoleon and the invasion*, p. 93.
14. *The London Gazette*, 8–12 May 1798, pp. 390, 391.
15. J.-J. Antier, *Histoire mondiale du sous-marin* (Paris: R. Laffont, 1968), p. 61; J. T. Flexner, *Steamboats come true: American inventors in action* (New York: Fordham University Press, 1993 {1944}), p. 273.
16. Fortescue, *British Army*, Vol. 4, p. 587.
17. Fortescue's above-cited account mentions two bomb-vessels, and Clowes's mentions none.

18. Fortescue, *British Army*, Vol. 4, pp. 588–589.
19. '[I]t took too long to haul the guns across the deck, and the weight of them all on one side gave the vessel a dangerous list. In an engagement in January 1799 she suffered many casualties as she was unable to bring her main armament into action; and when engaged by a French privateer in the Atlantic in 1804, she was swamped through her open gunports and sank': Randolph Cock, 'Schank [Schanck], John (1740–1823)', *ODNB*.
20. Cock, 'Schank [Schanck]', *ODNB*.
21. Wilkinson-Latham, *British artillery*, p. 75.
22. Wilkinson-Latham, *British artillery*, p. 75.
23. Ardesoif, *Marine fortification*, p. 104.
24. 'Pound shot was not used over 1,500 yards, because the spread was too great': Wilkinson-Latham, *British artillery*, p. 78.
25. Report signed by Robert Morse, Abraham D'Aubant, and William Twiss, 26 April 1804, quoted in http://parkscanadahistory.com/series/chs/15/chs15-1e.htm.

Chapter 9: 'My troops and my other armed subjects'

1. 'Should [Bonaparte's] troops effect a landing, I shall certainly put myself at the head of my troops and my other armed subjects to repel them': George III to Bishop Richard Hurd of Worcester, 28 May 1797, quoted in full in Wheeler and Broadley, *Napoleon and the invasion*, p. 14.
2. Gee, *Volunteer movement*, p. 284.
3. Maurice-Jones, *Coast artillery*, p. 91.
4. Gee, *Volunteer movement*, p. 52.
5. The raising of volunteer field artillery was actually prohibited (Maurice-Jones, *Coast artillery*, p. 102), presumably as being more of a danger to friend than foe.
6. Hanger, *Military reflections*, p. 10. Even the capture or destruction of Southwark, provided that London's bridges were held or destroyed, would not 'render us [...] a province to France', as London *per se* was 'the grand primary object beyond all others': *ibid.*, pp. 53, 56.
7. Longmate, *Island fortress*, p. 238.
8. Cookson, *Armed nation*, p. 45.
9. In Dirom's *Plans*, see esp. p. 12 on 'every field affording an intrenchment'; pp. 14–15 on the importance of mobility in defence; pp. 33–35, against strong coastal fortresses; and pp. 36–37, against open-air batteries with embrasures. '[F]ortification ought to be rendered subservient to the operations of the army, and to form only an inferior part in a system of general defence for the country': *ibid.*, p. 132.
10. Maurice-Jones, *Coast artillery*, p. 94. This district comprehended Devon, Cornwall and part of Somerset.
11. Dirom, *Plans*, pp. 35–36.
12. Cookson, *Armed nation*, p. 45.
13. Grey or Palmer, quoted in Longmate, *Defending the island*.
14. Dirom, *Plans*, p. 16; see also *ibid.*, pp. 60–61.
15. Hanger, *Military reflections*, pp. 49, 83.

16. This is the current version in the Royal Canadian Navy, though numerous small variations exist.
17. Wheeler and Broadley, *Napoleon and the invasion*, p. 100.
18. '[B]etween 1798 and 1806 the Army bought seven per cent of all slaves sold in the British West Indies': https://www.nam.ac.uk/explore/slaves-red-coats-west-india-regiment. The average price paid for a slave by the Army was around £77: https://www.bl.uk/west-india-regiment/articles/creating-the-west-india-regiments. Those still serving in 1807 became free upon the abolition of the slave trade.
19. In the RA and RE, commissions were achieved through education, and promotion by merit; but in the regular infantry and cavalry, both commissions and promotions could be, and usually were, secured by purchase from the early days of the Army's existence until 1871.
20. Dirom, *Plans*, p. 136.
21. Quoted in Longmate, *Island fortress*, p. 217.
22. Glover, *Britain at bay*, p. 43.
23. Dirom lamented in 1797 that the militia was 'composed almost entirely of substitutes', many of them with no ties to their regiments' counties: *Plans*, p. 93; to Glover, however, the fact that no British government ever banned substitution reflected 'the real freedom of the English people under even the old and unreformed parliament': *Britain at bay*, p. 127.
24. Longmate, *Island fortress*, p. 284; Glover, *Britain at bay*, p. 128, 133–134, 141.
25. Quoted in Longmate, *Island fortress*, p. 247.
26. Dirom, *Plans*, pp. 45, 53.
27. Gee, *Volunteer movement*, p. 73.
28. Gee, *Volunteer movement*, p. 54.
29. Wheeler and Broadley, *Napoleon and the invasion*, pp. 114–115, quotation at p. 114.
30. He had been replaced by Charles, Lord Cornwallis in 1795.
31. Walker, *Honourable Artillery Company*, p. 186; crowd size from Wheeler and Broadley, *Napoleon and the invasion*, p. 117.
32. Wheeler and Broadley, *Napoleon and the invasion*, pp. 117–118.
33. Gee, *Volunteer movement*, p. i.
34. Gee, *Volunteer movement*, pp. ii–iii.
35. Wheeler and Broadley, *Napoleon and the invasion*, pp. 112–113.
36. Gee, *Volunteer movement*, p. 1.
37. Knight, *Britain against Napoleon*, p. 81.
38. Though this came to be interpreted as any pattern of twelve hours: usually, two hours per day, Monday through Saturday.
39. Ireland's own militia were no better, and characterised by Sir Ralph Abercromby as 'in a state of licentiousness that must render them formidable to any one but the enemy': quoted in Rose and Broadley, *Dumouriez*, p. 228.
40. The RHA's original two 12-pounders per troop were replaced by two 6-pounders in 1800.
41. Longmate, *Island fortress*, p. 263 only mentions that this was done between Calais and Antwerp, but my own reading of various Royal Navy encounters suggests it was happening westward of Calais too.
42. Dirom, *Plans*, pp. 9–11, 70–71; Rose and Broadley, *Dumouriez*, pp. 257, 263.

43. There was a net loss of one company from Portsmouth, which had had two in 1798: Maurice-Jones, *Coast artillery*, pp. 100–101.
44. Maurice-Jones, *Coast artillery*, pp. 103–104.
45. Maurice-Jones, *Coast artillery*, p. 102.
46. McConnell, *British smooth-bore artillery*, p. 243.
47. Dirom, *Plans*, p. 83.
48. Fortescue, *British Army*, Vol. 4, pp. 597–598.
49. Longmate, *Island fortress*, p. 231.
50. Dirom, *Plans*, p. 91.
51. Dirom, *Plans*, p. 39; also *ibid.*, p. 102.
52. Maj.-Gen. G. Don, 'Preparatory General Orders', 4 May 1798, reproduced in full in Rose and Broadley, *Dumouriez*, pp. 61–65.
53. A shilling, one-twentieth of a pound sterling, was in 1798 worth £60–£66 in modern terms.
54. Knight, *Britain against Napoleon*, p. 82.
55. Nelson and Dumouriez both felt they would acquit themselves well; Glover broadly concurred, but noted that the results would have depended on 'how much close support [...] heavy ships could give the landing craft as they approached the shore': *Britain at bay*, p. 83.
56. The names of all the districts, including those added in Ireland and Britain between the resumption of the war in 1803 and the abolition of the Sea Fencibles in 1810, can be found at http://discovery.nationalarchives.gov.uk/details/record?catid=131&catln=3.
57. Dirom, *Plans*, pp. 17, 18–19.
58. Longmate, *Island fortress*, p. 217.
59. January 1798 troop numbers in this chapter are from Wheeler and Broadley, *Napoleon and the invasion*, p. 99, except for the lower figure given here for yeomanry in January 1798, which was 9,750 according to Cookson, *Armed nation*, p. 70. This could reflect an exclusion by Cookson of the splendid urban troops.
60. Dirom, *Plans*, p. 18.
61. Gee, *Volunteer movement*, p. iv.
62. *Island fortress*, p. 217.
63. May and Embleton, *British Army in North America*, p. 37.
64. For example, *Military reflections*, pp. 95–98.
65. Longmate, *Island fortress*, p. 258.
66. Lipscombe, 'Napoleon's obsession', p. 120.
67. Harvey, *War of wars*, p. 352.
68. The important exceptions were the two Trekroner Forts, which mounted a total of sixty-eight 24- and 36-pounders. These forts 'were still almost uninjured' after four hours of incessant combat, 'and were, moreover, considered to be too strong to be stormed' by Col Isaac Brock's 49th Foot and two companies of riflemen, embarked for the specific purpose of capturing shore batteries. Clowes, *Royal Navy*, Vol. 4, pp. 427–428, 430, 437, quotations at p. 437.
69. Harvey, *War of wars*, pp. 363, 365, 367.
70. Harvey, *War of wars*, p. 356; publicity for this cannibalism, whether or not it actually occurred, and whether or not Nelson actually endorsed it, was guaranteed by Fox ranting against it in Parliament: *ibid.*, p. 358.

71. Nelson lost 350 men killed and mortally wounded, to the Danes' 1,600 killed and more than 4,000 wounded and prisoners: Clowes, *Royal Navy*, Vol. 4, pp. 438–439.
72. Harvey, *War of wars*, p. 353.
73. Longmate, *Island fortress*, p. 259.
74. Wheeler and Broadley, *Napoleon and the invasion*, p. 139.
75. Wheeler and Broadley, *Napoleon and the invasion*, p. 151.
76. Quoted in Wheeler and Broadley, *Napoleon and the invasion*, p. 151, italics in original. This sentiment was closely echoed after the Peace of Amiens by Dumouriez. '[F]ar from fearing the muster [of invasion craft] in the Roads of St. Jean, one should rather desire it, provided of course that everything is in readiness': quoted in Rose and Broadley, *Dumouriez*, p. 244.
77. Clowes, *Royal Navy*, p. 445; boat types and numbers from Roger Knight, *The pursuit of victory: The life and achievement of Horatio Nelson* (Boulder, CO: Westview, 2007), p. 406.
78. Clowes, *Royal Navy*, p. 445; minimum number of British shells fired from Knight, *Pursuit of victory*, p. 406; length of the engagement from Wheeler and Broadley, *Napoleon and the invasion*, p. 154.
79. Clowes, *Royal Navy*, p. 445.
80. Maurice-Jones, *Coast artillery*, p. 92; see also Wheeler and Broadley, *Napoleon and the invasion*, pp. 137–140, who seem to see this phase of invasion planning more as a feasibility study than a plan *per se*.
81. Wheeler and Broadley, *Napoleon and the invasion*, p. 140.
82. Brownrigg, quoted in Wheeler and Broadley, *Napoleon and the invasion*, p. 152.
83. Wheeler and Broadley, *Napoleon and the invasion*, p. 139.

Chapter 10: Fathers of the Martello

1. Sara Georgini, 'Newly digitized maps explore the world of George III', smithsonianmag.com, 26 February 2020.
2. This was a *de facto* appointment that became *de jure* only three years later.
3. Clowes, *Royal Navy*, Vol. 4, pp. 408–409. The main cause of the surrender of eleven of these warships and the sloop appears to have been that the ordinary seamen mutinied in the name of the deposed Prince of Orange: *ibid.*, pp. 410–411.
4. As well as £140,000 in cash (£168 million at today's values), intended for soldiers' pay, when HMS *Lutine* of Lloyds Insurance fame sank in a storm. Under articles IV and VIII of the Convention of Alkmaar (18 October 1799), essentially an invasion-specific peace treaty, York's forces were allowed to leave Holland unmolested provided that they left the fortress guns they had captured in place, and that 8,000 French and Dutch prisoners of war be released. The captured ships, representing nearly half of the Dutch fleet as rebuilt following the Battle of Camperdown two years earlier, were all retained by the allies – making the operation a victory, at least in strict counter-invasion terms.
5. H. M. Stephens, revised by John Van der Kiste, 'Frederick, Prince, duke of York and Albany (1763–1827)', *ODNB*.

6. Glover, *Britain at bay*, pp. 39, 42.
7. Quoted in P. A. L. Vine, *The Royal Military Canal: An historical account of the waterway and military road from Shorncliffe in Kent to Cliff End in Sussex* (Newton Abbot: David and Charles, 1972), p. 24.
8. Vine, *Canal*, p. 24.
9. Glover, *Britain at bay*, p. 120.
10. Vine, *Canal*, pp. 38–39.
11. Glover, *Britain at bay*, pp. 31–32.
12. Sutcliffe, *Martello towers*, p. 51.
13. Farrell, 'Pratt, John Jeffreys', *ODNB*.
14. Quoted in Maurice-Jones, *Coast artillery*, p. 99.
15. Christopher Doorne, 'Pitt, John, second earl of Chatham (1756–1835)', *ODNB*.
16. Rose and Broadley, *Dumouriez*, p. 216.
17. J. A. Houlding, 'Dundas, Sir David (1735?–1820)', *ODNB*.
18. Cookson, *Armed nation*, p. 53.
19. Longmate, *Island fortress*, p. 243.
20. This was a complete turnabout from his defence plan of August 1796, which made the 'far too sanguine' assumption that any small-boat descent on Essex or Suffolk would fail, due to the strength of the Royal Navy at Yarmouth and the Nore: Rose and Broadley, *Dumouriez*, p. 219.
21. Quoted in Clements, *Martello towers worldwide*, p. 19.
22. https://sussexhistory.net/2018/12/08/the-martello-towers-west-of-seaford/.
23. Clements, *Martello towers worldwide*, p. 20.
24. Clements, *Martello towers worldwide*, p. 23.
25. Iain Gordon Brown, 'Brown, John (*bap.* 1756?, *d.* 1816)', *ODNB*.
26. Vine, *Canal*, pp. 35–37, quotation at p. 37.
27. Wheeler and Broadley, *Napoleon and the invasion*, p. 110.
28. Vine, *Canal*, p. 39.
29. Quoted in Glover, *Britain at bay*, p. 196.
30. Alastair W. Massie, 'Morse, Robert (1741/2–1818)', *ODNB*.
31. McConnell, *British smooth-bore artillery*, p. 249.
32. That being said, however, the roofs of the three 1790s proto-Martellos in Halifax, Nova Scotia, are said to have featured front-pivot traversing carriages, at least for their carronades: McConnell, *British smooth-bore artillery*, p. 222.
33. All quotations in this paragraph up to this point have been from Alastair W. Massie, 'Twiss, William (1744/5–1827)', *ODNB*.
34. Rose and Broadley, *Dumouriez*, p. 230, from which the quotation; Clements, *Martello towers worldwide*, p. 17.
35. Quoted in Vine, *Canal*, p. 24.
36. Quoted in Sutcliffe, *Martello towers*, p. 55.
37. http://www.kentpast.co.uk/dover_castle.html.
38. Sutcliffe, *Martello towers*, p. 55.
39. Vine, *Canal*, p. 51.
40. In particular, I am thinking of Hanger's 1795 diagram of a concave line of four mutually supporting redoubts for the defence of a particularly vulnerable stretch of the Essex shore: *Military reflections*, p. 29.

41. Quoted in Sutcliffe, *Martello towers*, p. 56.
42. Among these, especially fine examples are item wcl000935, 'Sketch of Dumplin Point with a project for a battery of 4 guns and a redout [*sic*] for 90 men; with a barrack in the battery'; wcl008474, 'Plan of Fort Brown, for 4 guns en barbette; with a small redout [*sic*], and a line for 60 men, and a barrack'; and wcl006126, 'Plan of the town and environs of Newport, Rhode Island [...] when the French fleet engaged and passed the batteries [... and] also the works proposed to be erected in the present year 1779'.
43. Quoted in Sutcliffe, *Martello towers*, p. 56.
44. Horatio Nelson to Lord Hood, 9 July 1794, in N. H. Nicholas, ed., *The dispatches and letters of Vice-Admiral Lord Viscount Nelson*, Vol. 1 (London: Henry Colburn, 1844), pp. 427–428.
45. Elizabeth Sparrow, 'Nepean, Sir Evan, first baronet (1752–1822)', *ODNB*. Their younger brother Nicholas began his working life as an officer of HM Marines in the American War, and after a stint as one of the first officers of the New South Wales Corps, was promoted brigadier-general, and went on to serve as *de facto* governor of Cape Breton Island in Canada, through his brother Evan's influence: https://www.geni.com/people/Lt-Gen-Nicholas-Nepean/6000000007087446220.
46. In semi-retirement, having served as the governor of Bombay, he would be appointed a Fellow of the Royal Society for his contributions to botany: Sparrow, 'Nepean, Sir Evan', *ODNB*.
47. Geoffrey S. Powell, 'Brownrigg, Sir Robert, first baronet (1759–1833)', *ODNB*.
48. John Sweetman, 'Moore, Sir John (1761–1809)', *ODNB*.
49. Stuart Reid, 'Hanger, George, fourth Baron Coleraine (1751–1824)', *ODNB*, which gives the date of the by-election as 1787. Townshend was eligible to sit in the Commons, 'Lord' being a courtesy title (his father being a marquess).
50. Hanger, *Military reflections*, pp. 29, 31. Lloyd repeatedly commended or recommended defensive formations in 'a curve, concave towards the enemy' such that 'the enemy could not advance at all, without presenting his left flank' to the right of the defenders' line: Lloyd, *History*, Vol. 1, p. 53.
51. Wilkinson-Latham, *British artillery*, p. 60.
52. Hanger, *Military reflections*, pp. 30, 32.
53. Hanger, *Military reflections*, p. 93.
54. Clowes, *Royal Navy*, Vol. 4, p. 455.
55. C. H. H. Owen, 'Elphinstone, George Keith, Viscount Keith (1746–1823), *ODNB*. A recent claim that the decisive naval figure in the Mortella and subsequent Martello efforts was Adm. Lord St Vincent is hard to fathom, as his appointment as head of the British Mediterranean fleet was not even considered until May 1795; and, more than four months prior to the Rochester Conference, he vacated the office of first lord of the Admiralty. Moreover, he was one of the leading proponents of the idea that French invaders would be defeated on the high seas or not at all: cf. Roger Millward, *An assessment of the east coast Martello towers* (Swindon: National Monuments Record Centre, 2007), p. 6 and P. K. Crimmin, 'Jervis, John, earl of St Vincent (1735–1823)', *ODNB*. I can only suppose that Millward confused St Vincent for Keith.

56. Rose and Broadley, *Dumouriez*, p. xi.
57. Rose and Broadley, *Dumouriez*, p. 380.
58. Millward, *East coast Martello towers*, pp. 8–9; Dumouriez's own account of these frustrations is quoted at length in Rose and Broadley, *Dumouriez*, pp. 255–256.
59. Millward, *East coast Martello towers*, pp. 8–9.
60. Dirom, *Plans*, pp. 35–36.
61. Rose and Broadley, *Dumouriez*, p. 248.
62. Rose and Broadley, *Dumouriez*, p. 249.
63. Quoted in Rose and Broadley, *Dumouriez*, p. 250.
64. Quoted in Rose and Broadley, *Dumouriez*, p. 250.
65. Quoted in Rose and Broadley, *Dumouriez*, p. 253.
66. Rose and Broadley, *Dumouriez*, pp. 246, 285–286, 288.

Chapter 11: 'An all-encompassing attack'

1. Dumouriez, quoted in Rose and Broadley, *Dumouriez*, p. 59 (uppercase 'A' added).
2. Dumouriez, quoted in Rose and Broadley, *Dumouriez*, p. 59.
3. Dumouriez, quoted in Rose and Broadley, *Dumouriez*, p. 60.
4. Dumouriez, quoted in Rose and Broadley, *Dumouriez*, p. 49.
5. Rose and Broadley, *Dumouriez*, pp. 286–287.
6. Wheeler and Broadley, *Napoleon and the invasion*, p. 227.
7. Longmate, *Island fortress*, p. 262.
8. Glover, *Britain at bay*, p. 16.
9. Wheeler and Broadley, *Napoleon and the invasion*, p. 229.
10. Rose and Broadley, *Dumouriez*, p. 231. I am assuming the scale of these formations based on Dumouriez's opinion that nearly the whole of the government forces in Ireland should be concentrated at these four camps plus Dublin, and should total 75,000 men, i.e. 15,000 per location, in the unlikely event that no smaller detachments were placed anywhere at all: *ibid.*, pp. 231–232.
11. Quoted in Rose and Broadley, *Dumouriez*, p. 315.
12. Glover, *Britain at bay*, p. 43.
13. Quoted in Knight, *Britain against Napoleon*, p. 251.
14. Longmate, *Island fortress*, pp. 286–287.
15. However, arming all of the volunteers was as yet beyond the capability of the country's munitions industry: Glover, *Britain at bay*, p. 45. Glover's numbers would seem to be conservative estimates, as James Davey states that there were 116,000 militia at that time, and of the volunteers, 'around half a million were armed': 'Mutiny and insecurity', in Colville and Davey, eds., *Nelson navy and nation*, pp. 134–151, p. 147. It is possible that Davey's numbers include the 70,000 or so volunteers in Ireland, as well as militia who were not 'embodied'.
16. Cookson, *Armed nation*, p. 45.
17. Rose and Broadley, *Dumouriez*, p. 243.
18. Walker, *Honourable Artillery Company*, pp. 186–190, quotation at 188. '[I]n 1804, General Sir John Moore [...] was, under the Duke of York,

undertaking a complete reorganisation of army transport [...]. It had been realised that to meet a fast moving Napoleon[,] drastic changes were required to make the British Army more mobile': Glendinning, *Hammers of Invicta*, p. 62.

19. Knight, *Britain against Napoleon*, pp. 217, 238.
20. That is, 200 to 300 yards at a man-sized target, as compared to the 60 to 100 yards of the Brown Bess.
21. See especially Wheeler and Broadley, *Napoleon and the invasion*, pp. 142–145.
22. Gen. Sir David Dundas, 15 October 1804, quoted in Vine, *Canal*, p. 42. As the Duke of York also noted, 'an enemy [...] is never to be lost sight of by the light troops, every inch of ground, every field may to a degree be disputed, even by inferior numbers': quoted in Wheeler and Broadley, *Napoleon and the invasion*, p. 141.
23. Rose and Broadley, *Dumouriez*, pp. 256–257. Elsewhere, Dumouriez wrote that no less than three-eighths of British regulars should be 'rangers, sharpshooters and light infantry fighting irregularly': quoted in *ibid.*, p. 263.
24. Juha Mälkki, *The quest for manoeuvre: The English manoeuvre warfare theories and British military thought 1920–1991* (unpublished general staff course dissertation, National Defence College of Finland, 2002), p. 8.
25. Rose and Broadley, *Dumouriez*, p. 226.
26. *Preußische Gesetzessammlung*, sections 7, 8, 43, and 52.
27. The slackening of the importance of religion was reflected not only in non-adherence by Protestants to their own strictures of obedience, but in the fact that, in or by 1803, English Catholics had ceased to be suspected of enemy sympathies: Longmate, *Island fortress*, p. 293.
28. Quoted in Rose and Broadley, *Dumouriez*, p. 255.
29. Rose and Broadley, *Dumouriez*, p. 236.
30. Rose and Broadley, *Dumouriez*, pp. 236–237, 258, quotation from Dumouriez at p. 258.
31. Glover, *Britain at bay*, p. 113.
32. Quoted in Rose and Broadley, *Dumouriez*, p. 242.
33. Quoted in Rose and Broadley, *Dumouriez*, p. 245.
34. Longmate, *Island fortress*, p. 297. However, one of these devices subsequently sank a 'test ship' off Deal: Benjamin Armstrong, *Small boats and daring men: Maritime raiding, irregular warfare, and the early American navy* (Norman, OK: University of Oklahoma Press, 2019), p. 102. Fulton eventually went home to America and the successful commercialisation of river steamboats.
35. The lower figure is from Glover, *Britain at bay*, and the higher from Rif Winfield and Stephen S. Roberts, *French warships in the age of sail 1786–1861* (Barnsley: Seaforth, 2015).
36. Glover, *Britain at bay*, p. 95.
37. Glover, *Britain at bay*, p. 95.
38. Longmate, *Island fortress*, p. 261.
39. Glover, *Britain at bay*, p. 94.
40. Glover, *Britain at bay*, p. 98.
41. Glover, *Britain at bay*, p. 84.
42. Longmate, *Island fortress*, p. 260; Glover, *Britain at bay*, pp. 92–93.
43. All vessel numbers are from Glover, *Britain at bay*, pp. 98, 101 except as otherwise noted.

44. Glover, *Britain at bay*, p. 97.
45. Glover, *Britain at bay*, pp. 14–15, quotation at p. 15.
46. Quoted in Rose and Broadley, *Dumouriez*, p. 369.
47. Longmate, *Island fortress*, p. 260, from whom the higher troop figure; Glover, *Britain at bay*, p. 53, states that the number 'in 1804 was 120,000' and supports the higher number of tides required, by way of questioning a two-tide assertion made by C. J. Marcus in *The age of Nelson: The Royal Navy 1793–1815* (New York: Viking, 1971), p. 264.
48. Glover, *Britain at bay*, p. 83.
49. Glover, *Britain at bay*, p. 47.
50. Quoted in Rose and Broadley, *Dumouriez*, p. 291; even after the invasion threat of 1805 had passed, this number was reduced only to 20,000: *ibid.*, p. 369.
51. Quoted in Rose and Broadley, *Dumouriez*, p. 280.
52. Quoted in Rose and Broadley, *Dumouriez*, pp. 374–375.
53. Longmate, *Island fortress*, p. 292. The military retained the site until 1984: *ibid.*
54. Glover, *Britain at bay*, p. 85.
55. Glover, *Britain at bay*, p. 109.
56. Dumouriez, quoted in Glover, *Britain at bay*, p. 110.
57. Knight, *Britain against Napoleon*, p. 84.
58. Hanger, *Military reflections*, pp. 17–18, italics in original.

Chapter 12: Signed, sealed and delivered: the south coast towers

1. Sutcliffe, *Martello towers*, p. 57.
2. Sutcliffe, *Martello towers*, p. 51.
3. Quoted in Sutcliffe, *Martello towers*, p. 55.
4. Dirom, *Plans*, p. 37.
5. However, the last Martello to be planned and completed in what is now Canada within the Napoleonic period, at Lancaster west of Saint John, mounted two 24-pounder long guns and two 24-pounder carronades on the roof, as well as two 12-pounder carronades on the floor below. Begun in 1812, its construction included a conical shingled snow-roof, as well as 78,000 bricks imported from England for the interior vaulting and central pillar.
6. Glover, *Britain at bay*, p. 117.
7. A fourth redoubt at Rye Old Harbour reached an advanced state of planning before being cancelled: Sutcliffe, *Martello towers*, pp. 57–58.
8. Glendinning, *Hammers of Invicta*, pp. 31, 34.
9. Sutcliffe, *Martello towers*, p. 81.
10. Longmate, *Island fortress*, p. 278.
11. Sutcliffe, *Martello towers*, p. 103.
12. Sutcliffe, *Martello towers*, p. 78.
13. Glendinning, *Hammers of Invicta*, p. 54.
14. Sutcliffe, *Martello towers*, pp. 68, 77, quotation at p. 77.
15. Report of 3 September 1804, quoted in Sutcliffe, *Martello towers*, p. 92.
16. https://martellotowers.co.uk/kent.
17. Sutcliffe, *Martello towers*, p. 57.
18. Quoted in Vine, *Canal*, p. 51.

19. Sutcliffe, *Martello towers*, p. 48. There was also 'a scheme to flood the Lea valley [...] by Rennie': *ibid.*, p. 102. On road-destruction in particular, see especially the Duke of York's remarks quoted in Wheeler and Broadley, *Napoleon and the invasion*, p. 143.
20. Rose and Broadley, *Dumouriez*, pp. 226–227.
21. Vine, *Canal*, pp. 54–55; quotation from the *Sussex Weekly Advertiser*, 22 October 1804, at p. 55.
22. Vine, *Canal*, p. 74.
23. Vine, *Canal*, p. 74.
24. Quoted in Vine, *Canal*, p. 102.
25. Quoted in Sutcliffe, *Martello towers*, p. 50.
26. Ardesoif, *Marine fortification*, pp. 65–70. However, a British version was devised in America in the middle 1770s by John Schank, inventor of the drop-keel that bore his name.
27. Vine, *Canal*, p. 99. Longmate, *Island fortress*, p. 283, states that 'none were installed until 1812'.
28. Vine, *Canal*, pp. 89–90, quotation at p. 89.
29. Vine, *Canal*, p. 90.
30. Sutcliffe, *Martello towers*, p. p. 49.
31. Sutcliffe, *Martello towers*, p. 48.
32. Rose and Broadley, *Dumouriez*, p. 246.
33. Longmate, *Island fortress*, p. 291.
34. Maurice-Jones, *Coast artillery*, p. 94, does not name Campbell but ascribes the plan to the GOC Western District, an office Campbell held from 1793 until his retirement in 1803.
35. Sutcliffe, *Martello towers*, p. 159.
36. Wheeler and Broadley, *Napoleon and the invasion*, p. 232. Back in 1796, Sir David Dundas's team had likewise identified the country around Sandwich (five miles north of Deal and ten south of Margate) as one of the most vulnerable points on the English coastline: Rose and Broadley, *Dumouriez*, p. 217. It is possible to draw a straight line on the map from Dunkirk to Buckingham Palace via Deal and the Great Lines Heritage Park, suggesting that our would-be ruler was fond of rulers of a more pedestrian sort.

Chapter 13: Peak danger

1. To name just two typical examples, Maurice-Jones wrote that '[t]he fear of invasion ebbed and flowed according to the situation' but 'was never really and finally layed [*sic*] to rest until [...] Trafalgar Bay' (*Coast artillery*, p. 86); while Armstrong stated that '[a]fter the victory of the British fleet at Trafalgar [...] the probability of invasion waned and along with it the need for elaborate coastal defences' (*Small boats and daring men*, p. 101). A 2007 report for English Heritage by Roger Millward went so far as to describe the construction of the east-coast towers as ironic: *East coast Martello towers*, p. 2. For a sustained and cogent rejection of such views, see Glover, *Britain at bay*, esp. pp. 13–19 and 123.
2. Knight, *Britain against Napoleon*, p. 228.
3. Harvey, *War of wars*, p. 502.

4. The full text of the Berlin Decree in English translation can be found at https://www.napoleon.org/en/history-of-the-two-empires/articles/the-berlin-decree-of-november-21-1806/.

5. 'Most people (excepting a very few scholars) who read and think about the Revolutionary and Napoleonic wars today do not realize how vulnerable Britain was at this time; nor [...] of how much its civilians had to endure': Knight, *Britain against Napoleon*, pp. xxi–xxii, curved brackets in original.

6. Quoted in Rose and Broadley, *Dumouriez*, pp. 388–389.

7. The Battle of Maida in Italy on 3 July 1806 was also fought 'without London's knowledge' (Glover, *Britain at bay*, p. 22). Maida gave its name to a pub, which, in turn, gave its name to Maida Vale.

8. Harvey, *War of wars*, pp. 497–501.

9. Knight, *Britain against Napoleon*, p. 240.

10. Knight, 'Beyond Trafalgar', pp. 209–10.

11. Rose and Broadley, *Dumouriez*, pp. 213–232.

12. Vine, *Canal*, p. 16.

13. Knight, *Britain against Napoleon*, p. 239.

14. Glover, *Britain at bay*, p. 123.

15. Knight, *Britain against Napoleon*, p. 94.

16. Knight, *Britain against Napoleon*, p. 206.

17. Knight, *Britain against Napoleon*, p. xxxviii.

18. Lord Bathurst to Wellington, 31 December 1813, quoted in Cookson, *Armed nation*, p. 39.

19. Sutcliffe, *Martello towers*, p. 77.

20. Millward, *East coast Martello towers*, pp. 9–10, quotation at p. 10.

21. Millward, *East coast Martello towers*, p. 10.

22. Sutcliffe, *Martello towers*, p. 104. Weeley was built in 1803 and demolished in 1814: Millward, *East coast Martello towers*, p. 22.

23. Sutcliffe, *Martello towers*, p. 78.

24. Though Ardesoif (*Marine fortification*, p. 149) mentions only mortars in this context, their use in howitzers does not seem out of the question.

25. Rose and Broadley, *Dumouriez*, pp. 260–261, quotation from Dumouriez at p. 260.

26. Quoted in Rose and Broadley, *Dumouriez*, pp. 336–337.

27. Martin R. Howard, 'Walcheren 1809: A medical catastrophe', *British Medical Journal*, Vol. 319 (1999), pp. 1,642–1,645, p. 1,642.

28. Harvey, *War of wars*, p. 599.

29. For a typical example, see Harvey, *War of wars*, p. 631.

30. Martin R. Howard, *Walcheren 1809: The scandalous destruction of a British army* (Barnsley: Pen and Sword Military, 2012), unpaginated e-book.

31. J. W. Fortescue, *A history of the British Army*, Vol. 7 (n.p.: Pickle Partners, 2014 {1912}), unpaginated e-book.

32. Indeed, Dumouriez had been arguing for years that Walcheren was the 'key to Holland' and that Britain should take and hold it as a sort of beacon of counter-revolution, as much as for its practical value: quoted in Rose and Broadley, *Dumouriez*, p. 325.

33. Fortescue, *British Army*, Vol. 7, unpaginated.

34. Fortescue, *British Army*, Vol. 7, unpaginated.

35. Quoted in Fortescue, *British Army*, Vol. 7, unpaginated.
36. Fortescue, *British Army*, Vol. 7, unpaginated.
37. Since the expedition, Walcheren has been joined to Zuid-Beveland, and Zuid-Beveland to the mainland by landfill.
38. This is also now joined to the mainland, but on the opposite side of the Scheldt to where the Walcheren/Zuid-Beveland agglomeration joins it.
39. Fortescue, *British Army*, Vol. 7, unpaginated.
40. Fortescue, *British Army*, Vol. 7, unpaginated
41. John Webbe, quoted in Howard, 'Walcheren 1809', p. 1,643.
42. Howard, 'Walcheren 1809', pp. 1,643–1,644.
43. Fortescue, *British Army*, Vol. 7, unpaginated.
44. Howard, 'Walcheren 1809', p. 1,643.
45. Quoted in Rose and Broadley, *Dumouriez*, p. 325.
46. Adm. Keith dismissed out of hand a French attempt on the Isle of Wight in 1803, on the grounds that 'it would not be easy to get off it' onto the mainland unless control of the sea were maintained throughout: quoted in Glover, *Britain at bay*, p. 152.
47. Quoted in Rose and Broadley, *Dumouriez*, p. 280.
48. This is the exact number Bonaparte contemplated sending in September 1803, exclusive of medics, cooks, prostitutes and so on (Longmate, *Island fortress*, p. 265), and therefore assumes an implausible 100 per cent survival rate for the crossing and disembarkation.
49. Assuming an otherwise equal distribution of the Southern Military District's volunteers, yeomanry, and army of reserve across its two counties (Sussex and Kent), the forces in Kent on an average day in 1804 would have numbered just under 36,000, not counting the several thousand garrisoning Dover Castle. An additional 15,000 volunteers from London and Essex would have piled on if Kent were attacked: Glover, *Britain at bay*, p. 87.

Chapter 14: Endgame

1. Vine, *Canal*, p. 99.
2. Longmate, *Island fortress*, p. 205.
3. Vine, *Canal*, p. 16.
4. Harvey, *War of wars*, esp. pp. 307, 632, 707. This was largely because French officers generally winked at robbery, rape, and murder by their men, whereas most British officers would gladly have flogged half their own soldiers to death to prevent such occurrences: *ibid.*, p. 591. This was not only for moral reasons but also for operational ones, i.e. staying in the good graces of the civilian population as a means of securing food, fodder, and intelligence.
5. See also Glover, *Britain at bay*, p. 46.
6. Formed when the Electorate of Hanover was dissolved by the French in 1803, this was not a mercenary formation but a division-sized German-speaking wing of the British Army, incorporating infantry, cavalry, artillery, and engineers. Integral to coastal defence, the infantry were headquartered at Bexhill-on-Sea and the cavalry at Weymouth, though both would serve extensively abroad, particularly after 1808.

7. Fortescue, *British Army*, Vol. 7, unpaginated.
8. Knight, 'Beyond Trafalgar', p. 214. Heligoland's garrison, as established in early 1808, included thirty Royal Artillery Invalids led by a commissioned officer, and a full battalion of Invalid infantry: Maurice-Jones, *Coast artillery*, pp. 124–125.
9. Maurice-Jones, *Coast artillery*, p. 125.
10. Knight, 'Beyond Trafalgar', p. 214.
11. Knight, 'Beyond Trafalgar', pp. 214–215.
12. Andrew Lambert, 'Foreword', xvii–xx in Brian Arthur, *How Britain won the War of 1812: The Royal Navy's blockades of the United States 1812–1815* (Woodbridge: Boydell, 2011), p. xvii. A detailed review of the complexities of impressment at sea is provided by Glover, *Britain at bay*, pp. 66–73.
13. Lambert, 'Foreword', p. xvii.
14. Glenn A. Steppler, 'Roberts, Charles', *Dictionary of Canadian Biography* online (hereafter *DCB*).
15. Clowes, *Royal Navy*, Vol. 4, pp. 427–428.
16. John W. Spurr, 'Bruyeres, Ralph Henry', *DCB*.
17. https://www.battlefields.org/learn/war-1812/battles/york.
18. *The London Gazette*, 6–10 July 1813, pp. 1,331–1,332.
19. Virginia Department of Historic Resources, *Virginia's historical highway markers and the War of 1812* (Hampton, VA: n.p., 2014), pp. 3–4, quotation at p. 4.
20. J. K. Laughton, revised by Roger Morriss, 'Cockburn, Sir George, eighth baronet (1772–1853)', *ODNB*; for one of Westphal's adventures on the Chesapeake pre-Havre de Grace, see *The London Gazette*, 6–10 July 1813, p. 1,331.
21. https://www.battlefields.org/learn/war-1812/battles/fort-mchenry.
22. J. K. Laughton, revised by Michael Duff, 'Yeo, Sir James Lucas (1782–1818)', *ODNB*.
23. Laughton, 'Yeo', *ODNB*.
24. Laughton, 'Yeo', *ODNB*.
25. This figure does not include the two 68-pounder carronades carried by *Victory* or the four such weapons carried by *St Lawrence*, as non-gun artillery weapons were not counted for ship-rating purposes until after the war was over.
26. D. Bamford, *Freshwater heritage: A history of sail on the Great Lakes, 1670–1918* (Toronto: Dundurn, 2007), p. 127.
27. https://www.loc.gov/pictures/item/96510111/.
28. H. M. Chichester, revised by Roger T. Stearn, 'Pakenham, Sir Edward Michael (1778–1815)', *ODNB*.
29. https://projectarchaeology.org/2016/08/01/a-history-of-lighthouses/.
30. 'Between 1796 and 1815, 194 towers were built [...] in Britain and its dependencies': Millward, *East coast Martello towers*, p. 7.
31. Millward, *East coast Martello towers*, p. 7.
32. Millward, *East coast Martello towers*, p. 4.
33. Millward, *East coast Martello towers*, p. 2.
34. Two others were also intentionally destroyed in post-Napoleonic War artillery tests, and one in Pevensey Bay was lost to enemy action in the Second World War.

IMAGE CREDITS

Page 64. Bibliothèque Nationale de France. Declaration of commercial use submitted 13 October 2020.

Page 73. *The Landing of British Troops at Aboukir, 8 March 1801* by Philip James de Loutherbourg, scan © National Galleries of Scotland.

Page 78. 'Mill wheel', © 2016 by Cclionna, CC BY-SA 4.0.

Page 83. Alamy item no. 2BJ20MJ.

Page 85. 'Tour de la Mortella', © 2007 by M. Colle, CC BY-SA 3.0.

Page 91 (top). 'Tour du telegraphe, Chappe Saverne', © 2005 Hans-Peter Scholz, CC BY-SA 2.0 DE.

Page 91 (bottom). Alamy item no. AYKC99.

Page 93. 'Martello tower 01', © 2014 by Lennon Fletcher, CC BY-SA 3.0.

Page 94. AKG Images item no. 2325651.

Page 100 (top). 'Killiney Martello no. 7', © 2008 by Irlpol, CC BY-SA 2.0.

Page 103 (bottom). 'Dover Castle aerial view', © 2011 by Lieven Smits, CC BY-SA 3.0.

Page 105 (bottom). 'Remains of Martello Tower 19', © 2005 by Steve Popple, CC BY-SA 2.0.

Page 115 (top). 'Swedish galley (1749)', © 2010 by Peter Isotalo, CC BY-SA 4.0.

Page 115 (bottom). 'Udema *Ingeborg* 1', © 2010 by Peter Isotalo, CC BY-SA 4.0.

Page 121 (bottom). 'Eighteen-gun brig model', © 2007 by Rémi Kaupp, CC BY-SA 3.0.

Page 134. Alamy item no. T1HR2R.

Page 144. AKG Images item no. 5564689.

Page 163. 'Model of the Redoubt Fortress', © 2007 by Ksimisk, CC BY-SA 3.0.

Page 164 (top). 'Redoubt Fortress', © 2010 by Paul Gillett, CC BY-SA 2.0.

Page 164 (bottom). 'Redoubt Fortress Eastbourne, Casemates No. 2 and No. 3', © 2016 by Forscher SCS, CC BY-SA 4.0.

Page 165. 'Martello tower, Dymchurch', © 2011 by Kmtextor, CC BY-SA 4.0.

INDEX